Competitive Intelligence in the Digital Age:

Strategies for Business and Technology Leadership

Ricardo Marcão
ISLA Santarém, Portugal

Vasco Ribeiro Santos
Polytechnic Institute of Tomar and ISLA Santarém, Portugal

IGI Global
Scientific Publishing
Publishing Tomorrow's Research Today

Vice President of Editorial	Melissa Wagner
Director of Acquisitions	Mikaela Felty
Director of Book Development	Jocelynn Hessler
Production Manager	Mike Brehm
Cover Design	Jose Rosado

Published in the United States of America by
IGI Global Scientific Publishing
701 East Chocolate Avenue
Hershey, PA, 17033, USA
Tel: 717-533-8845
Fax: 717-533-7115
Website: https://www.igi-global.com E-mail: cust@igi-global.com

Library of Congress Cataloging-in-Publication Data

Names: Marcao, Ricardo, 1987- editor | Santos, Vasco, 1986- editor
Title: Competitive intelligence in the digital age : strategies for business and technology leadership / edited by Ricardo Marcão and Vasco Ribeiro Santos.
Description: Hershey, PA : IGI Global Scientific Publishing, [2026] | Includes bibliographical references and index. | Summary: "This book aims to provide a comprehensive exploration of competitive intelligence as a key enabler of strategic decision-making, innovation, and digital transformation"-- Provided by publisher.
Identifiers: LCCN 2025014122 (print) | LCCN 2025014123 (ebook) | ISBN 9798337326900 hardcover | ISBN 9798337326917 paperback | ISBN 9798337326924 ebook
Subjects: LCSH: Business intelligence http://id.loc.gov/authorities/subjects/sh85018300 | Leadership http://id.loc.gov/authorities/subjects/sh85075480
Classification: LCC HD38.7 .C6595 2025 (print) | LCC HD38.7 (ebook) | DDC 658.4/72--dc23/eng/20250606
LC record available at https://lccn.loc.gov/2025014122
LC ebook record available at https://lccn.loc.gov/2025014123

British Cataloguing in Publication Data
A Cataloguing in Publication record for this book is available from the British Library.

Table of Contents

Detailed Table of Contents

As organisations increasingly recognise the importance of sustainable development, corporate social responsibility has emerged as a pivotal strategy for fostering long-term success and gaining a competitive advantage in the marketplace. In this chapter, we dive into the relationship between competitive intelligence, sustainability, and corporate social responsibility to examine how firms can leverage competitive intelligence to create sustainability practices and CSR activities that help address social challenges and create advantages for the firm. Systematically, the examination addressed empirical evidence linking CSR to superior financial performance, competitive advantage, and investment efficiency. This would contribute significantly toward the paradigm shift of competitive intelligence for CSR, thus explicitly enabling capabilities for becoming knowledge-based, advocating the innovations, developing the reputation, and infusing organisational resilience.

Workforce effectiveness measures quality, utilization, and performance, which affect productivity. Performance evaluation is needed for organizational decision-making. Technology-driven businesses use new instructional methods. KPIs and appropriate performance measures for workforce effectiveness metrics must be linked since they impact performance management. HR decisions and procedures benefit from metrics and data. The project's main goal is a realistic 7SF Performance Metric Model. From an open-approach technique, a flexible 7-step conceptual framework for assessing workforce effectiveness utilizing HR metrics and performance indicators was created. In today's competitive workplace, HR managers want predictive analytics. To improve performance management, the chapter will identify relevant HR metrics from literature databases to measure workforce effectiveness linked to appropriate performance measures in an organization. Academics, organizations, practitioners, researchers, and students will be interested.

This article aims to explore the association among leaders ethics and the influence use of platforms founded on digital technologies in nurtures intelligence to compete within corporates. It addresses the challenge of bring into ethical leadership practices with technological advancements to improve competitive policymaking. The study employs quantitative surveys to gather data from various industries regarding leadership styles and technology exploitation. Key outcomes manifest that leaders ethics worthy influences the adoption of digital tools, which in turn augments intelligence to compete capabilities. Corporates with a strong ethical ethos are more likely to leverage data influence in their competitive processes. The outcomes depict that nurturing leader's ethics is fundamental for corporates seeking to improve their intelligence to compete. Future directions assimilate investigating the specific traits of leader's ethics and the influence of emerging technologies on policymaking practices. Recommendations emphasize the need for training programs and approaches of leadership.

In the ever-evolving organizational environment, the interplay between leadership, training, and employee motivation is pivotal for achieving success. This chapter delves into this dynamic, emphasizing the mediating role of training and development. By integrating theoretical frameworks and empirical evidence, it presents a model illustrating how leadership styles influence training initiatives and, in turn, affect employee motivation. The chapter underscores the importance of aligning leadership practices with organizational objectives and values, while also emphasizing how training enhances employee competencies and job satisfaction. Additionally, it explores moderating elements such as organizational culture. Offering both theoretical insights and practical recommendations, the chapter provides valuable guidance for leaders and HR professionals aiming to foster motivation and engagement within their organizations.

platforms effectively. Ultimately, it argues for a reimagined model of CI—one that is agile, inclusive, and grounded in a nuanced understanding of digital realities.

Preface

In today's hyper-connected marketplace, the ability to gather, interpret, and act on competitive intelligence (CI) defines industry leadership. Competitive Intelligence in the Digital Age: Strategies for Business and Technology Leadership arrives at a pivotal moment, offering a concise yet powerful preface to guide leaders, practitioners, and scholars through a world where data-driven insights and intelligent process automation intersect.

At Engibots (https://www.engibots.com/), our core expertise lies in designing and deploying advanced process automation solutions that transform back-office workflows and elevate strategic decision-making. We've seen how integrating CI frameworks with automated data collection, natural language processing, and machine learning can turn raw information into actionable insights, reduce human error, and free talent to tackle high-value, creative challenges. These real-world experiences inform our contribution here.

Within these pages, you'll find:

- Actionable frameworks crafted to embed competitive intelligence within automated processes and analytical pipelines;
- Real-world vignettes spanning precision agriculture, where automated data workflows optimize yields and sustainability, to smart transportation networks leveraging predictive analytics for cost and emissions reduction;
- Ethical guardrails emphasizing servant leadership, data privacy, and social responsibility, reflecting commitment to building automated systems that earn trust as well as performance gains.

This volume is more than a manual for deploying intelligent systems; it's a call to reimagine the role of the human collaborator. As automation assumes routine tasks, tomorrow's leaders will succeed by orchestrating hybrid teams – balancing algorithmic rigor with human empathy. Whether you're steering a legacy enterprise or launching a nimble startup, the strategies outlined here will empower you to craft resilient, insight-driven operations that outpace competition while upholding the highest standards of integrity.

We invite you to leverage these insights, adapt them to your organization's unique challenges, and join the mission in shaping a future where intelligence – both human and automated – drives sustainable growth and lasting innovation.

Ricardo Silva

CEO at Engibots

Acknowledgment

We would like to extend my sincere gratitude to the academic community of ISLA Santarém – Polytechnic University for their unwavering support throughout the development of this book. The insights, encouragement, and collaboration from both professors/ colleagues and students have been invaluable. Their enthusiasm for innovation, strategic thinking, and continuous learning served as a source of inspiration and critical reflection during the research and writing process.

To our colleagues and students – thank you for fostering an environment where ideas are challenged, refined, and transformed into meaningful contributions to the fields of management and competitive intelligence. Your commitment to academic excellence and practical relevance truly shaped the direction and depth of this work.

Chapter 1
Building an Intelligence Driven Organization for Sustainable Growth

Muhammad Nawaz Iqbal
https://orcid.org/0009-0006-4266-4720
Sir Syed University of Engineering and Technology, Pakistan

ABSTRACT

To uphold the tenets of sustainable growth, the digital revolution has metamorphosed competitive intelligence into a strategic necessity for businesses. This chapter focuses on the importance of intelligence-driven decision-making in maintaining organizational resilience and sustainability. It emphasizes the synthesis of artificial intelligence, big data analytics, and strategic foresight in a competitive intelligence framework. Other topical articles include building a culture of data-driven decision-making, using technology in market analysis, and ethical practice regarding intelligence. Case studies from organizations that have successfully pursued intelligence-driven strategies for a competitive edge will be examined. In this intelligence-led framework, agility in strategy, which ultimately contributes toward sustainable growth, will be enabled in the dynamic market environment.

DOI: 10.4018/979-8-3373-2690-0.ch001

1. INTRODUCTION

In the modern digital economy, organizations have large volume of data, very fast technology advances, and constantly changing market dynamics. To navigate this complex environment, not only does strategic foresight to exist, but it must be possible to turn intelligence into an asset. The building of an intelligence driven organization is not the option anymore but a strategic imperative for sustainable growth. These organizations use their data analytics, business intelligence and market insights that are embedded in their decision making processes to improve the performance, to adjust in the shortest possible time when the change occurs and to remain competitive.

This chapter presents the core elements of an intelligence driven organization focusing on how an intelligence can be brought into all functions and used to achieve sustainable growth. It elaborates upon how leadership, technology, organizational culture and talent development foster intelligence capabilities. The chapter also explores the real life examples of the intelligence driven processes and the best practices of businesses implementing such strategies.

1.1 Understanding Intelligence in the Organizational Context

Organizational intelligence is a capacity to collect, interpret and utilize information to choose efficiently. That means structured data that is financial metrics and customer databases as well structured data and unstructured data like social media feedback, market trends. Technologies do not hold our intelligence, but human insight, experiential knowledge and strategic intuition that comes without technology.

The contextual factors seen as technological, organizational, and environmental affecting the adoption process have been elaborated by Krieger et al. (2021) while focusing on AI approaches in auditing. AI techniques help in understanding client and audit risks as well. In hospitality AI social robots, AI and virtual reality in the fashion industry, and AI-driven digital twins in the infrastructure industry are revolutionizing these industries (Broo & Schooling, 2023; de Kervenoael et al., 2020; Silva & Bonetti, 2021).

To actually bring intelligence to bear on your organization, these systems and processes have to exist to enable real time data collection, analysis, and distribution. In order to do so, alignment with strategic objectives and quick and correct decision making, these capabilities must. Additionally, intelligence needs to be democratized within the organization to enable staff at each level to participate in decision making based on data.

1.1.1 Defining Organizational Intelligence

The concept of intelligence today is beyond a person's competence and has become a part of the organizations. Organizational intelligence is the collective organizational capacity to embrace the capability to take information, process it, and then make use of it to drive strategic and operational success. This is the ability of the organization as a whole, made up of people, systems, and culture, to understand and respond effectively to the action in dynamic environments, and to make sense of it.

Organizational intelligence is a systematic and distributed phenomenon and different from personal, cognitive, individual intelligence. It is composed of human resources, tools, data infrastructure, leadership practices, and communications systems. The organizational intelligence includes intelligence elements like learning, capability of adaptation, foresight, collaboration, and memory (institutional knowledge).

The companies of today, fighting to maintain relevance in this rapidly changing business environment, are constantly looking for avenues for enhancing performance and breaking out of the packs (Lyu et al., 2020). Culture lately has received a considerable amount of attention as one of the factors that influence the success of an organization (Suh, 2021). The learning culture has therefore developed into an important factor in the effectiveness of organizations. Basically speaking, an organizational learning culture is an atmosphere that promotes and nurtures learning in all employees (Lee & Choi, 2003). Such an environment should not be viewed merely as a series of training programs but rather as a wider approach that ensures the creation of knowledge, room for experimentation, teamwork, and continuous improvement (Kucharska & Bedford, 2020).

However, with the increased production of data and digitization efforts, organizations now have greater access to the insights about their business with analytic, artificial intelligence, and machine learning. Yet, there is no correlation between having data and intelligence. What separates raw data from actionable insights and how organizations extend insights into operations, culture and strategy is real organizational intelligence.

At a time when market conditions change rapidly, the competition is global, customer preferences are changing continually, all organizations should have a formidable intelligence framework for their own survival and growth. It is not only collecting data, but also collecting data that is accurate, time bound, and relevant. What is more, these data should be interpreted in some way, and people should be able to exchange insights across teams and weave learning into decision making.

Organizational intelligence also has a learning orientation, whereby past mistakes, successes and experiences are leveraged to learn in order to improve future action. It helps to establishing a continuous improvement, adaptability, and strategic responsiveness cycle. Knowledge changes rapidly in areas such as technology, finance, and healthcare, and there is fierce competition, so this concept is particularly important.

1.1.2 Strategic Value of Intelligence in Decision-Making

Intelligence can bring several strategic benefits in terms of incorporating intelligence into organizational decision making processes. It also allows organizations to make evidence based decisions and reduce dependence on guessing or practicing out of habit. In a world of data, but limited attention intelligence aids decision makers to get to the heart of the matter by boiling down complex information to the essential information.

Organizational intelligence is one of the most valuable outcomes because it enables us to be able to anticipate changes in the environment (emerging trends, customer behavior shifts, regulatory updates, competitor strategies, etc.) and be able to act proactively by using the data provided. With power of intelligent systems, leaders are gifted with the foresight to develop the resilient and agile strategies needed in advance. For example, a commercial bank that utilizes customer transaction data, can determine potential loan defaulters prior to default, which may prevent default and proactively minimize the institution's default risk.

According to Kuosa (2011), strategic intelligence refers to the collection and analysis of data and subsequent dissemination regarding the environment in which organizations develop their strategies. Strategic intelligence includes the definitions of rules, the objects and processes of financial affairs and tax, categories of political and economical extent, and human resources of the organizations. In other words, the social, political, and economical behavior of the organizations is concerned and analyzed as strategic intelligence. Strategic intelligence is judged by the factors such as the strategic vision, human and social resources, and the economical and political issues of the organizations (Gabber, 2007).

It also helps with alignment of strategy. Equivalently, when different departments and functions have a common understanding of the market landscape and internal capabilities, the actions make sense and are more synergistic. Culture of intelligence breaks silos down, fosters a culture of collaboration, facilitate flows of insights between units. The plus side of this collaborative approach is that it is better at coordination; it is better at innovation, and it is faster at execution.

On top of that, intelligence driven organizations are in a stronger position to personalize offers and do customer oriented play. For instance, in retail setting, customer preferences and customer buys history helps with dynamic pricing strategies, tailored marketing, and improving customer satisfaction. Intelligence of human resources can be used in determining the talent acquisition, needs of training, and personnel succession out of data concerning performance, the skills and potential.

It is also important to highlight that strategic intelligence is not within the purview of the upper echelon of management. It is empowering middle and frontline employees with access to relevant insights that allows the organization to be agile and responsive at all levels. A truly intelligence driven organization distributes knowledge in an actionable and embedded in the decision making of any great organization.

2. FOUNDATIONS OF AN INTELLIGENCE-DRIVEN ORGANIZATION

2.1 Leadership Commitment and Vision

The leadership commitment and the strategic vision are the heart of an intelligence driven organization. It is not a technical investment: senior leaders and executives must 'sell' organizational intelligence as a value add to be the driving force behind long term growth, innovation and competitiveness.

If leadership commitment exists, intelligence initiatives are positioned in parallel with business objectives, and the appropriate resources (budget, talent, time) are assigned for them. In this scenario, visionary leadership creates a culture where data driven insights are valued in the process of taking decisions and curiosity, learning and adaptability become an inherent trait across the organization at all levels.

Thus, in all of them, leadership is highlighted as one of the most important forces that would change employees' behavior (Northouse, 2016). This was the part of transformational leadership-having a direct bearing on commitment of employees to organizations across a number of organizational settings (Hoffman et al., 2011; Mesu, et al., 2015) . Yet another avenue of research is missing. While performance and attitudes of a work group indeed would be good indicators of the effectiveness of leadership itself (Dionne et al., 2004), most studies on transformational leadership have focused on the individual level, i.e., this theory of transformational leadership was originally conceived to understand effective leadership at the team and organization levels (Bass, 1985; Burns, 1978; Hoffman et al, 2011). Therefore, there is a need to examine transformational leadership and its work-related outcomes in an organizationally committed environment at the team level.

As intelligent organizations, leaders in these organizations understand data and also have the initiative to find ways to leverage it – for example to anticipate the market trends, mitigate risks and find opportunities. The role played by this leadership is important to the way in which it helps overcome resistance to change, leads digital transformation, and models the behavior that characterizes a learning oriented, insight driven culture.

Top leaders have a clear vision that intelligence is not fragmented, but the strategic integration of intelligence missions, values, and performance metrics into the organization's mission. Without such commitment, and never mind the power of data initiatives, they will fail to scale or deliver actionable value.

2.2 Technological Infrastructure

An intelligence driven organization must have a technological backbone. It has the data collection, storage, processing, analysis, and visualization tools, platforms, and systems. It empowers real time decision making, Predictive model and automation for organizations to operate and compete differently.

It includes the cloud computing, the big data platforms, the data warehouse, the business intelligence (BI) tools, the machine learning algorithms and the artificial intelligence applications as the core components of this infrastructure. These technologies let organizations consume massive quantities of structured and unstructured data from any number of sources including customer interaction, market data, financial system, social media and IoT devices.

With emerging technologies, much has improved with respect to strategic planning and inventive company models in recent times (Longo et al., 2017). The market today requires manufacturers to be able to machine agilely and produce superior-quality products that will satisfy their customer base at affordable pricing (Virmani et al., 2023). The technologies, which can be called major enablers of I4.0 practices, include the IoT, CPSs, AR/VR, ML, blockchain technology, AI, digital twin technologies, and BDA. It is speculated that the I4.0 technology adoption will greatly enhance industrial enterprises' social and economic sustainability in the country Bangladesh (Karmaker et al., 2023).

IT infrastructure is expected to be robust and scalable, ensuring interoperability, scalability, security and supporting the growing data needs and protecting sensitive information. APIs and data integrate solutions enable seamless connection between various departments to collaborate and have cross functional intelligence.

The organization has invested in modern analytics tools like Power BI, Tableau, or advanced AI models that help building insights and discover pattern that may even be missed by human analysis. Technology is the engine that drives data intelligence, but it works at the level of technology—the more it is aligned with organizational needs and strategy, the more its success will hinge on it.

2.3 Data Governance and Quality

No Intelligent initiative will walk anywhere without having a good data governance, quality managements basis. Data governance processes, policies and frameworks that make sure of the essence of the data like accurate, consistent, secure and used ethically is known as data governance. It lays out clearly whom owns, is accountable for, and what standards should be used for data at all stages of its lifecycle.

It can be defined as accurate, trustworthy, timely, current, and transparent. Faulty analyses, misguided decisions, eroded trust in organizational systems, all this is created by poor data quality. For this reason, organizations need to set up data validation mechanisms and methodologies for cleansing the data and also for managing metadata.

A good and appropriate definition of data governance would be the organizational practice dealing about data and information management and formalizing policy and procedures to consider the whole life cycle of the data from acquisition phase to usage and finally to disposal. Marco (2006) argues that the realization above is perhaps the greatest benefit of a data governance initiative: opening the eyes of organizations towards the understanding that data is a valuable and priceless asset of any enterprise. While, in fact, many organizations tend to overlook this, focusing more on managing financial and human resources, the fact remains that even the many models of governance of such corporations and information technology do not measure up and cannot show how business value is being realized from data, simply because for them data are viewed as being IT assets like computer and database technologies instead of seeing them as the core of business value (Khatri & Brown, 2010).

As an intelligence driven organization, data governance even tackles issues of compliance and regulation, especially when the data being handled is of personal, financial, or sensitive nature. This is more crucial when the data can be treated and processed using strict data privacy regulations (like GDPR or Pakistan's Personal Data Protection Bill) that exist in sectors such as banking, healthcare and insurance.

In addition, governance is effective in ensuring data democratization—making data available to authorized users all across an organization and managing the confidentiality of the data that may be classified as sensitive. If teams take appropriate trust in the data they use, it improves the probability of adopting a data driven approach to work.

2.4 Cultural Transformation

Cultural transformation is perhaps the most difficult yet critical foundation of a true intelligence driven organization. This is about refashioning mindsets, behaviors, and organizational values to encourage the continuous learning, experimentation and data driven thinking.

A culture of intelligence allows critical thinking, openness to insights, motivation to help, and collaboration among departments. When employees believe this is how the company operates, they are motivated to ask questions, test hypotheses, share knowledge, and use evidence over the likes of intuition or hierarchy when deciding. In such settings, failures are learning opportunities and curiosity is reinforced.

Business today in a rapidly changing digital ecosystem is embracing technical innovations for the purpose of innovation, productivity, and survival. Within and organization, Artificial Intelligence initiatives will cause an unavoidable impact on the culture (Chourasia et al., 2024). Benefits or disadvantages may arise. Digital is used to promote adaptability, collaborative spirit, and flexibility, sometimes in a complicated and contradictory coexistence of variables. But that definition itself is already a testament to the mighty influence technology can exert in this space (Chourasia et al., 2024).

However, to make cultural change possible, there is needed to have training, change management and internal communication. It must be up skilled to data literacy, analytical thinking, and digital tools for organizations. However, simultaneously management needs to create psychological safety so that employees are able to work on data and offer ideas.

Cultural transformation is important but locale (.com) is the same as it is in your country, cultural transformation must be inclusive and all employees at the company, be it from marketing, operations, HR or finance, must see the value of data and how it applies to their role. After a period of time, an organization emerges that embeds intelligence in the DNA of the entire enterprise and not just in a few analysts or departments.

3. KEY PILLARS OF AN INTELLIGENCE-DRIVEN ORGANIZATION

3.1 Business Intelligence and Analytics

The foundation on which an intelligence based organization thrives is BI and analytics. BI is a set of those processes, technologies, and tools for collecting and integrating business data for further analysis and then presentation so that better decisions are made. Next is analytics that takes it a step further by utilizing statistical, machine learning, and predictive modeling to interpret data, identify trends and pattern, suggest that there are some trends that may come through in the future, and in turn, derive actionable insights to act upon.

This is a pillar through which organizations are able to track key performance indicators (KPIs), monitor a company's operational efficiency, reduce a supply chain's costs and also measure a company's market dynamics. Using it, raw data is transformed into dashboards, visualizations, and reports that enable executive and manager to quickly detect weaknesses, and opportunities and their respective improvement areas on time.

Business intelligence (BI) is generally an umbrella term that refers to all that concepts and methods that improve the business decision from fact-based support systems. It includes all underlying architectures, tools, databases, applications, and methodologies. Its major objectives have to enable an interaction and straightforward access to miscellaneous data, permit maneuver and transformation of these data, and deliver business managers and analysts the ability to conduct and perform the relevant analyses and actions (Turban et al. 2008; Wixom et al. 2011). Every sector, from health industries and airlines, to the major companies in IT and telecommunication, has reported successful BI initiatives Anderson-(Lehman et al. 2004; Carte et al. 2005; Turban et al. 2008).

For example, a Takaful company in Pakistan can use BI to monitor claim ratios, policy sales, customer retention rates and agent performance in various geographic areas. It also enables real-time analytics to forecast the risk exposure, enhance underwriting accuracy and fine tuned marketing strategy with emerging trends.

A good BI and analytics framework democratizes data access, so that departments outside IT, such as Human Resource, Finance and Operations can make evidence based decisions. It helps being organized both how you should be and agile in light of the change in the market.

3.2 Customer Intelligence

Customer Intelligence is the procedure that involve collection and analysis of the data concerning customers interest, behavior, demographics, interaction in order to predict and understand what they want. It helps organizations build deep understanding of what really drives customer satisfaction, customer loyalty to purchase decisions.

In the Islamic marketing environment, the area of customer intelligence can assist the providers to design Shariah compliant products, personalized communications and experiences. So for example, customer pain points, preferred channels and service expectations are disclosed from digital touch points, such as mobile apps, social media, call centers.

According to France and Ghose in 2018, Ramaswamy and Ozcan in 2019, the flow of services puts greater emphasis on customer intelligence in enabling firms to optimally offer their services and service-oriented products. Customer intelligence in the age of big data means knowledge or insights on customers derived from the data mining process of integration, analysis, and interpretation of different sources of customer data (Dam et al., 2020b; Davenport & Spanyi, 2019). In turn, customer intelligence allows businesses to formulate service offerings, comprehend customer behaviors, and enhance marketing tactics within the service-based economy (Anshari et al., 2019; Yan et al., 2020; Zerbino et al., 2018). The service industry now constitutes most of the gross domestic product (GDP), particularly in developed countries, accounting for over two-thirds of the economy (Szirmai & Verspagen, 2015).

This pillar supports the development of customer personas, churn prediction model and segmentation based on valid Islamic ethics. Additionally, it helps companies looking to analyze customer lifetime value (CLV) and therefore optimize allocation of resources to higher potential segments and improve their relationship with existing clients.

But only when customer intelligence is leveraged well can it help in building trust; and making your brand viable, inseparable; and your retention high etc. especially in Financial services where trust is the key, and transparency is indispensable. This gives decision making a basis that goes beyond simply the average of the market, but granular, behavior based sales data.

3.3 Competitive Intelligence

Competitive Intelligence (CI) is a systematic process of information gathering of information regarding the competitors, industry trends, regulatory changes and technological advancements. It allows organizations to assess its performance, predict competitor moves and form strategies to acquire and lock sustainable competitive advantage.

Needless to say, this is a pillar in dynamic industries, such as insurance or banking, where new entrants, fintech disruptors or new ways of consumption can severely threaten incumbent players. The products can be tracking competitor pricing, partnerships, product launches, digital initiatives, customer feedback etc.

Competitive intelligence is not a business activity that is new; however, its study as an academic discipline is fairly recent (De Pelsmacker, et al., 2005). It is a complex phenomenon to define competitive intelligence.

Much like other fledgling academic subjects without an established consensus on their boundaries and content, definitions abound in regards to competitive intelligence; in addition, there exist certain definitions that would warrant the appellation 'universal' (Pellissier & Nenzhelele 2013).

Competitive intelligence in Takaful and Bancassurance sectors contributes to formulation of strategies through insights of market gaps, demand for Islamic financial products and how competitors position themselves in digital ecosystems in Pakistan's market. In this way, it can also assist Islamic financial institutions in obtaining differentiators based on unique value propositions, while staying aligned to regulatory regimes and sensitivity of religion.

CI is being used by organizations to carry out SWOT analysis, to assess the industry risk and opportunities for innovative, merger or market entry. It is much more about structured, ethical knowledge gathering for the benefit of strategic decision making and agility, not espionage.

3.4 Talent Intelligence

The term Talent Intelligence describes an approach of using the data analytics to make better decisions in workforce planning, recruitment, development and retention. It helps to understand the current capabilities and gaps of the workforce and future requirements of the business.

This pillar is based on internal data (performance reviews, engagement surveys,HRIS records) and external labor market data (LinkedIn trends, job postings and industry benchmark) such that they can determine employee potential, employee mobility and employee satisfaction. Given the fast changing characteristics of the digital world, talent intelligence is used to make sure you have the right people on the right roles doing the right things with the right skills.

With changing time and growing organizations, recruitment and talent acquisition techniques have evolved over time, and AI-driven talent intelligence (TI) and talent acquisition (TA) today take their place in most organizations. It is believed that AI implementation in managing employees has enormous benefits in organizational efficiency (Charlwood & Guenole, 2022).

Within Islamic financial services, one should have a workforce that can see the need of Shariah principles, digital pulse, and customer empathy, especially in Takaful and Bancassurance. Talent intelligence is useful to find such niche skills and connect them to the organizational roles. Also, it will help identify high potential people in the company who can be used in becoming successors or in development of leadership.

Also, it helps promote building of a varied and creative work culture that values innovation and learning. Creating an HR analytics view using mixing AI with human inputs will help organizations to predict attrition risks, close skill gaps & may give birth to scholars who are resilient & future ready workforce.

4. INTEGRATING INTELLIGENCE INTO STRATEGIC PLANNING

At its core, strategic planning in an intelligence-based organization is based on data. Unlike intuition or past practice, leaders gather data insights to judge market conditions, customer needs, operational performance and then make decisions based upon these. Data analytics gives an additional edge to scenario planning, forecasting, risk analysis, so the strategies can be more resilient and adaptive.

Agile planning methods also have to be adopted by organizations, as they continuously revise and revise strategies based on the new intelligence. And to achieve this, it calls for the collaboration of cross functional people, transparent communication and feedback driven.

4.1 Leveraging Data for Informed Decision-Making

With the advent of the business world in the modern day, intelligence is no longer a requirement but a need. To be strategic, planning needs to be based on real time, data driven insights and if not, it will be too slow to change, off target, and not competitive. Intelligence here implies the gathering of data from different syndromes including the market trends, customer behavior, competitive strategies, internal operations, and financial performance systematically and then bringing it together in a systematic manner.

Data-driven decision-making represents a significant new development. Data-driven decision-making aims to create an evidence-based management culture by providing a basis for strategy and operations decisions through rigorous analysis and interpretation of data (McAfee et al., 2012). In contrast to classic decision-making processes that often relay on gut feeling or experience, data-driven decision-making stresses the importance of empirical evidence drawn from data (Chen et al., 2012). This fundamental change from intuitive to data-centric decision-making emphasizes the ability to enhance accuracy, reduce risk, and direct optimum outcomes across all functions of business (Russom, 2011).

Today, organizations have available to them large volumes of structured and unstructured data from internal and external sources, including customer interaction on social media, transaction records, and CRM databases, reports of competitors, industry publications, and regulatory announcements. This then enables decision makers to extract this raw figure out of these business intelligence tools and analytics platforms.

Market intelligence can be used for instance, by a new market entry into a new market segment as they would analyze demand patterns, pricing architectures and demographics of customers. Likewise, performance data can be used in resource allocation decisions and investment priorities, risk management, etc. Thus, intelligence enables leadership to verify its assumptions, diminish uncertainty and correspond strategy with market realities.

4.2 Aligning Intelligence Functions with Strategic Objectives

Integrating intelligence into strategic planning involves making sure intelligence functions are in line with the organization's main aims. To be fair, this requires a known structure of where intelligence comes in the decision making process. Along with this is putting the governance in place to help departments work together, such as marketing, sales, finance, operations, and the human resources.

The best capability comes when intelligence units are not in silos. This time, they need to work cross functionally to take a holistic view of both internal and external landscapes. For instance, competitive intelligence shouldn't just be used by the marketing team, but it should also influence how to design & develop product, how price to charge, and how to engage customers. Customer intelligence should also impact the brand positioning, service innovation and the loyalty building programs.

Artificial intelligence (AI) has been redefining the pace at which organizations need to align their objectives with technology innovation. From feature significance and efficiency on large datasets perspective, Mohammed (2025) examines the real-time AI-enabled business decision-making process. Machine learning assessment methods will provide organizations with high adoption in AI, improved operational efficiencies, and the maintenance of their competitive edge (Mohammed, 2025).

In fast moving and highly regulated industries, finance, healthcare, and telecommunications to name a few, this alignment is important, and exactly what your software is doing, in the services that you are providing. For example, there are organizations that have to keep both demand side and Shariah compliance in their strategic planning within the Islamic financial sector. For developing and implementing feasible and ethical strategies, intelligence concerning the consumer's preferences, religious sentiments and regulatory changes needs to be tightly integrated.

Secondly, this makes it easy for scenario planning and forecasting since one has an idea of the intelligence to be acquired and how to align it with strategic objectives. It supports a company to simulate different future states based on data and trends and thus give leadership a head start in the unforeseen un clarity and capture the new possibilities. However, this proactive approach increases resilience and is in the long term sustainable.

4.3 Embedding Intelligence into Organizational Culture and Processes

Intelligence integration into the strategic planning, though, starts with cultural and structural shift in the organization itself. It should not be treated like an annual input to the strategy meetings. The best way to do/address this is to embed it into local processes, local mindsets of institutions, leading to continuous learning, real time monitoring and adaptive decision making.

Particularly, leadership drives this cultural transformation. Leadership that instills this kind of culture improves when they continuously prioritize the importance of data driven insights and use evidence to justify their decisions. Middle managers and frontline employees are more likely to produce insights, to bring up issues, and to offer improvements when their input is appreciated and actually put to use.

Traditionally, Information Systems research has concentrated on information as a means of providing support to decision-making processes. The data-processing view, in this sense, relegated the decision-maker to a rather passive recipient of information. This perspective is being challenged as organizations increasingly start to become concerned with the production of knowledge. Organizations seek intelligence (Cronquist, 2004). This pursuit involves the processing of information, interpretation of environments, generation of strategies and decisions, and monitoring experiences and learning from them. Organizational Intelligence (OI) is in particular concerned with the systematic processing of information from external environments in order to improve the ability to predict the future and react accordingly (Cronquist, 2004).

At the same time, technological infrastructure also has a very enabling role. Integrating platforms that promote the flow of data, view-ability, and interactivity needs to be an investment for the organizations. It covers analytics tools with artificial intelligence, business intelligence systems which can be used across the department, dashboards etc. Diluting intelligence and making it more obtainable and digestible facilitate its broader usage and exchange within the strategic dialogues.

Up skilling is also important and so is employee training. Giving analytical capabilities to all parts of the workforce makes it such that data gets collected, and it gets interpreted meaningfully and ethically. Hence, in areas where insurance is offered through banks or to banks (Bancassurance as well as Takaful), those who are familiar with more powerful strategic suggestions, which are closer to the customer, and that are also more aligned with religious values, will be more powerful and compliant.

When intelligence is embedded into the culture and operation of the organization, strategic planning becomes a living, growing process that changes to the new data, feedback and environmental shifts. It redefines strategy as a living means for guiding the organization to keep itself on course while navigating a very complex and rapidly changing world.

5. CHALLENGES IN BUILDING INTELLIGENCE-DRIVEN ORGANIZATIONS

While benefits of building an intelligence driven organization are good, it does have its own set of challenges:

5.1 Organizational Silos and Resistance to Change

Overcoming internal silos and resistance to change have to be one of the most prominent challenges of building intelligence driven organizations. In most traditional business arrangement, the departments work in isolation with no interaction across departments. This happens because such a plethora of vital data and insights are usually isolated and fractured, which makes it hard to have a clear intelligence strategy. In addition to impeding the information flow through the organization, these silos prevent the organization from maximizing the collective intelligence based on the gathering of information and using that information to develop strategic foresight and shared meaning.

Silos exist in almost all organizations as vertical divisions or horizontal functions. In fact, they produce the most pragmatic way for organizations to operate efficiently in the very best cases; at the very worst, in fact, they create the silo mentality (de Waal et al., 2019), with departments unwilling to exchange knowledge or information, and as a result internal collaboration and organizational learning are impeded, thereby inhibiting the highest performance and sustainability of the organization. The issue of the silo mentality has been acknowledged as a very long time tangible problem that needs to be tackled (de Waal et al., 2019).

Employees and managers alike may reject changes to the status quo with workflows, and especially when they perceive these changes as the product of new technology or the threat of data-driven decision making altering their respective space in the regard. It may also come from not understanding why business intelligence tools or analytics is valuable. Even the most advanced intelligence tools can fail to deliver with a lack of a shift in mindset, and a lack of strong leadership advocacy. This challenge has to be over come by either a clear change management and communication strategy and leadership commitment to the culture that values data and collaboration.

5.2 Data Quality, Accessibility, and Integration Issues

Any intelligence driven organization depends on high quality data, yet the obstacle of achieving consistency, accuracy and timeliness in data is quite significant. Most of the time, organizations are faced with multi source of disparate data that are not in consistency of format, they have legacy systems that are not of real time analytics. If the data quality is poor (regardless it may be duplicate records, outdated information or incomplete dataset), it will end up with wrong conclusions, in turn causing mistaken decisions and incorrect signals.

Without data, AI is lifeless and helpless since that is the only substrate on which all machine-learning algorithms learn and hence make predictions and improve their performances over time. So, while training an AI model, a huge amount of data is needed to let the model learn to recognize patterns, make predictions, and improve with time (Aldoseri et al., 2023).

Two key human elements with which AI algorithms deal are data and learning from data to establish patterns and make predictions or decisions. In AI, machine learning refers to algorithms that train machines to automatically select patterns and make predictions from a given data set without being programmed to do so explicitly (Dahiya et al., 2022). The use of these techniques is hence widespread in applications such as natural language processing, image and speech recognition, and recommendation systems. Generally, the more data available to an AI algorithm for learning, the more accurate will be the predictions or decisions of the algorithm. There are various approaches to propounding other ways of putting data to use in training AI systems (Dahiya et al., 2022; Marr, 2018)

There is also another massive issue of data accessibility and integration on different platforms. This means that most organizations have their operations, customer relationship management (CRM), finance and human resources on many unconnected software systems. The disconnected systems inhibit a compilation of a complete performance picture. However, in regulated industries of Takaful and Bancassurance in Pakistan where there exist data privacy regulations, compliance issues, and the imperative to keep the customer's information intact, the issue is much more compelling. These problems need to be mitigated by organizations given by investing in data governance frameworks, combined IT infrastructure, and on tracking of data processes in a continuous manner.

5.3 Skills Gaps and Talent Constraints

Another important challenge is in having enough qualified people who can understand, and carry out, the managing and interpreting the complex data. While the collection and, by extension, the processing of vast amounts of information is enabled by technology, it is only people analyzing this information that gives value to intelligence. Unfortunately, there is a growing dearth of professionals that possess the appropriate combination of domain knowledge, analytical power and technological capability, particularly in emerging economies.

It also goes to decision makers. Data teams and AI teams don't always know how to present data at executive level and how to use the insights, or understand or interpret predictive models created from AI. As an example of Islamic financial institutions like Takaful operators and Bancassurance channels, there is an element of complexity to align data insights with

Shariah principles, under the context of aligning both of financial analyses and Islamic jurisprudence.

Organizations have to put effort towards capacity-building initiatives like, up skilling of current staff, hiring data-literate people and making intelligence educators a part of the leadership development courses. Developing an intelligence ready workforce can also be accomplished in partnership with universities, certification programs, hands on training workshops, etc.

6. SUSTAINABLE GROWTH THROUGH INTELLIGENCE

Happening in modern organizations, this sustainable growth is not only limited to the short term money target, but it relies and balances innovation, operational efficiency, risk management and engagement of human capital within the long run. Intelligence driven organizations use advanced analytics, in real time data savvy and predictive model for continuous evolution and to keep up with the market trends while active in environmental, social and governance goals. The other approach guarantees that it can be fast and competitive and simultaneously resilient and responsible. Companies through incorporation of intelligence at each level of business planning and execution can predict disturbances, personalize customer engagement, optimize resources, and assist processes of transitioning into sustainability and scalability in the future.

6.1 Informed Innovation

When intelligence is the guide to innovation it thrives. Informed innovation is using data to gain insights that will develop new products or services, processes, or business models. Rather then make intuition or tradition, organizations use market intelligence, consumer behavior analytics, trend forecasting and competitive benchmarking so that they ideate and validate new solutions. This also includes the development of forming digital financial Shariah compliant products in the areas of Takaful and Bancassurance to cater to the new customers' needs.

Artificial intelligence and machine learning also helps companies find white spaces in customer service and creates tailored solutions that make customer value better. The innovation becomes a constant loop of learning from data, doing something to the product based on that information, measuring impact, and repeating. By being data driven, this approach reduces the risk of failure, time to market, and that innovations support consumers and strategic goals.

6.2 Operational Efficiency

In fact, intelligence widens the gap between the inefficient and efficient. With real time data and advanced analytic organizations can identify bottlenecks, keep performance under control and automate a lot of the tasks that were not possible earlier. For instance, there is BI tools that will provide insight into inefficiencies in claims processing in Takaful & understanding of how to fix it or identifying the underperforming selling channels in Bancassurance where changes can be done to reduce the gap & make it more efficient.

Additionally, both intelligent automation, such as robotic process automation (RPA) and intelligent document processing (IDP), reduces manual labor and error rates to a large extent. All these include predictive maintenance, the optimization of logistics, and resource allocation analytics to leaner operations. Therefore, companies not only reduce costs but also enhance customer satisfaction in the process as companies ensure that they deliver faster and more accurate services.

6.3 Risk Management

An intelligence driven organization is using risk in a proactive basis as opposed to a reactive one. For Takaful and Bancassurance companies, this includes assessing geopolitical risks that impact the market dynamics and watching out for fraudulent claims, and monitoring the compliance with Islamic finance principles.

Organizations use the risk models based on historic data, the current trends and external indicators to develop contingency plans to simulate different scenarios. Real time monitoring systems of potential threats are also supported by intelligence which alerts the decision makers of the same when they pertain. Organizations embed intelligence into Enterprise Risk Management (ERM) that strengthen the structure and enable organizations to adapt to uncertainty and maintain stability.

6.4 Employee Engagement

Intelligence is a vital pillar to sustained business success; the cornerstone being the engagement of the employee. People Analytics and talent intelligence allow the organization to find out employee satisfaction, performance trends, turnover risks and training needs. This allows the HR populations to make data driven strategies for recruitment, development, and ensuring that the revolving doors of employee movement slow down.

Furthermore, intelligent platforms can make learning and development paths personal for users, recommend what career progression opportunities will benefit employees and make sure that employee feedback is actually being acted on as soon as it is provided. Put in a broader terms, a culture of intelligence is an attitude that allows employees to excel, knowing that they were given the freedom to access data they need to make informed decisions. The likelihood of employees getting engaged naturally goes up when they experience their voices being heard and when their initiative aligns with organizational goals.

7. FUTURE DIRECTIONS AND EMERGING TRENDS

And as technology progresses on its intelligence route, the intelligence of the organizations will also evolve. Emerging trends include:

7.1 AI-Powered Decision-Making

Decision making based on Artificial Intelligence (AI) is radically changing decision making by organizations on how to analyze the data and make important decisions. This is in contrast to traditional decision making models using humans making judgments and looking back on results, AI systems provide forecasting and prescription possibilities to organizations that are able to forecast trends, evaluate results, and make real time decisions more accurately. Those systems based on algorithms, learn from the data patterns and keep improving each passing minute.

For instance, the Takaful and Bancassurance are, AI can analyze customer profiles to predict most appropriate insurance plans or those that hints of claim fraud. In terms of resources optimization, financial forecasting and customer segment, AI helps with more strategic planning. With evolving AI capabilities, the role of humans in the decision making is shifting toward the role as overseeing, giving strategic guidance and giving ethical governance whereas AI is handling its complex data driven assessment and suggestions itself.

7.2 Augmented Analytics

That next level of business intelligence is known as augmented analytics. This tool uses ML, NLP to automate data preparation, data driven insight discovery and data visualization. It allows users, technical and non, to interact with data in ways that are more intuitive and thus faster and more accurate to derive the needed insight.

Augmented analytics tools do not need the user to dig through enormous datasets to identify key trends, anomalies or opportunities; Automatic highlighting of trends, anomalies or opportunities is done. An example would be an insurance manager getting an insight from AI about the sudden reduction of policy renewal in a particular area which might lead to immediate action. This technology expedites the data to decision time by shortening the technical barriers that might otherwise hinder the capture of meaningful insights and have them buried in silos.

7.3 Data Democratization

Data democratization means to create data accessible for non technical users within the organization without the need of data science or analytics expertise. A focus is placed on destroying the silos and giving every employee — from CEO to front line worker — the ability to access pertinent, real time data to make informed decisions.

Employees gain access to the insights that are valuable to their departments through the self service analytics platforms, dashboards and mobile access. This enables departments like marketing, HR, finance and operations to become more independent, take more agile decisions and add greater value to the strategic outcomes. Data democratization is crucial in the case of industries including Islamic finance where compliance, ethics and responsiveness are necessary and decisions should be made in time and based in the context while heads should be aligned with Shariah principles.

7.4 Ethical Intelligence

Given that today's organizations are increasingly adopting AI and advanced analytics, ethical intelligence is fast becoming an absolutely non-negotiable element of future strategy. As an example of the environment where ethical considerations like fairness, transparency, accountability and cultural sensitivity are baked into their governance of data and AI, ethical intelligence is another excellent example bordered between trade and fair regulation. This encourages the development of intelligent systems that both achieve results and enforce morality, laws and societal norms.

For the Islamic financial service of Takaful and Bancassurance, ethical intelligence also means compliance with Shariah principles of the risk sharing, fairness and non exploitation. The companies must guarantee that AI algorithms do not discriminate, violate privacy or inadvertently inflict hurt on extremely powerless populations. It includes creating the diverse dataset, auditing the AI model for bias, protecting customer data and incorporation of these ethics committees of Shariah boards into the mix.

8. CONCLUSION

To build an intelligence driven organization is a multi faceted endeavor of bringing together technology, culture, leadership and strategy. By transforming decisions, made about customers and how value is created. Intelligence embedded into the core of the organization can make businesses grow resiliently, sustainably and therefore with a lasting competitive edge in the constantly changing environment.

An intelligence driven organization utilizes technology, data and a human touch to gain sustainable competitive advantage using their data. Indeed, what is showcased in this chapter, again and again, is that changing over to such organization would not be straightforward—there is more than technological upgrading needed; cultural reorientation and leadership commitment would also be necessary. For businesses, structured data governance with an ecosystem of intelligence created by advanced analytics and supportive infrastructure can help to anticipate change, to be proactive by adapting, and lead with innovation.

The phenomenon of intelligence in strategic planning combines historical performance and real time insights and predictive models as part of each decision. The business model is transformed into a forward looking, agile system that is able to cope with uncertainty and exploit new ones. Intelligence increases the ability of the organization to respond efficiently and strategically to whatever is being term of new markets, optimizing internal operation, or addressing customer needs more precisely.

In addition, core pillars like customer intelligence, competitive analysis, and talent intelligence are better embedded to achieve alignment of the cross functional teams and a unified business strategy. The convergence of business intelligence with today's new technologies like artificial intelligence, augmented analytics and data democratization allows more stakeholders within the firm to converge to an informed, inclusive, and accountable culture. Equally as important is the attention given to the ethical intelligence aspect, which prevents the integrity of data usage and AI deployment from being breached with respect to the societal values and numerous regulatory frameworks.

In a volatile, complex, and fast changing global economy, intelligence driven organizations are especially placed to lead and perform. Future growth within businesses will depend on their capacity to weave technology into human judgment, innovation with ethics, and insights with strategic action. This chapter outlines a blueprint of an intelligence roadmap which can build resilience and add value for all the stakeholders of the enterprise and create long term sustainable growth.

This chapter provides a detailed map that can be followed by organizations to move intelligence to a strategic asset. Intelligence driven organizations will be not only able to survive today, but also to shape the future with the right foundation and continuous innovation.

9. POLICY IMPLICATIONS

This chapter ends on the need for the policy frameworks that will support the development of such intelligence driven organizations. Policies which help governments and regulatory bodies to encourage the adoption of advanced technologies such as artificial intelligence, data analytics, Cloud Computing and other technology etc. must be given priority while also ensuring equitable access to these across all industries. Tax benefits, innovation grants and infrastructure development subsidies can put in place a good atmosphere for the digital transformation. Also, public private partnerships need to be promoted to promote the knowledge sharing, workforce up skilling and cross sectoral collaboration so that even small and medium enterprise (SME) can build intelligence capabilities.

The governance and the ethical use of data is a policy implication. Correct now is that Data privacy, security, and transparency regulations are becoming important with time as we more depend on data-driven decisions for organizations. To protect the consumer rights, meanwhile policymakers should hint and clear guidelines regarding the responsible data usage, AI accountability and ethical analytics. To ensure sustainability, the data sovereignty laws, cross border exchange standards and sector specific compliance frameworks need to be developed and harmonized to promote infant growth of new innovations under the purview of public trust and legal integrity.

Finally, there need to be an investment at the level of workforce transformation in policy agendas to guarantee that the shift to intelligence centered operations is inclusive and sustainable. Vocational training institutions and education systems should come up with realignmenting their curriculum to focus on digital literacy, critical thinking and interdisciplinary skill sets. To be ready for the intelligent demands of a work organization and the decentralized recruitment, lifelong learning policies, industry-academia partnerships, as well as re-skilling programs should become institutionalized. Such policies not only fill the digital skills gap, but also promote employee's meaningful contribution in an innovation-based, intelligence amplified business environment.

REFERENCES

Aldoseri, A., Al-Khalifa, K. N., & Hamouda, A. M. (2023). Re-thinking data strategy and integration for artificial intelligence: Concepts, opportunities, and challenges. *Applied Sciences (Basel, Switzerland)*, *13*(12), 7082. DOI: 10.3390/app13127082

Anshari, M., Almunawar, M. N., Lim, S. A., & Al-Mudimigh, A. (2019). Customer relationship management and big data enabled: Personalization & customization of services. *Applied Computing and Informatics*, *15*(94), 101. DOI: 10.1016/j.aci.2018.05.004

Bass, B. M. (1985). Leadership: Good, better, best. *Organizational Dynamics*, *13*(3), 26–40. DOI: 10.1016/0090-2616(85)90028-2

Broo, D. G., & Schooling, J. (2023). Digital twins in infrastructure: Definitions, current practices, challenges and strategies. *International Journal of Construction Management*, *23*(7), 1254–1263. DOI: 10.1080/15623599.2021.1966980

Burns, J. M. (1978). *Leadership*. Harper & Row.

Carte, T. A., Schwarzkopf, A. B., Shaft, T. M., & Zmud, R. W. (2005). Advanced business intelligence at Cardinal Health. *MIS Quarterly Executive*, *4*(4), 413–424.

Charlwood, A., & Guenole, N. (2022). Can HR adapt to the paradoxes of artificial intelligence? *Human Resource Management Journal*, *32*(4), 2022. DOI: 10.1111/1748-8583.12433Chen, H., Chiang, R. H., & Storey, V. C. (2012). Business intelligence and analytics: From big data to big impact. *Management Information Systems Quarterly*, *36*(4), 1165–1188. DOI: 10.2307/41703503

Chourasia, S., Dhama, A., & Bhardwaj, G. (2024). AI-Driven Organizational Culture Evolution: A Critical Review. In *2024 International Conference on Communication, Computer Sciences and Engineering (IC3SE)* (pp. 1839-1844). IEEE. DOI: 10.1109/IC3SE62002.2024.10592949

Cronquist, B. (2004). *Organizational intelligence: A dynamic knowledge creating activity embedded in organizational routines. Informatics Research Group*. Kristiansted University.

Dahiya, N., Sheifali, G., & Sartajvir, S. (2022). A Review Paper on Machine Learning Applications, Advantages, and Techniques. *ECS Transactions*, *107*(1), 6137–6150. DOI: 10.1149/10701.6137ecst

Dam, N. A. K., Le Dinh, T., & Menvielle, W. (2020b). *A Service-based Model for Customer Intelligence in the Age of Big Data*. Academic Press.

Davenport, T. H., & Spanyi, A. (2019). Digital Transformation Should Start With Customers. *MIT Sloan Management Review*.

de Kervenoael, R., Hasan, R., Schwob, A., & Goh, E. (2020). Leveraging human-robot interaction in hospitality services: Incorporating the role of perceived value, empathy, and information sharing into visitors' intentions to use social robots. *Tourism Management*, *78*, 104042. DOI: 10.1016/j.tourman.2019.104042

De Pelsmacker, P., Muller, M. L., Viviers, W., Saayman, A., Cuyvers, L., & Jegers, M. (2005). Competitive intelligence practices of South African and Belgian exporters. *Marketing Intelligence & Planning*, *23*(6), 606–620. DOI: 10.1108/02634500510624156

de Waal, A., Weaver, M., Day, T., & van der Heijden, B. (2019). Silo-busting: Overcoming the greatest threat to organizational performance. *Sustainability (Basel)*, *11*(23), 6860. DOI: 10.3390/su11236860

Dionne, S. D., Yammarino, F. J., Atwater, L. E., & Spangler, W. D. (2004). Transformational leadership and team performance. *Journal of Organizational Change Management*, *17*(2), 177–193. DOI: 10.1108/09534810410530601

France, S. L., & Ghose, S. (2018). Marketing analytics: Methods, practice, implementation, and links to other fields. *Expert Systems with Applications*, *119*, 456–475. DOI: 10.1016/j.eswa.2018.11.002

Gabber, H. (2007). Competitive intelligence topology analyze for improved plan operation. *Industrial Management & Data Systems*, *107*(2), 198–236.

Hoffman, B. J., Bynum, B. H., Piccolo, R. F., & Sutton, A. W. (2011). Person-organization value congruence: How transformational leaders influence work group effectiveness. *Academy of Management Journal, 54*(4), 779–796. DOI: 10.5465/amj.2011.64870139

Karmaker, C. L., Al Aziz, R., Ahmed, T., Misbauddin, S. M., & Moktadir, M. A. (2023). Impact of industry 4.0 technologies on sustainable supply chain performance: The mediating role of green supply chain management practices and circular economy. *Journal of Cleaner Production, 419*, 138249. DOI: 10.1016/j.jclepro.2023.138249

Khatri, V., & Brown, C. V. (2010). Designing data governance. *Communications of the ACM, 53*(1), 148–152. DOI: 10.1145/1629175.1629210

Krieger, F., Drews, P., & Velte, P. (2021). Explaining the (non-) adoption of advanced data analytics in auditing: A process theory. *International Journal of Accounting Information Systems, 41*, 100511. DOI: 10.1016/j.accinf.2021.100511

Kucharska, W., & Bedford, D. A. D. (2020). Love your mistakes!—They help you adapt to change. How do knowledge, collaboration and learning cultures foster organizational intelligence? *Journal of Organizational Change Management, 33*(7), 1329–1354. DOI: 10.1108/JOCM-02-2020-0052

Kuosa, T. (2011). Different approaches of pattern management and strategic intelligence. *Technological Forecasting and Social Change, 42*(6), 458–467. DOI: 10.1016/j.techfore.2010.06.004

Lee, H., & Choi, B. (2003). Knowledge Management enablers, processes and organizational knowledge: An integrative view and empirical investigation. *Journal of Management Information Systems, 20*(1), 179–228. DOI: 10.1080/07421222.2003.11045756

Longo, F., Nicoletti, L., & Padovano, A. (2017). Smart operators in industry 4.0: A human-centered approach to enhance operators' capabilities and competencies within the new smart factory context. *Computers & Industrial Engineering, 113*, 144–159. DOI: 10.1016/j.cie.2017.09.016

Lyu, C., Yang, J., Zhang, F., Teo, T. S. H., & Mu, T. (2020). How do knowledge characteristics affect a firm's knowledge sharing intention in inter firm cooperation? An empirical study. *Journal of Business Research, 115*(381), 48–60. DOI: 10.1016/j.jbusres.2020.04.045

Marco, D. (2006). Understanding data governance and stewardship, part 1. *DM Review, 16*(9), 2006.

Marr, B. (2018). *Artificial Intelligence in Practice: How 50 Successful Companies Used AI and Machine Learning to Solve Problems*. John Wiley & Sons.

McAfee, A., Brynjolfsson, E., Davenport, T. H., Patil, D. J., & Barton, D. (2012). Big data: The management revolution. *Harvard Business Review, 90*(10), 60–68. PMID: 23074865

Mesu, J., Sanders, K., & Riemsdijk, M. V. (2015). Transformational leadership and organisational commitment in manufacturing and service small to medium-sized enterprises: The moderating effects of directive and participative leadership. *Personnel Review, 44*(6), 970–990. DOI: 10.1108/PR-01-2014-0020

Mohammed, I. A. (2025, February). Managing AI-Driven Innovations: Aligning Technological Advancements with Strategic Business Objectives. In *2025 First International Conference on Advances in Computer Science, Electrical, Electronics, and Communication Technologies (CE2CT)* (pp. 950-955). IEEE DOI: 10.1109/CE2CT64011.2025.10941386

Northouse, P. G. (2016). *Leadership: Theory and practice* (7th ed.). Sage.

Pellissier, R., & Nenzhelele, T. E. (2013). Towards a universal definition of competitive intelligence. *South African Journal of Information Management, 15*(2). Advance online publication. DOI: 10.4102/sajim.v15i2.559

Ramaswamy, V., & Ozcan, K. (2019). Digitalized Interactive Platforms: Turning Goods and Services into Retail Co-Creation Experiences. *NIM Marketing Intelligence Review, 11*(1), 18–23. DOI: 10.2478/nimmir-2019-0003

Russom P. (2011). Big data analytics. TDWI best practices report, *fourth quarter. 19*(4):1-34.

Silva, E. S., & Bonetti, F. (2021). Digital humans in fashion: Will consumers interact? *Journal of Retailing and Consumer Services, 60*, 102430. DOI: 10.1016/j.jretconser.2020.102430

Suh, B. (2021). Workplace learning: How to build a culture of continuous employee development. *The Learning Organization, 28*(4), 457–459. DOI: 10.1108/TLO-05-2021-269

Szirmai, A., & Verspagen, B. (2015). Manufacturing and economic growth in developing countries, 1950–2005. *Structural Change and Economic Dynamics, 34*, 46–59. DOI: 10.1016/j.strueco.2015.06.002

Turban, E., Sharda, R., Aronson, J. E., & King, D. (2008). *Business Intelligence: A Managerial Approach*. Pearson Prentice Hall.

Virmani, N., Sharma, S., Kumar, A., & Luthra, S. (2023). Adoption of industry 4.0 evidence in emerging economy: Behavioral reasoning theory perspective. *Technological Forecasting and Social Change, 188*, 122317. DOI: 10.1016/j.techfore.2023.122317

Wixom, B. H., Watson, H. J., & Werner, T. (2011). Developing an enterprise business intelligence capability. *MIS Quarterly Executive, 10*, 2.

Yan, Y., Huang, C., Wang, Q., & Hu, B. (2020). Data mining of customer choice behavior in internet of things within relationship network. *International Journal of Information Management, 50*, 566–574. DOI: 10.1016/j.ijinfomgt.2018.11.013

Zerbino, P., Aloini, D., Dulmin, R., & Mininno, V. (2018). Big Data-enabled customer relationship management: A holistic approach. *Information Processing & Management, 54*(5), 818–846. DOI: 10.1016/j.ipm.2017.10.005

KEY TERMS AND DEFINITIONS

AI in Business Strategy: Artificial Intelligence in Business Strategy is to incorporate Artificial Intelligence technologies in strategic information and operationalization to create innovation, enhance processes, and boost customer engagement. This allows the businesses to automate decision making and create competitive advantages, as well as predicting market behavior.

Business Sustainability: Business Sustainability is simply the ability of the business to operate in a way that allows it to comply with present business needs without already compromising the ability of the subsequent generations to do the same. The framework covers the economic, environmental, and social dimensions of [doing business] which urge businesses to achieve profitability while being environmentally, reflecting the social responsibly.

Competitive Intelligence: Competitive Intelligence (CI) is defined as the process of describing, gathering, analyzing, but most importantly utilizing information about competition, trends in the market and the external business environment in order to support strategic decision making. It enables organizations to define what goes on 'inside', plan for the future, benchmark performance and identify such opportunities or threats in their industry landscape.

Data-Driven Decision Making: Data Driven Decision Making (DDDM) is a strategic business decision making approach by which the decisions are made on the basis of data analysis for matured interpretation of data than intuition or observation alone. This method increases the accuracy, increases the prospective, and diminishes the risks by utilizing the created from structured data and unstructured data.

Digital Transformation: Digital Transformation is the integration of digital technologies in all business processes and functions of an organization aiming to alter its structure, strategy and transformation operations, so as to provide value to customers. Innovations which include adopting tools such as, cloud computing, AI, IoT and Data analytics to increase efficiency, customer experience, innovation and agility to increase the power of doing and thinking in a digital world.

Market Intelligence: Market Intelligence is defined as the process of gathering and analyzing information relating to market modus operandi and application. It helps to create a detailed market strategy, new product plan and marketing efforts through a deep understanding of the market landscape.

Organizational Resilience: Organizational Resilience is the ability of a company to realize it can anticipate, prepare for, respond to and adapt to incremental and sudden disruptions to live and survive. Flexibility, risk management, crisis response and continuous improvement make up its fold.

Strategic Foresight: Strategic Foresight is the discipline encompassing the visionary and analytical practice of anticipating and prepping for future situations by means of long term thinking and trends, uncertainties and risks. It is used by organizations to develop adaptive strategies that improve resilience and competitiveness in a high dynamic environment.

Chapter 2
Case Studies in Competitive Intelligence:
Real-World Applications in Global Industries

Mustafa Kayyali
https://orcid.org/0000-0003-3300-262X
Maaref University of Applied Sciences, Idlib, Syria

ABSTRACT

This chapter explores the practical landscape of competitive intelligence (CI) through a series of global industry case studies that illustrate how data, strategy, and decision-making intersect in real-world scenarios. As businesses face increasing volatility and digital acceleration, CI has evolved from a peripheral analytical tool into a central pillar of strategic foresight. Drawing from sectors including manufacturing, finance, healthcare, and emerging tech, the chapter dissects how firms collect, process, and act on intelligence to secure market advantage. It also examines the fine line between ethical intelligence gathering and invasive surveillance in a data-saturated world. Beyond tools and frameworks, the focus is on lived practice—what actually works, where it fails, and why context

DOI: 10.4018/979-8-3373-2690-0.ch002

matters. This work invites both scholars and practitioners to rethink how intelligence is conceptualized and operationalized in an age where information is abundant, but actionable insight remains scarce.

INTRODUCTION

In today's volatile and data-saturated world, the rules of competition have fundamentally changed. No longer is market leadership determined solely by internal capacity or product superiority—it is now shaped, perhaps even dictated, by the quality of a firm's insights into its competitors, customers, industry shifts, and emerging risks. Competitive intelligence (CI) has emerged as both a compass and a radar—helping organizations navigate uncertain terrain while simultaneously detecting opportunities and threats before they surface in mainstream discourse (Kanellopoulos & Ioannidis, 2024). And yet, despite its growing centrality to strategic decision-making, competitive intelligence remains a misunderstood and unevenly applied discipline, often obscured by jargon or diluted into simplistic tools and software dashboards. This chapter begins with a conviction: that competitive intelligence must be reclaimed as a deeply human process—rooted not just in data, but in context, judgment, and disciplined curiosity. The tools of CI—yes, they matter—but tools are only as powerful as the minds that wield them and the questions they are tasked with answering. In that spirit, this chapter is not an abstract treatise on CI theory, nor a rehash of familiar frameworks. Instead, it is an inquiry into how CI actually plays out on the ground, in diverse industries, across cultural and regulatory landscapes, and under varying levels of technological sophistication.

What happens, for instance, when a healthcare firm in Singapore uses competitive intelligence to anticipate a regulatory shift before its rivals? Or when a legacy manufacturing company in Germany leverages CI to successfully pivot into a niche green market? Or when a North American tech startup uses CI not to copy competitors, but to better understand customer pain points that its rivals are missing? These are not hypotheticals—they are real-world examples of how intelligence, when gathered ethically and applied strategically, can become a force multiplier. In the digital age, intelligence is not scarce—but insight is. Organizations are drowning in information, and yet many still struggle to draw out the signals from the noise (Singireddy, 2025). This disconnect, often born from a failure to contextualize or synthesize data meaningfully, is what separates reactive organizations from those that lead markets. Competitive intelligence, at its best, bridges that gap. It draws upon disciplines as diverse as anthropology, data analytics, behavioral economics, and strategic management. And it refuses to settle for surface-level analysis; it demands depth, agility, and reflexivity. This chapter is structured around a series of case studies that illustrate how CI has been used across industries and contexts to make informed, often bold, decisions. But it also steps back to reflect critically: What patterns can we see? Where does CI deliver its greatest value? And where do organizations falter—either through ethical missteps, strategic blindness, or over-reliance on tools that promise much but deliver little? In a world where algorithms increasingly shape perception and decision-making, CI must not become another automated checkbox. It must be practiced as an interpretive, ethical, and adaptive craft. The stories that follow are intended not only to illuminate best practices, but to provoke deeper questions about the evolving role of intelligence in shaping business futures. This is a field not merely of knowledge, but of vigilance, synthesis, and foresight. And it is only becoming more vital.

Unpacking Competitive Intelligence: From Theory to Tactical Edge

In consulting workshops, and graduate classrooms around the world, the term *competitive intelligence* is frequently invoked—often as a catch-all for business insight, market awareness, or strategic foresight. Yet, for all its popularity, the term is rarely unpacked with the depth and care it deserves. Too often, it's framed either as a toolkit—defined by the latest digital dashboards—or as a vague philosophical concept, full of promise but lacking operational clarity. But competitive intelligence, when stripped of jargon and restored to its true form, is something far more nuanced, more indispensable, and frankly, more human (Wing, 2025). It is less about *knowing everything* and more about *knowing what matters*—and doing so early enough to act on it meaningfully. To understand CI is to understand the intersection of perception and action. At its heart, CI is about making sense of the external environment in a way that empowers internal choices (Heath, 2022). It is about gathering signals—some loud, some barely audible—interpreting them within context, and translating them into decisions that sharpen competitive advantage. In this sense, CI is not merely reactive; it is anticipatory. It is not only about competitors, but about customers, technologies, regulations, social norms, and emerging behaviors. In other words, competitive intelligence is a strategic lens—it helps organizations not just see the world more clearly, but see what's coming next. But to get there, we must resist the temptation to reduce CI to tools and tactics. Intelligence is not software. It's not a database subscription. It's not a report with color-coded charts. These things support CI, but they are not its essence. Real intelligence begins with curiosity and discipline. It asks: *What do we not know? What are we assuming? What would we need to see to challenge our current strategy?* These are not easy questions, and they cannot be answered by simply scanning competitor websites or pulling up keyword alerts. They require a mindset that is both humble and rigorous—aware of complexity, yet always searching for clarity.

Historically, the roots of CI go far deeper than the digital age. In fact, the origins of competitive intelligence can be traced back to ancient statecraft and military strategy (Madureira et al, 2023). Think of Sun Tzu's *Art of War*, or the intelligence operations of Renaissance courts, or even the commercial espionage of 19th-century European trading companies (Olah, 2024). The core idea—that knowledge of one's rivals and environment is essential to strategy—is ancient. What has changed is not the principle, but the pace. Today, the competitive landscape shifts by the hour, and the sources of intelligence are more diverse and decentralized than ever. From social media posts to patent filings, satellite imagery to podcast interviews, intelligence today is embedded in a kaleidoscope of open and closed channels. The challenge is no longer access to data—but discerning what data to trust, how to interpret it, and when to act. This brings us to a critical distinction: intelligence is not information. While the two are often used interchangeably, conflating them is a mistake. Information is raw. It can be vast, noisy, and confusing. Intelligence, by contrast, is processed, contextualized, and actionable. It is not just what you know—it's what you understand. This transformation from information to intelligence requires human judgment. No matter how advanced our analytics become, it is people—experienced, curious, and strategically grounded people—who determine what matters, why it matters, and what should be done about it.

In the real world, this process is rarely linear. Intelligence gathering often begins in the margins. A sales manager hears from a client that a competitor is offering new pricing structures. A researcher notices an unusual spike in patent activity in a niche technology space. A policy analyst flags a quietly proposed regulation that could reshape logistics in a key region. These fragments alone mean little. But when stitched together with other data points, trends, and strategic priorities, they form a mosaic that can guide critical decisions. This is the work of CI—not glamorous, not always conclusive, but immensely powerful. Still, intelligence is only useful if it leads somewhere. And here lies another challenge. In many organizations, CI functions exist in isolation—overburdened, under-integrated, and occasionally ignored. Reports are written but not read. Insights are gathered but not translated into strategy. The value of CI, then, is not simply in what it reveals, but in its *uptake*—how it is communicated, championed, and embedded into leadership thinking (Fannon et al, 2022). This means CI professionals must do more than analyze; they must influence. They must become storytellers, framing their insights in ways that resonate with decision-makers and align with organizational goals.

To make this possible, CI must be built into the fabric of an organization's culture. Leaders must learn to ask better questions. Teams must be trained to spot early signals. Cross-functional communication must become standard practice. And perhaps most importantly, CI must be seen not as a luxury, but as a discipline of survival and adaptation. The world is moving too quickly—and the stakes are too high—for intelligence to be relegated to the sidelines. That said, the field is not without its tensions. Ethical dilemmas abound. Where is the line between competitive research and corporate spying? How can organizations respect privacy while still engaging in robust monitoring of the competitive landscape? What about the use of AI to scrape and analyze data at scale—where does that cross into manipulation or surveillance? These questions are not theoretical. They are playing out in real time, as regulators, companies, and civil societies wrestle with the implications of a hyperconnected, data-rich world. CI practitioners must be at the forefront of these debates, not only because their work touches on sensitive areas, but because the credibility of their insights depends on the integrity of their methods.

Moreover, in unpacking CI, one must also acknowledge its blind spots. Intelligence, no matter how sophisticated, is shaped by the biases of its collectors and interpreters. What we choose to monitor, how we frame our competitors, what assumptions we bring into our analysis—these shape the outcome. A firm too focused on short-term rivals may miss the long-term disruptor. A team too enamored with data may overlook cultural signals. A leader too confident in current success may ignore weak signals of decline. The greatest threat to good intelligence is often not the lack of data, but the illusion of certainty (Lee, 2024). This is why the best CI operations are reflexive—they audit their own thinking, challenge their own conclusions, and remain open to surprise. They foster environments where dissent is welcome, where uncertainty is acknowledged, and where intelligence is not expected to predict the future, but rather prepare the organization to meet it with clarity and agility. Unpacking competitive intelligence, then, is less about defining a method and more about cultivating a stance. It is about remaining intellectually agile in the face of complexity. It is about respecting both data and intuition, structure and flexibility. And above all, it is about embracing the uncomfortable truth that the most powerful intelligence often comes not from what everyone is watching, but from what others overlook.

In sum, CI is neither purely analytical nor purely creative—it is both. It requires systems for gathering and tools for analysis, but also imagination to ask better questions and foresight to make connections others miss. It is both science and art, both discipline and instinct. In an age where change is constant and disruption is the norm, this blend of capacities becomes not just useful, but essential. Competitive intelligence, properly understood and rightly practiced, is not just a business function. It is a strategic necessity. As the chapter progresses into specific case studies, the aim is to illustrate how these principles play out in concrete contexts. Not every company gets it right. But when intelligence is embedded into the core of decision-making—when it is understood as a living, human process—then it becomes more than a strategic tool. It becomes a competitive edge that is hard to replicate, because it is not rooted in software, but in culture, mindset, and disciplined reflection.

Strategic Listening in Practice: Sectoral Case Studies Across Borders

Strategic listening is not a new concept, yet in competitive intelligence, it takes on a more layered and essential role than most disciplines tend to recognize (Tanev, 2024). It is not simply the act of monitoring what competitors say, nor is it limited to scraping data or setting up keyword alerts. Strategic listening, at its core, is the art and discipline of *tuning into what matters*, especially when it's not being said directly. It is about interpreting silences, tracing undercurrents, and connecting fragments of insight that, on their own, might seem trivial but together offer a map of impending change. And nowhere is this practice more visible—and more vital—than in the real-world case studies of companies operating across industries and borders, where stakes are high and the margins for error are razor thin. To understand how strategic listening operates in practice, we must move away from abstraction and into context (Kluger & Itzchakov, 2022). In this section, we step into the shoes of companies in different regions, navigating their own specific market dynamics, cultural sensibilities, regulatory climates, and strategic urgencies. We look not just at what they did, but *how they paid attention*—and how that shaped their trajectory. Each case is less a showcase of perfect strategy than a window into how intelligence, when truly practiced as listening, becomes a transformative force.

Let's begin with an instructive case from the healthcare sector in Southeast Asia. A mid-sized pharmaceutical company in Singapore, traditionally focused on generics, found itself in a tight spot: pricing pressure was intensifying, local regulations were evolving, and multinational giants were beginning to edge into its domestic territory. Rather than rush to react tactically, the company stepped back. It began a six-month project not of launching new products or cutting costs, but of listening. The team mapped regulatory chatter, not only through formal channels but by attending overlooked industry forums and analyzing parliamentary records. They tracked competitor hiring trends—specifically, sudden increases in regulatory affairs roles—and inferred that competitors were preparing for a significant compliance shift. They also listened, in a very literal sense, to patients—commissioning interviews and community focus groups that uncovered concerns about over-medication and demand for holistic care. This disciplined listening paid off. The company realized that a regulatory move toward integrated health services was coming—something not yet on the radar of larger firms. Acting early, they partnered with wellness platforms, diversified their service model, and positioned themselves as a "health outcomes" company, not just a pharmaceutical supplier. Within 18 months, they were not only compliant with new regulations but ahead of them. Strategic listening, in this case, wasn't just about knowing what was happening—it was about *hearing what the future was whispering*, and acting before others even noticed the conversation.

Contrast this with a case from the automotive sector in Germany. A family-owned manufacturing firm specializing in precision components for combustion engines had long been known for its craftsmanship but had resisted shifting toward electric vehicle (EV) markets. The firm believed that the EV wave was overhyped and that their niche would hold steady for at least another decade. However, a newly hired intelligence analyst took a different approach. Instead of diving into conventional industry forecasts, she turned her attention to supply chain patterns. She noticed a sharp increase in small-scale R&D investment by their long-time clients—particularly in battery tech and lightweight materials. She also monitored job boards, LinkedIn profiles, and patent databases, tracking a quiet exodus of engineering talent from internal combustion projects toward hybrid powertrain development. What was critical here was not just the information—but the *connections* she made. She presented a simple but powerful insight to the leadership: your best clients are preparing to leave you behind. This insight, backed not by high-level strategy slides but by evidence that felt real and grounded, changed the tone in the executive suite. The company initiated a partial pivot, not abandoning its core, but setting up a parallel innovation unit focused on high-precision EV components. Within four years, this unit accounted for 30% of its revenues. The shift was not dramatic, but it was timely—and it was driven by someone listening to the future through non-obvious channels. One of the most compelling examples of strategic listening comes from the finance sector, specifically a fintech startup operating out of Lagos, Nigeria. In a crowded and fast-evolving financial landscape, the startup initially focused on digital wallets and micro-loans. While growth was steady, the market was beginning to saturate, and their leadership was feeling pressure from more heavily funded competitors. The firm's CEO decided to do something unusual: she asked her intelligence team to ignore the usual KPIs and start mapping informal economies—particularly rural and semi-urban communities that didn't show up in most conventional datasets.

The team went beyond market research. They embedded themselves in local markets, attended village banking co-op meetings, and spoke to informal vendors who handled cash flows larger than some registered businesses. They listened not with the intent to sell, but to understand. What they found was revelatory: there was enormous financial activity happening outside the formal system, but trust—not technology—was the missing link. Armed with these insights, the startup built a product designed not just for mobile use, but for *relationship-building*. They added human agents into their digital system—community representatives who vouch for transactions and mediate loans (Bisht et al, 2025). The result wasn't just a product innovation; it was a market strategy grounded in cultural intelligence. Today, they are one of the fastest-growing inclusive finance platforms in West Africa—not because they chased trends, but because they listened to the *unbanked* before others saw their value. These stories may feel worlds apart—in sector, geography, and context—but they share something profound: they are all anchored in the practice of *strategic listening* as a living, daily discipline. They did not depend on big consultancy reports or flashy AI dashboards. They relied on the ability to notice, to piece things together, to listen at the edges of the map. They made listening a core business function, not a side activity delegated to junior staff. They treated signals not as trivia, but as early warnings or hidden openings. In short, they practiced CI not as a reactive posture but as an *active engagement* with the world around them.

Another striking pattern is the role of empathy in these case studies. Strategic listening is not mechanical. It is relational (Hinz et al, 2022). It means putting oneself in the shoes of customers, regulators, competitors, and even critics. It requires humility—the recognition that what an organization thinks it knows may not be what truly matters. In many of these cases, breakthroughs happened not because teams had the most data, but because they were *present* in the right conversations. They earned access to insights through credibility, relationship-building, and consistent curiosity.

That's hard to quantify—but it's invaluable. At the same time, strategic listening is not immune to risk. The problem of misinterpretation, of jumping to conclusions, or of confirmation bias is always present. Listening becomes dangerous when it turns into eavesdropping without context, or when every signal is treated as a crisis. This is why organizational culture matters. Teams must be trained not just in collection, but in interpretation. They must know when to push and when to pause. They must learn to read nuance—because sometimes, the loudest voice in the room isn't the most important. Often, it's the quiet shift at the margins—the drop in sentiment, the change in tone, the new silence—that tells you everything.

Moreover, there's a subtle danger of over-digitizing strategic listening. As more companies adopt AI-powered monitoring tools, there's a growing belief that machines can do the listening for us. While these tools are useful—indeed, many of the above cases used digital aids—it is crucial to remember that machines can collect, but they cannot care. They can highlight anomalies, but they cannot understand context. They can filter noise, but they cannot hear intention. That's the role of people. And that is why competitive intelligence, no matter how digital it becomes, must remain a *human-centered* craft. In a globalized world, where business is shaped not only by economics but by politics, culture, environment, and social sentiment, strategic listening is not a luxury—it's a necessity. Markets shift before balance sheets reflect the change. Consumer sentiment hardens long before quarterly earnings show the impact (Lagerborg et al, 2023). Regulatory trends can be felt years before they are formalized into law. Those who listen early, listen deeply, and listen well—across borders, sectors, and social layers—gain not just an informational advantage, but a *strategic one*. They get to shape their future rather than simply react to it. As we move toward more case studies in the following sections, it is important to carry this sensibility forward: intelligence is not about speed alone. It is about sensitivity. It is about presence. It is about *how* we pay attention—not just where. These examples from Singapore, Germany, Nigeria, and beyond remind us that the real currency of the future may not be data—but the capacity to hear what others have not yet noticed.

Digital Disruption and the New Language of Intelligence Gathering

There was a time when competitive intelligence followed a rhythm that, while intricate, was largely predictable (Zhao et al, 2024). Intelligence professionals collected news clippings, monitored trade journals, attended industry conferences, and relied heavily on networks of insiders to piece together the direction of market shifts. Intelligence gathering was often analog, discreet, methodical. It had its codes, its cadence, and its couriers. It was a practice shaped by scarcity—scarcity of access, of data, of transparency. Then came the digital deluge. In the span of just two decades, the world has gone from information scarcity to information saturation. Digital disruption has not merely changed how we gather intelligence—it has rewritten the language through which we understand competition itself. Everything now speaks. Devices speak. Platforms speak. Consumers speak. Algorithms speak, though not in voices we always understand. The signals are no longer subtle—they are relentless. Yet, the irony is inescapable: as the noise grows louder, true insight has become harder to hear. This is the paradox at the heart of competitive intelligence in the digital age. We are awash in data—clickstreams, sentiment analysis, mobile app behaviors, transaction logs, satellite imagery, facial recognition, real-time geopolitical trackers, and so much more. Every movement leaves a digital footprint. Every choice is a data point. In theory, we should know more than we ever did. In practice, we often feel more overwhelmed than ever before. The tools have evolved. But the human challenge remains the same: how do we turn noise into knowledge, and knowledge into timely action?

One of the most profound shifts brought by digital disruption is the breakdown of traditional boundaries (Gkeredakis et al, 2021). In the past, intelligence gathering operated along clear lines: public vs. private, domestic vs. international, internal vs. external. Now, those distinctions have blurred beyond recognition. Public discourse happens in private platforms. Domestic companies are influenced by global memes. External threats emerge from internal cultural blind spots. Intelligence is no longer about mapping a known field; it's about navigating an ever-shifting terrain where the boundaries change faster than the maps can be redrawn. Take, for instance, the transformation of social media into an intelligence goldmine—an unpredictable, chaotic, but undeniably rich source of real-time insight. Platforms like Twitter (or X), Reddit, TikTok, and LinkedIn are no longer just communication tools; they are cultural barometers, rumor mills, trend accelerators, and, at times, early-warning systems (Kayyali, 2025). Companies have been blindsided not by competitors' product launches, but by viral backlash from a single influencer post. Entire market valuations have shifted in hours due to social sentiment. In this environment, strategic listening—discussed previously—must now include cultural decoding, an ability to read between emojis and hashtags, to understand tone, irony, and the layered politics of digital identity. But beyond social platforms, digital disruption has opened the gates to unprecedented surveillance capabilities—some welcome, others unsettling. From scraping open-source code repositories to monitoring cross-border e-commerce flows in real time, intelligence professionals now wield tools that would have seemed like science fiction just a decade ago. And yet, the availability of tools does not automatically yield clarity. In fact, the abundance of tools can sometimes obscure the deeper work that intelligence demands. Dashboards can seduce us into thinking we understand trends. Real-time updates can make us reactive instead of reflective. There's a growing risk that CI becomes about *monitoring everything* rather than *understanding anything*.

This is where the "new language" of intelligence becomes vital—not just linguistically, but cognitively and culturally. Digital disruption has forced intelligence teams to learn a new grammar: a grammar of networks, of code, of data structures, and of digital behaviors. Understanding a competitor's strategy now might require analyzing app updates, patent filings in machine-readable formats, developer community conversations, or sudden changes in machine learning model parameters (Trabucco, 2024). In sectors like cybersecurity, biotech, fintech, and logistics, intelligence now speaks in APIs, in blockchain ledgers, in edge computing logs, and in predictive algorithmic modeling. But language is not just about symbols; it's about context, power, and meaning. The new language of intelligence requires fluency not only in technical terms but in the socio-political ecosystems that produce and interpret them. It's not enough to know what a new tool does; we must understand who is building it, what they believe, what constraints they face, and how their cultural assumptions shape their code. A facial recognition algorithm trained in one region may fail catastrophically in another, not because of flaws in data volume, but because of cultural mismatch in data diversity. Intelligence, then, must become *cross-disciplinary* by necessity. It is no longer enough to be a business strategist or a data analyst. The most effective intelligence practitioners are those who are part anthropologist, part coder, part ethicist, and part storyteller.

Let's consider a compelling case from the retail industry. A global fashion brand, long praised for its trend-spotting ability, began to notice a worrying decline in its market relevance in Southeast Asia (Gabriel, 2024). On paper, their supply chain was optimized. Their designs were aligned with global trends. Their pricing was competitive. But something wasn't landing. Traditional market research yielded few insights. Focus groups were inconclusive. So, the company took a new approach: they embedded an intelligence team not in the region's high-end malls, but in its digital ecosystems—peer-to-peer reselling apps, streetwear forums, and fan-made style mashup communities. What they found was a vibrant, dynamic fashion language that was not captured by trend forecasts or influencer campaigns. It was grounded in local nostalgia, recycled aesthetics, and hybrid cultural symbols that made no sense to Western fashion consultants. Armed with this digital ethnography, the brand partnered with local artists and reimagined its Southeast Asia collection—not as an export, but as a dialogue. Sales surged. But more importantly, trust returned. This wasn't just a win in branding; it was a triumph of listening to the digital language of a region on its own terms. It was intelligence not just as surveillance, but as cultural empathy.

Another illustrative example comes from the world of agritech, where digital disruption has radically changed how agricultural intelligence is gathered. A South American agribusiness cooperative, traditionally reliant on meteorological data and on-the-ground crop reports, began to experiment with satellite imaging and AI-powered soil analysis. The results were impressive—but what truly changed the game was their decision to open-source their intelligence tools and invite feedback from smallholder farmers. This act of transparency created a feedback loop that not only improved their predictions but unearthed hyper-local knowledge previously inaccessible through any digital system (Cruickshank, 2021). Here, disruption was not just technological—it was organizational and ethical. Intelligence became collaborative. The new language was one of inclusion, decentralization, and trust-building. The cooperative moved from a top-down model to a distributed one—less about control and more about coordination. And in doing so, it became more resilient, more adaptive, and more aligned with its broader community. Of course, digital disruption also brings with it profound ethical dilemmas. The boundary between insight and intrusion is thin. In some industries, particularly those where surveillance is embedded into business models—like e-commerce, social media, and smart devices—the line is not just thin, it is blurred by design. Companies track consumer behaviors with alarming granularity. Cookies, biometric data, voice patterns, location trails—all are harvested in the name of personalization, efficiency, and of course, competitive advantage.

Yet in this landscape, the question CI practitioners must ask is not "Can we gather this data?" but "Should we?". The new language of intelligence must include ethics as a fundamental syntax. It must account for consent, for bias, for unintended consequences. A CI operation that sacrifices trust for short-term advantage is building on sand. Reputation, once lost, is not easily regained (Levine, 2021). Consumers, regulators, and civil society are increasingly aware of data practices. Intelligence that ignores this broader shift toward digital accountability is not just unethical—it is *strategically naive*. As we grapple with these complexities, it's important to remember that digital disruption is not a single event—it is a continuous condition. It evolves. It mutates. What is cutting-edge today is obsolete tomorrow. New platforms emerge overnight. Algorithms are updated without notice. Competitors can pivot with startling speed. In such an environment, the role of competitive intelligence is not to establish fixed truths, but to maintain navigational clarity. CI becomes less about answers and more about *readiness*—the ability to see early, to act responsibly, and to adapt fast. This calls for a new kind of CI leadership. Leaders must not only invest in tools but build cultures of inquiry. They must foster diversity in their intelligence teams—not only in skillsets but in perspectives. They must break silos, reward questions, and value ambiguity. And they must empower their people not just to *collect information*, but to *challenge assumptions*. That's the real gift of digital disruption: not just more data, but more *possibilities*. But only if we have the courage and humility to rethink how we listen, how we learn, and how we lead. The new language of intelligence is not simply digital—it is adaptive, ethical, and human at its core. Digital disruption has changed the tempo, the vocabulary, and the channels through which intelligence flows. But it has not changed the ultimate aim: to understand the world well enough to make wiser choices in uncertain times. That task, timeless and urgent, remains ours to carry—with tools in our hands, yes, but with questions in our minds and integrity at our core.

Ethical Dilemmas and Data Boundaries in the Global Intelligence Arena

Ethics in competitive intelligence isn't a footnote—it's the heart of the discipline (Guessoum et al, 2022). In a world where access to information is easier than ever and the tools for surveillance grow more sophisticated by the hour, the ethical foundation of intelligence work is not just a matter of professional conduct—it is a matter of identity, of purpose, of trust. To ignore ethics in this domain is to reduce intelligence to espionage, insight to intrusion, and strategy to manipulation. And yet, in the global intelligence arena, where cultures, regulations, and corporate imperatives collide, ethics is rarely simple. It is contextual, fluid, and often contested. The digital age has blurred the lines between what is possible and what is permissible. Competitive intelligence professionals today operate within a borderless ecosystem, where the rules of one country may be considered invasive in another, and where what is legally allowed may still be morally troubling. We're no longer talking about the discreet collection of public information from annual reports and industry publications. We're talking about real-time behavioral tracking, sentiment mining from personal social media, geolocation data harvested from mobile apps, and even predictive models that infer private intentions from public actions. The ethical dilemmas now are not occasional—they are structural, constant, and embedded in the very architecture of how intelligence is gathered.

What complicates things further is the accelerating asymmetry between technological capacity and ethical oversight. The speed at which data can be collected, stored, analyzed, and acted upon far outpaces the ability of governments, institutions, or even companies themselves to fully understand or regulate it (Lin, 2025). And in the absence of clear, universal norms, much is left to interpretation, to organizational culture, to individual judgment. The boundaries of what's considered acceptable shift with each new platform, each new scandal, each geopolitical flare-up. Let's begin with a simple but profound question: what should be off-limits? This question alone invites a whirlwind of perspectives depending on who is answering. For some, anything publicly available on the internet is fair game. If a competitor posts product details on its website, or if an employee updates a LinkedIn profile with new job responsibilities, that's considered open-source intelligence. But is it ethical to use automated bots to scrape thousands of profiles without consent? Is it ethical to track social media behavior and build psychological profiles of employees at rival firms? Is it ethical to simulate customer experiences on competitor platforms simply to reverse-engineer their user experience? These are no longer edge cases—they are increasingly normalized practices. And just because they are common, or even legal, does not mean they are right.

One of the most persistent ethical grey zones in CI is the use of deception. In traditional intelligence operations—military, governmental, covert—the use of cover identities, misdirection, and psychological manipulation has been part of the toolkit. But in the corporate world, such tactics raise serious red flags. Consider the case of a Western tech firm that, in its effort to gain insight into a new Chinese market entrant, posed as a research institute to conduct "anonymous" interviews with mid-level employees of the rival. While no laws were broken and consent was technically obtained, the manipulation of identity and purpose breached ethical trust. The fallout wasn't immediate, but once revealed, the damage to the firm's reputation in Asia was deep and enduring. Trust, once lost in intelligence circles, is rarely regained. The ethics of CI are not only about tactics; they are also about power. Who has the right to collect data? Whose privacy is sacrificed for insight? Whose voices are excluded from the intelligence process, and whose narratives are privileged? These questions become even more pressing in cross-border contexts where data sovereignty, surveillance culture, and political regimes differ widely. A global consumer brand operating in Europe may be bound by GDPR regulations that emphasize user consent, transparency, and the right to be forgotten (Bharti & Aryal, 2023). But the same brand operating in less regulated markets may find itself in possession of data that would be illegal to collect back home. What then? Should the brand apply its home ethics universally? Or is it justified in adapting its intelligence practices to local legal laxity? Too often, companies choose the path of least resistance. But this is shortsighted. Ethics is not only a moral compass; it is a strategic asset. Organizations that develop internal CI policies aligned with the highest standards, rather than the loosest legal loopholes, are more likely to build sustainable competitive advantages rooted in integrity and resilience. In an era of rising consumer consciousness, stakeholder scrutiny, and whistleblower activism, intelligence that is gained through questionable means can backfire spectacularly. Ethical lapses in CI are no longer internal matters; they become public scandals, fuel for competitors, and catalysts for regulatory crackdowns.

The internal culture of intelligence teams matters deeply. In some organizations, CI professionals operate in isolation, with little oversight or ethical guidance. The pressure to deliver actionable insights can lead to a kind of moral erosion—where the end justifies the means, and "everyone else is doing it" becomes a mantra. This is dangerous. Ethics in CI must be proactive, not reactive. It must be taught, modeled, and embedded into every phase of the intelligence cycle—from planning to collection to analysis to dissemination. Transparency is another ethical frontier in CI. How transparent should organizations be about their own data practices? In B2B contexts, companies routinely monitor competitor pricing, procurement patterns, and innovation cycles (Hall, 2022). But what if the roles were reversed? What if your competitor is analyzing your internal hiring patterns or tracking the digital movements of your executives? Are you comfortable being scrutinized under the same light? Ethics often asks us to consider how we would feel if the same methods were applied to us. This brings us to the principle of reciprocity—a deeply human, often forgotten lens in the ethical evaluation of intelligence. Reciprocity reminds us that intelligence gathering does not happen in a vacuum. It creates a relational dynamic. How you listen, how you observe, how you interpret others sends a signal about how you expect to be treated. And in competitive markets where partnerships, joint ventures, and alliances are common, this ethical signaling matters. A company that engages in ethically questionable CI practices may win a short-term edge, but lose long-term trust with potential partners.

Another subtle, but equally important dimension is the ethics of interpretation. Intelligence is not just about collection—it's about meaning-making. And meaning can be distorted by bias, assumption, or manipulation. Misinterpreting a competitor's move, projecting malice where there is none, or framing data to support a predetermined narrative are all forms of ethical failure—not because they involve illegal activity, but because they corrupt the very purpose of intelligence: to see clearly. Ethics in CI is not only about what you gather, but how you think about what you've gathered. To navigate these complexities, some organizations are beginning to formalize ethical charters for competitive intelligence, setting clear boundaries for acceptable behavior and reinforcing values such as integrity, discretion, respect, and transparency. These charters are not legal documents—they are cultural compasses. They send a message internally and externally that the pursuit of insight will not come at the expense of dignity or fairness. But more often than not, these are still rare. The field of CI still lacks universally accepted codes of conduct akin to those in journalism or medicine. This absence is problematic, particularly as intelligence becomes more digitized, more automated, and more vulnerable to misuse.

AI brings its own ethical baggage. Algorithms are increasingly being used to collect, sort, and analyze intelligence (Esposito, 2022). But AI systems inherit the biases of their creators, and their opacity makes accountability difficult. If an AI-driven monitoring tool flags a competitor's "aggressive hiring strategy" based on flawed criteria, and that leads to a strategic overreaction, who is to blame? The algorithm? The analyst? The decision-maker? Ethics in the age of automation requires new frameworks of responsibility—ones that acknowledge both human and machine agency. We must consider the ethical burden of *inaction*. Intelligence is often framed as power—but it is also a responsibility. What happens when a company uncovers intelligence that reveals exploitation, corruption, or systemic harm by a competitor? Does it remain silent to protect its competitive position? Or does it act—through whistleblowing, regulatory reporting, or public accountability? These moments test the ethical soul of an organization. They reveal whether intelligence is being used solely to win—or also to lead. Ethical competitive intelligence is not about being perfect—it is about being principled. It's about navigating ambiguity with self-awareness. It's about resisting the easy shortcuts and embracing the harder path of transparency and trust. It's about remembering that behind every data point is a person, a system, a consequence. The global intelligence arena is vast, complex, and full of opportunity. But the boundaries within it are not marked by barbed wire or legal codes—they are drawn by the conscience of those who operate within it. Those who respect these boundaries, who pause before crossing the line, who ask the harder questions—*they* are the ones who will not only succeed, but endure.

Lessons from the Field: Patterns, Pitfalls, and Practical Frameworks

There's something unique about wisdom that emerges from lived experience. In competitive intelligence, it's not the models in textbooks or the theories in boardrooms that reveal the whole story—it's the quiet truths learned in the trenches: the failed assumptions, the subtle shifts, the insights that come too late or arrive just in time. Real competitive intelligence, when practiced well, is messy, iterative, human. It does not always follow linear logic or neat frameworks (Oosthuizen, 2022). Instead, it lives at the intersection of judgment and uncertainty, often shaped more by questions than by answers. And the only way to truly understand its power—and its limits—is to listen to what the field has taught us. Over the years, across geographies and industries, certain patterns have emerged that point to recurring truths in the practice of CI. These are not rules, but rhythms—observations that appear time and again, regardless of sector or strategy. The first is deceptively simple: the best intelligence is often already inside the organization—it's just not being heard. Sales teams hear things on the ground long before the data shows a trend. Customer service agents pick up on dissatisfaction that competitors might soon exploit. Regional teams spot subtle regulatory signals that could shift the strategic landscape. But too often, this intelligence is unstructured, unvalidated, or simply overlooked. Many organizations still treat intelligence as something that flows downward from analysts to executives, when in reality, it should flow laterally and upward—a conversation, not a report.

This means that building a CI function isn't just about hiring experts—it's about designing a listening culture where information is shared, context is valued, and curiosity is encouraged. The pattern is clear: companies that treat intelligence as a *distributed mindset*—rather than a centralized function—tend to identify opportunities earlier and respond to threats with greater agility.

Another recurring lesson is that timing is everything. Intelligence has a half-life. A brilliant insight delivered too late is as useless as ignorance. The problem is that many organizations confuse perfection with relevance. Analysts are pushed to gather "just a bit more data" or to wait for more confirmation before delivering their findings. But intelligence is not academia. It doesn't wait for peer review. The most successful practitioners understand that speed and imperfection are often more useful than slow precision. They deliver insights when they are actionable, not when they are fully confirmed. This doesn't mean sacrificing accuracy—it means accepting that in fast-moving markets, a reasonably accurate signal now is worth more than a perfect signal too late. Then there are the common pitfalls—those recurring traps that even seasoned professionals fall into. One of the most dangerous is the tendency to overvalue competitive benchmarking (Zerbato, 2024). While it's tempting to constantly track what rivals are doing, there is a fine line between awareness and mimicry. Too many companies fall into the trap of strategic imitation, making reactive moves based on competitor behavior without fully understanding the underlying context. The result? Homogenization. Everyone starts to look the same, and true innovation suffers. The field reminds us, again and again, that competitive intelligence is not about *copying competitors*—it's about *understanding them*, so you can do something different and better. Closely related is the pitfall of confirmation bias. This is especially common when CI teams are under pressure to validate a decision that leadership has already made. Instead of exploring the landscape with open curiosity, the intelligence process becomes a search for evidence to support a pre-existing narrative. The field teaches a hard truth here: intelligence must be allowed to surprise us, to challenge our assumptions, even to contradict our intentions. Otherwise, it becomes theater—an exercise in false legitimacy rather than genuine discovery.

Another recurring misstep is failing to operationalize intelligence. Many companies invest heavily in data gathering and analysis, only to leave insights stranded in reports, slide decks, or digital dashboards (Bobylev, 2023). There's a mistaken belief that the job ends with insight delivery. But insight alone changes nothing. For intelligence to drive value, it must be woven into the decision-making process—not occasionally, but systematically. This means building feedback loops between CI teams and business units. It means aligning intelligence outputs with specific strategic decisions—whether related to pricing, market entry, innovation, or risk management. The practical lesson is clear: an unused insight is wasted potential. Yet despite the challenges, the field has also given us practical frameworks—not rigid formulas, but flexible approaches that help make intelligence more usable, humane, and impactful. One such framework is what many practitioners call the "3C loop": Context, Curiosity, and Consequence. At the heart of this model is a simple idea: good intelligence is always rooted in an understanding of the broader context—it doesn't just answer *what* is happening, but *why* it matters, and *what could follow*. Curiosity drives the process forward, keeping teams alert to the unexpected, the peripheral, the emerging. And consequence reminds us that intelligence is not academic—it exists to inform decisions that carry real-world implications.

Another useful lens is the "Signal-to-Decision Pathway"—a mental model that encourages practitioners to trace how weak signals move through the organization and become actionable. Where does the signal originate? Who hears it first? How is it validated, shared, interpreted, and finally acted upon? Mapping this pathway often reveals bottlenecks, blind spots, or organizational habits that dilute or delay intelligence. By improving the flow from signal to decision, organizations increase their strategic responsiveness—not by working harder, but by working smarter. The most resilient CI practices are also deeply adaptive. They don't cling to rigid taxonomies or outdated templates (Bajpai et al, 2024). They evolve with the business, with the market, and with the tools available. And above all, they stay close to the people who will ultimately act on the intelligence. One pattern that surfaces repeatedly in field interviews is that CI professionals who spend time with decision-makers—not just delivering insights, but understanding their needs, timelines, and pressures—produce more relevant and more impactful work. It's a reminder that intelligence is not a product—it's a relationship. There is also a growing recognition that CI must become interdisciplinary. The days when competitive intelligence could be managed solely by MBAs or data scientists are gone. Today's intelligence professionals must speak the language of behavioral economics, geopolitics, cultural studies, ethics, and even design. They must understand how social movements impact consumer behavior, how political instability disrupts supply chains, how algorithmic changes shape digital visibility. The field reminds us that intelligence is not confined to spreadsheets—it breathes in the cultural and human dynamics that shape every market move.

One of the most humbling lessons from the field is the realization that you can do everything "right" and still be blindsided (Dubiel, 2022). The intelligence was gathered. The warning signs were there. The analysis was solid. But no one listened. Or no one acted. Or the moment passed. This happens more often than most would like to admit. And when it does, it reminds us that competitive intelligence is ultimately an *invitation*, not a guarantee. It invites organizations to see more clearly, to prepare more wisely, to choose more intentionally. But it cannot force those choices. The final mile—where insight meets action—is always the hardest. And perhaps the most human lesson of all is that CI is a long game. It is not about scoring quick wins or feeding the next quarter's strategy slides. It's about building institutional memory. About developing a way of thinking that resists panic, embraces complexity, and asks better questions over time. The best CI teams do not measure their value solely by how many reports they produce, but by how they shape conversations, how they expand awareness, how they challenge complacency. In this sense, intelligence becomes less about answers and more about perspective. To close, the field of competitive intelligence is not a science, nor a pure art. It is a discipline, a craft, and, in its highest form, a culture. The patterns, pitfalls, and practical frameworks shared here are not ends in themselves—they are starting points. What matters most is how they are lived: with integrity, humility, creativity, and care. Because in the end, the value of intelligence lies not in the data, nor even in the insight—but in the people who choose to listen to it, learn from it, and act with wisdom.

CONCLUSION

As we reach the final reflections of this chapter, it becomes increasingly clear that competitive intelligence is not a peripheral function—it is a defining capability in the digital age. The case studies presented have demonstrated that organizations which embed CI into their strategic core—treating it not as a report, but as a way of thinking—are the ones that remain adaptive, resilient, and forward-looking in a constantly shifting marketplace. Whether in banking, biotechnology, e-commerce, or traditional industries, the same lesson echoes: the firms that see further are those who listen more closely—not just to their competitors, but to their customers, regulators, and even cultural shifts that precede market trends. The chapter also surfaces a sobering truth. Many organizations still fall short—not for lack of tools or technology, but because they underestimate the complexity of intelligence work. There is a persistent temptation to automate insight, to compress nuance into dashboards, to prioritize speed over sense-making. In doing so, companies risk acting on fragments rather than the fuller picture. They may identify a competitor's move but misread its intention. They may collect data on customer behavior but miss the deeper emotional triggers that drive loyalty or defection. What the case studies underscore is that competitive intelligence must be both rigorous and reflective. It must draw from both hard data and soft signals, blending quantitative evidence with qualitative judgment. And perhaps most critically, it must be practiced ethically. In an era when digital surveillance is becoming normalized and data privacy increasingly contested, the lines between intelligence and intrusion are thin. The best CI professionals—regardless of industry—understand this tension. They know that trust, integrity, and strategic restraint are not weaknesses but long-term assets.

Another key insight that emerges is the importance of organizational culture in sustaining effective CI. Intelligence cannot thrive in silos. It must be integrated into daily conversations, strategic planning sessions, and innovation processes. In high-performing organizations, CI is not outsourced to a distant analyst or confined to a monthly report—it is distributed, alive, and responsive. Executives ask sharper questions. Teams challenge assumptions. And decision-making becomes not only faster but more grounded. Looking ahead, the future of competitive intelligence will likely be shaped by two forces in tandem: technological advancement and human insight. Machine learning, natural language processing, and predictive analytics will continue to evolve CI capabilities—but they will not replace the need for human discernment. On the contrary, as machines get better at collecting data, humans must get better at asking the right questions, framing problems, and interpreting signals with humility and depth. This chapter ultimately makes a case for rehumanizing competitive intelligence. In an age where noise is abundant and trust is fragile, intelligence must be more than clever tactics or slick reports—it must be an ethical, strategic, and meaning-driven pursuit. The organizations that embrace this ethos won't just win markets. They will shape them.

REFERENCES

Bajpai, G., Schildmeijer, M., Mishra, M., & Piwosz, P. (2024). *CI/CD Design Patterns: Design and implement CI/CD using proven design patterns*. Packt Publishing Ltd.

Bharti, S. S., & Aryal, S. K. (2023). The right to privacy and an implication of the EU General Data Protection Regulation (GDPR) in Europe: Challenges to the companies. *Journal of Contemporary European Studies*, *31*(4), 1391–1402. DOI: 10.1080/14782804.2022.2130193

Bisht, N. S., Noronha, E., & Tripathy, A. K. (2025). Digital technologies exacerbating mission drift in microfinance institutions: Evidence from India. *Information and Organization*, *35*(1), 100541. DOI: 10.1016/j.infoandorg.2024.100541

Bobylev, T. (2023). Dashboard for data-driven decision support in small and medium enterprises: a web-based approach.

Cruickshank, P. (2021). Evaluation of engagement with hyperlocal e-participation systems by citizens and representatives (Doctoral dissertation).

Dubiel, M. (2022). The blind side of art: Visual impairment as a resource in the work of Mexican artists. *Przegląd Socjologii Jakościowej*, *18*(3), 120–137. DOI: 10.18778/1733-8069.18.3.07

Esposito, E. (2022). *Artificial communication: How algorithms produce social intelligence*. MIT Press. DOI: 10.7551/mitpress/14189.001.0001

Fannon, S. R., Munive-Hernandez, J. E., & Campean, F. (2022). Mastering continuous improvement (CI): The roles and competences of mid-level management and their impact on the organisation's CI capability. *The TQM Journal*, *34*(1), 102–124. DOI: 10.1108/TQM-03-2021-0083

Gabriel, A. K. (2024). *Cultural Intelligence for Marketers: Building an inclusive marketing strategy*. Kogan Page Publishers.

Gkeredakis, M., Lifshitz-Assaf, H., & Barrett, M. (2021). Crisis as opportunity, disruption and exposure: Exploring emergent responses to crisis through digital technology. *Information and Organization, 31*(1), 100344. DOI: 10.1016/j.infoandorg.2021.100344

Guessoum, M. A., Djiroun, R., & Boukhalfa, K. (2022, May). Causality analysis method and model related to why-question answering in business intelligence context. In *International Conference on Computing Systems and Applications* (pp. 15-26). Cham: Springer International Publishing. DOI: 10.1007/978-3-031-12097-8_2

Hall, S. (2022). *Innovative B2B marketing: new models, processes and theory*. Kogan Page Publishers.

Heath, J. B. (2022). Making sense of security. *The American Journal of International Law, 116*(2), 289–339. DOI: 10.1017/ajil.2021.63

Hinz, J., Stephens, J. P., & Van Oosten, E. B. (2022). Toward a pedagogy of connection: A critical view of being relational in listening. *Management Learning, 53*(1), 76–97. DOI: 10.1177/13505076211047506

Kanellopoulos, A. N., & Ioannidis, A. (2024). Leveraging competitive intelligence in offensive cyber counterintelligence: An operational approach for the Shipping industry. *Security and Defence Quarterly, 48*(4), 80–92.

Kayyali, M. (2025). E-Learning Platforms and Their Influence on Lifelong Learning. In Impact of Digitalization on Education and Social Sustainability (pp. 155-176). IGI Global.

Kluger, A. N., & Itzchakov, G. (2022). The power of listening at work. *Annual Review of Organizational Psychology and Organizational Behavior, 9*(1), 121–146. DOI: 10.1146/annurev-orgpsych-012420-091013

Lagerborg, A., Pappa, E., & Ravn, M. O. (2023). Sentimental business cycles. *The Review of Economic Studies, 90*(3), 1358–1393. DOI: 10.1093/restud/rdac053

Lee, E. A. (2024, October). Certainty vs. Intelligence. In International Conference on Bridging the Gap between AI and Reality (pp. 20-32). Cham: Springer Nature Switzerland.

Levine, D. K. (2021). The reputation trap. *Econometrica, 89*(6), 2659–2678. DOI: 10.3982/ECTA17891

Lin, X. (2025). A Model of Big Data-Based Governance: China's National Government Big Data Platform and an Analysis of Its Governance Competence. *Chinese Political Science Review*, •••, 1–40. DOI: 10.1007/s41111-025-00279-1

Madureira, L., Popovič, A., & Castelli, M. (2023). Competitive intelligence empirical validation and application: Foundations for knowledge advancement and relevance to practice. *Journal of Information Science*, •••, 01655515231191221. DOI: 10.1177/01655515231191221

Olah, D. (2024). Subversion as the Modus Operandi-China's integration of influence operations into the Belt and Road Initiative as a mode of disrupting geopolitical powers in Vietnam and Pakistan.

Oosthuizen, J. H. (2022). A fourth industrial revolution integrated intelligence taxonomy and measurement framework for top management.

Singireddy, J. (2025). *Smart Finance: Harnessing Artificial Intelligence to Transform Tax, Accounting, Payroll, and Credit Management for the Digital Age*. Deep Science Publishing.

Tanev, S. (2024). Design Thinking for Competitive Intelligence in a Digital Business Transformation Context. Journal of Intelligence Studies in Business, 14(Special Issue 1), 57-85.

Trabucco, T. G. (2024). Artificial intelligence as a tool for research and development in European patent law.

Wing, C. (2025). *Four Future Seasons: How to anticipate and prepare for multiple potential futures*. Penguin Random House South Africa.

Zerbato, G. (2024). Relative Valuation for Value Investing: theoretical aspects and empirical evidence.

Zhao, J., Wang, X., Yao, X., & Xi, X. (2024). Digital-intelligence transformation, for better or worse? The roles of pace, scope and rhythm. *Internet Research*. Advance online publication. DOI: 10.1108/INTR-12-2023-1125

Chapter 3
Competitive Intelligence in Sustainability and Corporate Social Responsibility (CSR)

Michael Oyedele Oyenuga
https://orcid.org/0000-0001-9921-5711
Woxsen University, Hyderabad, India

ABSTRACT

As organisations increasingly recognise the importance of sustainable development, corporate social responsibility has emerged as a pivotal strategy for fostering long-term success and gaining a competitive advantage in the marketplace. In this chapter, we dive into the relationship between competitive intelligence, sustainability, and corporate social responsibility to examine how firms can leverage competitive intelligence to create sustainability practices and CSR activities that help address social challenges and create advantages for the firm. Systematically, the examination addressed empirical evidence linking CSR to superior financial performance, competitive advantage, and investment efficiency. This would contribute significantly toward the paradigm shift of competitive intelligence for CSR, thus explicitly enabling capabilities for becoming knowledge-based, advocating the innovations, developing the reputation, and infusing organisational resilience.

DOI: 10.4018/979-8-3373-2690-0.ch003

INTRODUCTION

As consumers, regulators, and other stakeholders place increasing expectations on companies to operate sustainably, integrating Corporate Social Responsibility (CSR) into their corporate strategies is increasingly becoming critical for businesses. CSR includes a company's promise to direct its processes so that it has an overall positive impact on society. No longer being considered merely as a compliance issue or a means to improve the reputation of the company, CSR is now recognised as being an essential part of the competitive strategy and operational resilience of the company (Yu et al., 2017; Khương et al., 2021; Joo et al., 2017). Carefully orchestrated CSR practices in institutions foster the realisation of societal goals and maintain the competitive advantage by the development of better relations with stakeholders, a reputable brand name, trust, customer faithfulness and so on (Choi et al., 2019; Anokye et al., 2022; Tu n, 2013).

CI is the legal and ethical set of practices that collects and analyses information on competitors, boosts market capacity and studies technology performance (Bartes, 2015; Li et al., 2024). It provides firms with an opportunity for the energetic foresight of their rivals' behaviour and triggers a corresponding response to changes within their dynamic environment (Dela et al., 2024; Yu et al., 2017). As an example, CI is practised within the sustainability domain, providing practitioners with insights that can aid in monitoring changing trends, stakeholder expectations, unmet needs, patterns of innovation, and gaps in the real-world implementation of CSR activities. Consequently, competitive intelligence can be incorporated into firms' CSR model, by making it possible to adopt a perspective that is dynamic, proactive, and that favours the acceptance of innovative solutions that are profitable and socially responsible (Lu et al., 2020; Zhao & Du, 2017).

CSR practice could enhance the investment strategy of firms (Li et al., 2024) and prevent operating risk (Dela et al., 2024), and had an impact on the financial flexibility of firms (Ding-song & Li, 2023). Furthermore, insertion of robust CSR enables achievement of not only better financial performance in corporations but also a more competitive market; rather, consumers' sense of responsibility may yet matter for their purchasing

(Fernández-Kranz & Santaló, 2010; Yu & Liang, 2020). CI serves as the interface between CSR strategies and the competitive advantage perspective that can be used to assess competitive firms' practices towards CSR forms both in compliance-based and distinctiveness-based terms, with regards to being socially responsible and innovative in their businesses (Belu & M nescu, 2013; Kan & Xiang, 2023; Yadav & Sinha, 2021).

This chapter thus has the objective to illuminate the symbiotic relationship among the three phenomena: competitive intelligence, sustainability and corporate social responsibility. This chapter aims to examine the theoretical foundations, the available empirical knowledge, and actual case studies of how CI can be employed as a vehicle to advance sustainability and corporate social responsibility (CSR) agendas, with positive consequences to firm performance and societal well-being.

Understanding Competitive Intelligence and Sustainability

Competitive intelligence (CI) is an ongoing and, in some cases, increasingly systematic process for gathering, analysing and, in some cases, disseminating information on a competitor's external operating environment (local, regional, national or foreign) as well as that of industry or market. CI has emerged as a strategic lever to assist companies in these sustainability challenges and opportunities, and as a mechanism to integrate sustainable practices into a competitive set of capabilities that are required to win in the industry. This enables firms to monitor the sustainability initiatives of their competitors, monitor stakeholder expectations and discover ESG trends that are taking place (Nasri 2011). For instance, firms can consider competitor CSR strategies to benchmark their implementation and adoption of sustainability practice, not to fall behind on following consumer expectations about responsible business actions (Al-Omoush et al., 2023). Based on the intelligence from CI, organisations generate new solutions that address not just environmental sustainability requirements but also market wants, as well as enhanced brand loyalty and competitive placement (Kim et al., 2024).

As CI and business intelligence interact synergistically by providing the framework to build knowledge development or generating a sustainable competitive edge, the integration of business intelligence and competitive intelligence enables firms to adopt focused routines with which to build sustainability initiatives, whose nuances are to large degrees shaped by wise business decisions (Nixon & Thato, 2016). This is crucial because, in lending the latter the efficiencies to carry out such economically and socially responsible initiatives that would promote the firm's conduct practices that reduce waste and reduce their carbon footprint while helping to enable their profit optimisation through better resource allocation (Rith & Spinelli, 2024).

CI also contributes to building the resilience of organisations, which is important when uncertainty is a part of sustainability (Al-Omoush et al., 2023). The capability for rapid strategy agility, as a function of intelligence, is increasingly their key to survival in the long run, as companies are affected by external pressure from factors like regulation and consumer behaviour. This is more of a priority, in part because of rapidly developing sustainability standards and a changing competitive landscape.

Competitive intelligence also helps to build a bridge between CSR actions and broader business goals. With the help of CI, companies can demonstrate CSR opportunities in line with the needs of pertinent stakeholders without compromising their corporate ethics, ensuring sustainability projects are about being proactive as well as reactive (Bhattacharyya & Jha, 2020). This would significantly enhance CSR-impact and enhance the corporate reputation as well as stakeholder confidence (Frishammar et al., 2012; Omale et al., 2024; Oyedele, 2025).

Evolution of Corporate Social Responsibility and Sustainability

While Corporate Social Responsibility (CSR) is not a novel approach, it has developed with time due to changes in social attitudes, economic conditions, and the environment. It goes back to the early 20th century, when the ideas that would develop into ethical business practices and a corporation's responsibility to society were solidifying. CSR was seen as a philanthropic engagement where organisations made donations and elevated their social image for a positive brand image. On the other hand, with the emergence of global challenges (such as poverty, climate change or social inequality), CSR would evolve and move into a more strategic dimension, for its integration into a staged approach of corporate sustainability (Vorozheykina et al. 2019). Consequently, CSR has become a strategic factor necessary for gaining competitive advantage, improving the reputation of the corporate brand (Oyenuga et al., 2021), and ensuring the loyalty of customers (Trivellas et al., 2019; Oyenuga & Fredrick, 2023).

In contrast to classical CSR, modern CSR highlights that a corporation has an obligation not only to its shareholders but to multiple stakeholders, including employees, customers, suppliers and the societies in which it operates (Chernev & Blair, 2015). Increasingly, companies are being called to go beyond compliance and deepen social and environmental considerations into the core of how they do business and contribute to sustainable development. As an example, businesses that implement green technologies and marketing practices not only reduce risk exposure to environmental factors but often achieve improved financial performance as a result of efficiency gains and consumer demand for sustainable products (Glavas, 2016; Oyedele et al., 2023).

Furthermore, as stakeholders increasingly call for businesses to adopt sustainable practices, CSR approaches will have to be holistic and quantifiable. In this environment, advanced frameworks of CSR initiatives focusing on transparency and accountability, are being adopted towards improved corporate governance in general (Deitiana, 2015). Companies should report their sustainability footprint and key measures in social, economic and environmental impact. This trend is in line with increasing demands for transparency and accountability in corporate practices (Kang & Chiu, 2016; Xia et al., 2018).

Against this backdrop, CSR has become a core aspect of business operations as corporations seek to integrate it into their governance frameworks. CSR without this kind of supportive culture isn't effective because a supportive culture in the workplace encourages employees to engage, which creates greater employee engagement, better brand loyalty, and stronger community relations; all of which contribute to a holistic corporate ideology focusing on long-term goals (Kai-xing & Sun, 2021 and Guo, 2020).

Hence, CSR is no longer considered just as a cost but as an investment, which causes different businesses and companies to be concerned about embedding the companies' strategic social responsibility in their operational model (Chung et al., 2018).

Having said that, as little as Corporate Social Responsibility have turned into part of the corporate lifestyle. CSR has made a long journey from being a component of philanthropy to now an integral part of sustainability, with its role spanning practices designed to affect social and environmental outcomes. Organisations evolve in response to both societal expectations and conditions of grappling with environmental challenges in the years ahead; the CSR and sustainability relationship will continue to carry weight for organisational success.

Intersection of Competitive Intelligence, Corporate Social Responsibility, and Sustainable Business Strategy

Connecting Competitive Intelligence (CI), corporate social responsibility (CSR), and sustainable business strategy is a key component in contemporary organisational management. As part of this shift, access to data has led to the increasing demand of stakeholders for businesses to act more responsibly within society and the planet, especially considering the numerous environmental and social challenges we are facing today, making understanding the relationships among the three aspects crucial for firms that want to gain a competitive advantage. Competitive Intelligence is a systematic development of information about rivals and the competitive environment for short- and long-term decision-making (Nasri, 2011). Its main form of application in the field of CSR is as a tool for organisations to assimilate stakeholder expectations to discover the best forms of sustainability.

The integration of new and modern technologies such as CI into the existing CSR frameworks enables organisations to obtain a clear picture of the impact of their social responsibility initiatives, achieve compliance with the evolving regulations on sustainability and CSR, and keep a competitive edge in the market. For instance, firms that analyse their competitors' approach on the Accountable Sustainable Development (ASD) level discover a voiding strategy in their policies and practices and conform to emerging sustainability criteria (Al-Omoush et al., 2023).

Sustainable practices need to be integrated as they are crucial for the survival and competitiveness of businesses, as businesses become aware of measuring their impact on the environment and society (Lazarenko et al., 2021). By adopting a focused CI approach, organisations can identify innovation avenue pockets that add to operational efficiency and sustainability. Such alignments enhance corporate reputation and stakeholder trust, both of which are key factors in sustainable business longevity (Giannoni et al., 2017).

Moreover, there is a need to merge CSR and Sustainable strategy to foster an organisational culture of responsibility, utilising the insights provided by CI. Hence, this interdependence allows organisations to transition from mere compliance to the implementation of sustainability initiatives. When business intelligence with competitive intelligence as the engine generates business intelligence, the establishment of correlative CSR strategies could use the data as a basis, when high-quality CSR construction has become the basic business strategy of enterprises, it will promote the implementation of sustainable development of the enterprises, in this way CSR construction is not only beneficial to the creation of value in society, but also brings competitive benefits to enterprises (Liu & Xu, 2022). Thus, organisations that successfully employ CI as part of their CSR and sustainability strategies not only instil a sense of purpose but also income resilience. Such resilience stems from its adaptive flexibility and agility, allowing firms to respond to variations in the market and stakeholders (Al-Omoush et al., 2023; Nixon & Thato, 2016).

Moreover, leveraging CI in CSR initiatives creates a feedback loop that drives organisations to do better. The CI–based measures may be viewed as a means for firms to conduct assessments of their CSR program impacts into the social environment (negative CSR impacts, again, are between the lines for competitive intelligence) and speed up the time line for them to develop to keep apace of stakeholder (not competitor) expectations, thus contributing to economic futures (Muntean, 2018). By having this program in place, efficiency is added to the CSR program, which helps companies to enjoy and sustain an edge over the competition in the long run.

That's not to say competitive intelligence, corporate social responsibility, and sustainability-focused business strategy are not at the heart of every company that wishes to survive and thrive in the 21st-century marketplace. CI performs an iterative forward-looking "close up" and is built on scenario-building and trend-forecasting tools that anticipate stakeholder needs and facilitate system-wide innovations. Through further acknowledging the value of such aspects, they are in addition not only able to position themselves for long-term success, but also affect a positive, lasting impression on society and the environment.

Theoretical Foundations and Key Concepts

Competitive Intelligence (CI) has emerged as an influential strategic discriminator defining key business decisions over the past two decades and, more recently, positively influencing sustainability and Corporate Social Responsibility (CSR).

CI is an iterative process that links the gathering of data with analysis and strategy formulation to categorise institutional objectives and competitive environments (Maungwa & Laughton, 2023; Biran et al., 2013). For CI to be effective, information and intelligence should be seamlessly translated into actionable data. It is this cycle that allows organisations to readily respond to these novel sustainability and CSR trends adaptively, thus fostering the capacity to build resilience (Martins et al., 2023; Obonyo & Kilika, 2020). Theoretical development on intelligence domains can be described as follows: strategic intelligence, operational intelligence and marketing intelligence.

Strategic intelligence enables organisations to foresee competitive change, figure out what market shifts mean, identify where to play and how to win, and forge and act upon a plan. By assimilating strategic friendship in their organisations, firms can develop a proactive strategy to meet their objectives, manage risks and exploit new opportunities. It isn't simply data analysis but also harvesting information, interpreting it, and incorporating it into executable plans to underpin higher-level decisions ("Impact of Marketing Intelligence on Effectiveness of Decision Making: An Empirical Study," 2023).

Operational intelligence is the way to analyse real-time information and data from different operating processes in a company. This is the intelligence that makes operations more efficient and effective by making in-the-moment decisions more informed. Using operational intelligence, enterprises can streamline processes, allocate resources more effectively, and make their workforce more productive through data-driven decision-making. This type of intelligence frequently imploys business intelligence tools and analytics to follow performance metrics, to recognise bottlenecks, and to support process enhancements (Rayed, 2019; Lies, 2019).

Marketing intelligence is about the routine collection and analysis of information that will lead to market understanding, informed actions and decisions, and the consideration of the competitive experience. This information is utilised by companies to discover customer needs and wants, competitor capabilities and strategies and effective promotion tactics. These companies using market research can develop and refine more market-friendly products and services, and increase customer satisfaction, resulting in larger sales and profits. Serialisation of marketing intelligence will enable firms to make decisions concerning campaign development, pricing economics and market positioning (Ismaeel et al., 2023).

These domains collectively give a full view of competitive context and help the companies to explore novel directions for sustainability (Amaral et al., 2012). CI is not only applicable to information gathering, but also a set of policies for developing strategies to ensure the survival of the organisation while maximising shareholder value (Cavallo et al., 2020; Nenzhelele, 2016). Research suggests that firms that have sounder CI systems in place are more likely to undertake proactive sustainability efforts, that is, to be market-leading (Tarnovskaya, 2023).

Additionally, the association between sustainability and competitive advantage is guided by the concept of SCA (sustainable competitive advantage). In their pursuit of sustainability, organizations often find new opportunities for innovation and new core competencies (Wang, 2021; Tarnovskaya, 2023). SCA is not only relevant for companies with sustainability programs as a tool to obtain brand loyalty but it is a way to profitability, creating value and solving market problems, as companies would take over competitors not doing so in the market place with no other competitors to give such solutions (Stoyanova & Angelova, 2018; Nawangsari & Sutawidjaya, 2021).

Further, CI practices and sustainability projects add a lot of value to the organisation in terms of stakeholder expectation comprehension and business strategy harmonisation with societal trends (Palilingan & Batmetan, 2019; Cavallo et al., 2020). Not only do organisations comply with regulatory frameworks by engaging in competitive intelligence well, but they also position themselves as leaders in sustainable business. Such tensions are in congruence with theories on environmental management and resource-based perspectives that argue firms ability to combine resources is of the fundamentals underpinning the results of sustainability performance as well as competitive landscape (Wang et al., 2023; Srivastava et al., 2013; Liao et al., 2016).

RELEVANT THEORIES INTERSECTING COMPETITIVE INTELLIGENCE, CORPORATE SOCIAL RESPONSIBILITY, AND SUSTAINABLE BUSINESS STRATEGY

Multiple theoretical lenses have shaped the development of Corporate Social Responsibility (CSR), Competitive Intelligence (CI) and sustainable business strategy that govern organisation behaviour and approach to decision making. Theories like Stakeholder Theory, the Triple Bottom Line, and Shared Value accentuate the importance of integrating social responsibility into the core of business ventures.

Stakeholder Theory

Stakeholder Theory asserts that organisations have responsibilities to all their stakeholders, not just to the owners of their stock. This theory emphasises the obligation of businesses to consider multiple stakeholders, including employees, customers, suppliers, and the community, in strategic decision-making (Darnall, et al., 2010; Dmytriyev, et al., 2021). The application of stakeholder theory in businesses is more comprehensive, since CSR is integrated into the corporate strategy. Following the principles of

Stakeholder Theory, firms can use competitive intelligence for recognising the requirements and perceptions of their stakeholders and tend to adapt their CSR activities when needed (Dmytriyev et al., 2021; Hörisch et al., 2014). This is desirable for companies because they can take advantage of it, for example by claiming and strengthening their image (and relationship with stakeholders), which can evolve into a competitive advantage in the long term (Tinonetsana & Musariwa, 2024; Hörisch et al., 2014).

Triple Bottom Line (TBL)

The TBL is an accounting framework with three dimensions: social, environmental and economic. The TBL advocates for the idea that when it comes to evaluating the performance of firms, three criteria must be considered- People, Planet, and Profit (Geissdoerfer et al., 2017; Lazarenko et al., 2021; Oyetunde et al., 2023). This model aligns well with the sustainable business strategy ideal, in which companies are to pursue practices that are good for the company, good for people and good for the planet. CI, hence, helps companies to search for best practices and benchmark their performance along these three dimensions. For instance, when companies and institutions exploit CI insights to improve their resource utilisation, they can profit from enhanced operational efficiencies, which is in line with TBL goals (Lazarenko et al., 2021; Muntean, 2018). situation in the real world of economics and business (Fink & Yol, 2019). The TBL models emphasise the fact that organisations must generate value along several dimensions, in exchange for ensuring balanced corporate performance.

Shared Value

According to the Shared Value, companies can generate economic value by providing societal value and solving societal problems (Padgett & Moura-Leite, 2012; Frynas & Yamahaki, 2016). From this perspective, it urges organisations to adopt policies where social issues are mainstreamed in their business strategy, turning CSR into a driver of innovation and competitive advantage. Through competitive intelligence, companies can recognise the social issues in societies in which they operate and develop viable solutions to meet this societal need while achieving corporate objectives (Nixon & Thato, 2016; Muntean, 2018). This alignment between corporate goals and social imperatives allows firms to develop offerings that do more than profitably engage customers, but offer sustainable business strategy in embodying and delivering the essence of social good.

Integrative Insights

This approach enhances the theoretical understanding of the interplay between CI, CSR, and sustainability-focused business models. Through stakeholder theory, organisations can implement intelligence collection on their stakeholders, which ensures that the organisations are not losing public support over environmental and community values related to their CSR initiatives. The TBL additionally promotes a greener economy by encouraging companies to measure their bottom line not only by economic, but also social and environmental factors; meanwhile, the shared value principle emphasises how integrating social responsibility into core business strategy would mutually benefit society and the company itself.

So, organisational leaders are enhancing their use of competitive intelligence as it relates to decision making, sustainability programs, and stakeholder engagement through the frames of Stakeholder Theory, the Triple Bottom Line, and Shared Value. As the marketplace continues to evolve, the ability to adapt these theories into practical operations will not only promote competitive success but also drive a more sustainable future.

The Role of Competitive Intelligence in Driving Sustainability

As organisations seek to leverage CI to better respond to the evolving expectations of stakeholders for transparency and accountability in environmental and social matters, having the ability to collect, analyze, and interpret data on the competitive landscape equips firms to better anticipate the demands of the market, meet the preferences of consumers, and succor their Corporate Social Responsibility (CSR) initiatives (Nixon & Thato 2016).

There are several major ways CI contributes to sustainability. To begin with, it helps businesses recognise changes in market dynamics as driven by sustainability trends. Through systematic analysis of data on competitor behaviours and consumer attitudes towards sustainability, companies can better design their sustainability strategies (Ilić et al. 2022; Dobraca & Garib, 2022). Also, the integration of CI in the conditions of circular economy as a way both for the firms to get tools for innovation and orientation towards ecological marks. CI can be essentially characterised as an enabler which enables organisations to design their product lines in a better way, utilises resources in a positive sense, and aligns to sustainable activities that appeal to their customers (Khương & Nguyen, 2022).

Further, it serves as a strong base for regulatory excursion and sustainability reporting. As environmental laws continue to change, businesses need to be vigilant when it comes to monitoring the direction of regulation, and to have a competitive intelligence system that can monitor the movement of these laws and analyse their potential effects to update their plans. This kind of behaviour not only helps keep away from penalties by regulatory bodies, these firms are also portrayed as benchmarks of environmental sustainability in their sector (Battaglia et al., 2014). In this scheme, the responsible use of CI can help enhance reputation and trust and eventually lead to a competitive advantage in terms of responsible management (Cavallo et al., 2020).

In addition, by integrating CI with sustainability programmes, a learning-oriented environment is established that could provide improved organisational decision-making abilities. Organisations can begin benchmarking and establishing best practices for sustainability in their sector to set targets and metrics to gauge performance. Innovative companies benchmark against these sustainability goals themselves, so they put that pressure on themselves for that one step up (Cioffi et al., 2020). Implementing CI for insights on emerging technologies and sustainable practices allows organisations to identify opportunities for improvement and differentiation.

Additionally, CI and CSR share a symbiotic relationship, wherein competition and industry insights can help firms develop focused CSR initiatives. A better understanding of the "hot" environmental and social issues for consumers and other stakeholders can also help point businesses to the most effective CSR priorities (Mohammadalian et al., 2013). This convergence both increases the effectiveness of CSR objectives and works toward the establishment of a competitive advantage, evidenced in the resources-based perspective on competitive strategy (Yin et al., 2023).

Aligning CSR Initiatives with Competitive Positioning

CSR has shifted from being an optional business activity towards something integrated with strategic management, reframing how an organisation outlines its purpose and its measure for success. Companies now acknowledge that responsible corporate behaviour can improve their overall competitive positioning through increased brand reputation, customer loyalty, and operational efficiency (Afeltra & Goeldi, 2022; Chang & Yoo, 2023). Strong CSR initiatives help organisations set themselves apart from their competition to stand out competitively in fields of practice where ethics matter in order to compete.

For instance, Afeltra et al.(2022) show that firms that integrate sustainable innovation in business models can enhance their operational performance drastically while complying with the principles of the Triple Bottom Line, which include achieving objectives based on economic, environmental, and social needs. Not only does this address stakeholder calls for smart practices, but it also spurs innovation and, in the long run, can provide a competitive edge for a firm.

Utilising Competitive Intelligence for Effective CSR Alignment

Embracing CI in CSR strategies supports firms to understand what stakeholders expect, how the market is shifting and even what their competitors are doing. Such awareness allows organisations to drive CSR that positively complements wider business goals rather than being focused on mere compliance, using CSR as a strategic mechanism to tap into new business opportunities (Chang & Yoo, 2023; Anlesinya & Abugre, 2021). Among multinational companies, strategic alignment of CSR with business objectives improves the creation of business value (Anlesinya & Abugre, 2021). Through this alignment of CSR and strategic orientation, businesses can even use their act of social responsibility for competitive advantages, thereby enhancing their market competitiveness and brand value.

Creating Shared Value through CSR

The idea behind Shared Value is that organisations can generate economic value in a way that also produces value for society. Integrating CSR with the strategic pillars of the company creates a harmony of social and organisational well-being (Kurniawan & Arief, 2023). CSR initiatives that improve brand loyalty and customer engagement can significantly lower operational risks and enhance financial performance (Grant, 2024). By CSR communication, companies can also gain an advantage in that they are reaching out to socially conscious consumers, thereby enhancing their competitive positioning in the marketplace.

Challenges in Aligning CSR with Business Strategy

Even though they provide this advantage, it is not easy to align CSR to competitive positioning. Companies may face hurdles, including internal resistance to change, difficulties in measuring the impact of CSR initiatives, and complexities of integrating ethical practice into traditional business models (ElAlfy et al., 2020; Yousfi et al., 2023). Additionally, organisations are required to address the expectations of stakeholders regarding CSR and avoid using it as a marketing tool, which can threaten the organisation's reputation (Vázquez & Fornés, 2015). In addition, companies need to ensure transparency in their CSR report so that they avoid complaints of 'greenwashing' or the extent to which the company speaks falsely about its business practices being environmentally friendly to the public (Ardiansyah & Alnoor, 2024).

CASE STUDIES AND INDUSTRY INSIGHTS

Competitive Intelligence in the Energy and Natural Resources Sector (ENRS)

A focus on CI in the CSR initiatives of energy and natural resources firms has become increasingly integral as pressures mount on industries to deal with environmental issues, along with stakeholder expectations.

The Role of CI in Enhancing CSR Initiatives in the ENRS

In the energy and natural resources industry, companies need to deal with changing regulatory demands and increasingly complex societal views on environmental sustainability. High-quality CI will help companies to recognise the links between regulatory changes, market movements and attitude of stakeholders in a way that allows them to shape and enhance their CSR strategies (Jaén et al., 2021). Put in the context of stakeholders' theory, the company can accommodate varying perspectives of a diverse array of stakeholders, such as local communities, enviropolítica groups and consumers. and thus CSR programs to address anything that raises concern (Kartikasary et al., 2023). For instance, CI can help firms to benchmark their sustainability performance in their industry, identify best practices in CSR, and identify gaps and weaknesses in their efforts. This includes monitoring carbon emissions, as well as evaluating resource extraction, community engagement and environmental stewardship plans. Aligning CSR initiatives with stakeholder interests and industry standards can help companies strengthen their reputations and obtain their social license to operate (Sarjana & Khayati, 2016).

Driving Innovation through Sustainable Practices in the ENRS

CI plays an even more significant role among factors influencing strategy, especially with respect to innovation and CSR. Studies show that while bringing CSR and innovation as separate parts of business never equals a dominant competitive advantage, but if both are considering and carrying out together, both CSR and innovation will affect enormously (Benyaminova et al., 2019). In energy and natural resources, similar alignment can be found when such companies engage in eco-innovation (Pan et al., 2020), which involves new technologies or processes that minimize the company's impact on the environment, while potentially creating operational efficiencies.

Additionally, organizations can also derive their R&D efforts in line with CSR objectives by using CI to detect market requirements and technological trends. Balance in this operational ecosystem unlocks higher innovation outputs leading to efficiency and economic wealth while lowering the environmental footprint (Chakrabarty, 2020). This is an empirical study through which Grumbach explains this phenomenon of increasing strategic CSR initiatives will enhance sustainability in the energy sector that is inclusive of corporate performance and stakeholder trust (Grumbach, 2015).

Addressing Challenges and Gaining Competitive Advantage in the ENRS

It is important to pay attention to challenges to overcome while CI is being integrated into CSR strategies. Energy companies deal with complicated regulations in their industry and are often criticised for their environmental performance. In this respect, making use of CI as a proactive strategy for CSR and practice can reduce the threat of reputational damage and regulatory attention (Benyaminova et al., 2019). Firms, for example, are required to respond to this phenomenon with full carbon emission disclosures to fulfil legal requirements as well as provide information transparency to the stakeholders (Kartikasary AR et al., 2023). The adoption of these measures may be particularly important, given the current era of competitive consumer and investor markets geared towards sustainability (Latif et al., 2020).

Furthermore, socially responsible HRM is necessary to develop successful CSR initiatives as sustainability has to be also embedded into the organisations (Barrena-Martínez et al., 2018). Windows can create culture and both literate and integrate CI through their strategic HRM in the way in which this aligns organisational objectives with stakeholder expectations in the HRM system (Taylor et al., 2018).

Competitive Intelligence for CSR in the Fashion and Retail Industry (FRI)

The convergence of Competitive Intelligence (CI) and Corporate Social Responsibility (CSR) in fashion and retailing is emerging as a core requirement, as eco-conscious consumers are increasingly asking brands to be more ethical and sustainable. With the intense competition in this sector, it is not only required for the companies to adhere to the laws, but they also need to actively participate in acts of CSR which align with the consumers' likes and aspirations. By using CI effectively, companies can collect valuable information to create informed CSR strategies for interested parties and create and maintain brand loyalty, improving/cultivating their competitive position and be innovative.

The Role of Competitive Intelligence in Shaping CSR Strategies in FRI

As more consumers are demanding ethical and sustainable behaviour from brands, fashion and retail companies around the globe have reintroduced a focus on CSR and CI. In a competitive industry such as the textile industry, not only do companies need to act responsibly, but also take measures which will contribute to CSR, which is in alignment with consumers' motivations. CI aid companies generate strategic insights, which are vital in identifying CSR, which leads to brand loyalty, improved competitive standing and ultimately innovation. Fashion, retailers and brands who want to analyse market trends, stakeholder expectations and competitor strategies use it to facilitate them with competitive intelligence. CI communicates with large firms whose CSR barometers are consumer expectations and regulatory standards, and firms can see where they are and fill that gap (Kwon & Lee, 2021). Kwon & Lee (2021) also show that CSR advertising on social media platforms instils into society an image of the brand being transparent, honest and concerned about the well-being of their stakeholders. By examining competitors' communications, including concentrating purely on the strategic messages or themes, they can then tailor their communications strategy to better align with their target audiences.

Furthermore, CI offers a tool for firms to keep abreast of developments regarding sustainability and the ethical consumer, and firms can act based on such trends, rather than react to the trends (Feng & Ngai, 2020). One example is that many retailers have transformed their product offerings, as well as their sourcing practices, to align with consumer desires about sustainability, driven by an increasing consumer demand for ethical and sustainable fashion (Szegedi et al. 2023). Firms can better react to consumer expectations and use the feedback to inform stakeholder perceptions to inform the CSR strategy.

Strategic Alignment of CSR with Competitive Positioning in FRI

A key aspect of CSR that firms should lock on to is aligning broader CSR initiatives with their overall competitive positioning. The fast fashion industry, however, has witnessed a notable shift, with companies like Zara and H&M focusing on CSR as an integral aspect of their brand strategy (Jiang, 2022) and adopting practices that target social issues, including labour conditions and environmental sustainability. By leveraging CI to shape their CSR strategies, these brands gain a competitive edge that resonates with socially conscious consumers.

For example, Jiang (2022) demonstrates that CSR directly impacts brand competitiveness in the fast fashion market. This link demonstrates that when brands invest in CSR, they benefit from consumer loyalty, offering differentiation, and a sound corporate image.

In addition, CI allows retailers to identify and leverage CSR-driven market opportunities. One of the key challenges for retailers is about selling their CSR commitments at competitive price points (Mas et al●, 2021). By utilising CI, retail businesses will be able to pinpoint avenues in which CSR can be integrated in such a way that entices consumers whilst also being strategically priced to ensure longevity in the marketplace.

Innovation and CSR Integration in FRI

Integration of CI with CSR can unlock avenues for compliance and innovation for the firms. These reactions are reflected in the findings of Feng and Ngai (2020), who show how the fashion domain modifies its CSR communication considering major social and environmental crises suggesting a transition to sustainable practices as a source for innovation. Companies that utilise CI to dissect the market forces surrounding sustainability can encourage innovative solutions that improve their operational activities, all the while tackling societal and environmental challenges.

The significance of their contribution to CSR through these emerging practices should be recognised in the context of CSR by the size and capacity of the organisation. Branding and social media strategies have been identified as one promising way of implementing CSR work among SMES and making them participate and compete with a declared ethical attitude (Szegedi et al., 2023). Therefore, through aggressive CSR, SMES will be positioned to forge strong ties with community groups such as communities within their surroundings, which have the potential to positively influence a firm's competitive position.

COMPARATIVE REGIONAL PRACTICES IN CSR: INSIGHTS FROM AFRICA, EUROPE, AND ASIA

Corporate Social Responsibility (CSR) practices vary significantly across regions, influenced by cultural, economic, and regulatory contexts.

CSR Practices in Africa

CSR is part of the African society as a cultural practice and a community-based CSR model, which applies to African businesses. For example, in Kenya, CSR practices have largely been influenced by local stakeholders' perceptions of community development, environmental protection corporate accountability (Muhandi, 2024). Many African companies (particularly those in extractive industry sectors) have progressively shifted attention in their CSR activities toward vital social concerns such as poverty eradication and educational uplift. Nevertheless, issues of transparency, governance and the possibility of a more systematic approach to CSR have been challenged (Muhandi, 2024). Furthermore, some African industries have also begun to recognise the significance of CSR as a strategy for achieving a competitive advantage in an increasingly interdependent global economy. Yet, a significant gap exists in robust data on the effectiveness of CSR initiatives in promoting sustainable business practices in different countries in the region (Muhandi, 2024).

CSR Practices in Europe

CSR is mainly structured by regulation in Europe and is driven by stakeholder expectations. European companies are more likely to follow clear CSR disclosures, bolstering transparency and accountability toward different stakeholders (Sambharya, 2024). The CSR landscape varies widely across regions due to socio-economic factors, with Northern European countries usually producing better sustainability results and outperforming those of Southern Europe (Sambharya, 2024).

Firms have been motivated to operate responsibly and prove their contributions to sustainability and contribute positively to society because of governing instruments like the European Union's and the Non-Financial Reporting Directive (Sambharya, 2024). Even Europe, where CSR is becoming a marketing tool and a way to differentiate itself in competitive markets, thus improving the company's image and customer loyalty.

CSR Practices in Asia

In Asia, CSR practices are evolving, too, with several companies adopting CSR models based on regional culture and government. In some countries like China, CSR behaviours are going through a radical shift under the growing pressure from the public and demands for corporate accountability (Feng & Ngai, 2020). Although the approach is often frequent in different levels toward regions (Li et al., 2019), the firms in

China are more focused on their CSR on environmental sustainability and social project initiatives.

Local contexts, corporate governance structures, and economic conditions distinctly shape the CSR landscape.

Meanwhile, some firms operating in economically less developed areas or low-income countries do not strongly pursue social responsibility and are strategically motivated towards economic goals (Li et al., 2019). With increasing globalisation, Asian companies are starting to adopt Western CSR models, resulting in hybrid practices combining local culture with global practices (Yang et al., 2020).

CSR in America

Corporate Social Responsibility epitomises the ethical operating code, sustainability and formation of community seen as vital for American businesses. CSR is good business in the United States, where it is perceived as both a moral obligation and a strategic tool that can strengthen corporate reputation and build customer loyalty, thereby assisting the corporation to be profitable over time (Jia, 2019; D'Amato & Falivena, 2019). The evolving nature of pooling is driven by consumer demand; holders of social value prefer brands that lead the charge in sustainable, social initiatives. Companies that give priority to CSR are more likely to have high customer retention and achieve superior financial performance (Jia, 2019; D'Amato & Falivena, 2019). Firms like Patagonia, Starbucks, and Coca-Cola have undertaken different corporate social responsibility activities, including technology firms working vigorously to eliminate their carbon footprints, while others are supporting local educational and disaster relief initiatives (Faoziyah, 2022).

Openness in CSR reporting has also been on the rise as stakeholders are calling for accountability. Comprehensive report Practices can also enable companies to gain trust and show their commitment to responsible operations (Lailiyah, 2021). In addition, CSR-oriented firms have shown resilience in crises such as COVID-19 (Mattera et al., 2021). The effect of CSR on the performance of the firms is significant in terms of the brand, the retention of employees and the expansion of the market. However, its effectiveness varies according to industry dynamics and strategic implementation, it requires tailored approaches (Jia, 2019; Faoziyah, 2022). And as CSR progresses, businesses need to embed it as a long-term approach for enduring success.

Implications of Competitive Intelligence in Sustainability and Corporate Social Responsibility (CSR)

CI is a compass that tells firms the direction they should take based on stakeholder needs, competitive dynamics, and emerging trends. According to Nixon & Thato (2016), integration of CI with business intelligence results in the formation of niche intelligence frameworks through which organisations ultimately gain sustainable competitive advantages. This is of great importance for the companies that want to align their CSR initiatives with the competitive positioning, without losing track of their offered products and services.

Abad-Segura et al. (2024) emphasises the role of facilitating factors for sustainable actions, such as investments and policies favouring sustainability that could arise from competitive intelligence. That alignment will lead to a strong CSR framework that provides long-term value to the organisation.

Also, by analysing the industry landscape, an organisation can identify opportunities and risks, which leads to CI integration within its CSR initiatives, and fosters innovation (Chaudhuri et al.,2021). The characteristics of eco-innovative food business models, such as firms utilising CI, are in a strong position to engage with actors in their obtaining chain to further increase their advantage while striving for sustainability outcomes. And by analysing and engaging with the stakeholders, companies can create green and sustainable products which meet the needs of consumers, and subsequently use innovation as a strength of their social responsibility, as well as their advantage to bridge the consumer gap.

In addition, competitive intelligence allows firms to benchmark against best practices and successful CSR practices adopted by competitors, giving firms new ideas to create sustainable innovations. CSR, which in essence involves the intervention of the business in the society for its betterment, is no more just an ethical responsibility that organizations claim to fulfill, it has turned into a big competitive tool which promises the organization improved competitive efficiency, and allows it to take advantage of the opportunities which the society has to offer and is derived from the competitive intelligence which organizations possess. Such change enables organisations to create a change in CSR practices, evolving from guideline-based growth to being one of the prime strategic performance factors for organisations.

Also, organisations that can address the needs and concerns of all relevant stakeholders can optimally align their CSR strategies to maximise social value and improve community relations. CI facilitates management to remain sensitive to the demands of the stakeholders and the co-creation of CSR efforts with them, creating a maximising environment. Moreover, the organisations that use CI successfully in their CSR strategy will see an increase in consumer trust and brand loyalty. Waithaka (2021) also avers that competitive intelligence is a tool that can help track CSR activities, to increase transparency and aid stakeholders who perceive the corporate commitment to social and environmental responsibility. Psychologists understand that stakeholder engagement principles reflect the perception that socially responsible engagements of firms are more appealing to consumers and deliver increased consumer brand equity and increased market differentiation.

CONCLUSION

Transitioning organisational change in industries energy, retail, and fashion from the strategic implementation of Competitive Intelligence (CI) to Corporate Social Responsibility (CSR) and sustainability priorities is a game changer. Given that industries are facing new pressures as a result of environmental degradation and social inequalities across the globe, organisations must ensure that their CI approach aligns with their CSR, with stakeholder requirements and market conditions. Competitive intelligence (CI) is vital for sound decision making and strategic alignment, so that organisations can have a meaningful understanding of competitive environments and social issues as well. Through interacting with stakeholders, firms are also able to guarantee the pertinence and usefulness of their CSR programs to their serving community, whereas this can lead to longer-term relations based on trust and loyalty. CI adoption similarly leads to innovation by inventing economically sustainable practices and products to make sure it pays to meet ethical requirements.

There are serious consequences for CSR embracing CI. Enterprises that do use CI will increase their operational effectiveness and risk management, but will also stake their claim as royalty of corporate responsibility as consumers and regulators become more sceptical. It's the organisation that becomes adept at mastering and making sense of that complexity, and delivering genuine social and environmental value in return, that will succeed in the 21st-century marketplace and at the heart of this trinity arrangement between CI, CSR and sustainability goes beyond ticking boxes into building resilient business models that grow and deliver real societal value, a win-win for both the bottom line and the higher social good.

REFERENCES

Afeltra, G., Alerasoul, S., Minelli, E., Vecchio, Y., & Montalvo, C. (2022). Assessing the integrated impact of sustainable innovation on organisational performance: An empirical evidence from manufacturing firms. *Journal of Small Business Strategy*, *32*(4). Advance online publication. DOI: 10.53703/001c.38515

Al-Omoush, K., Ribeiro-Navarrete, B., & McDowell, W. (2023). The impact of digital corporate social responsibility on social entrepreneurship and organizational resilience. *Management Decision*, *62*(8), 2621–2640. DOI: 10.1108/MD-11-2022-1613

Amaral, R., Faria, L., Oprime, P., Gregolin, J., & Alliprandini, D. (2012). Perfis de competências relativas à inteligência competitiva: Um estudo exploratório no brasil. *Ciência da Informação*, *40*(2). Advance online publication. DOI: 10.18225/ci.inf.v40i2.1306

Anlesinya, A., & Abugre, J. (2021). Strategic CSR practices, strategic orientation and business value creation among multinational subsidiaries in Ghana. *Society and Business Review*, *17*(2), 257–279. DOI: 10.1108/SBR-02-2021-0021

Anokye, C., Hajmasy, G., & Raffay-Danyi, Á. (2022, November). The impacts of CSR of hotels on the socio-economic development of the South Tongu District of Ghana. *Euro-Asia Tourism Studies Journal*, *3*(November 2022). Advance online publication. DOI: 10.58345/MELK1969

Ardiansyah, M., & Alnoor, A. (2024). Integrating corporate social responsibility into business strategy: Creating sustainable value. *IIJB*, *1*(1), 29–42. DOI: 10.62569/iijb.v1i1.5

Barrena-Martínez, J., López-Fernández, M., & Fernández, P. (2018). Drivers and barriers in socially responsible human resource management. *Sustainability (Basel)*, *10*(5), 1532. DOI: 10.3390/su10051532

Bartes, F. (2015). The objectives of competitive intelligence as a part of corporate development strategy. *Acta Universitatis Agriculturae et Silviculturae Mendelianae Brunensis*, *62*(6), 1243–1250. DOI: 10.11118/actaun201462061243

Battaglia, M., Testa, F., Bianchi, L., Iraldo, F., & Frey, M. (2014). Corporate social responsibility and competitiveness within SMES of the fashion industry: Evidence from Italy and France. *Sustainability (Basel)*, *6*(2), 872–893. DOI: 10.3390/su6020872

Belu, C., & M nescu, C. (2013). Strategic corporate social responsibility and economic performance. *Applied Economics*, *45*(19), 2751–2764. DOI: 10.1080/00036846.2012.676734

Benyaminova, A., Mathews, M., Langley, P., & Rieple, A. (2019). The impact of changes in stakeholder salience on corporate social responsibility activities in russian energy firms: A contribution to the divergence/convergence debate. *Corporate Social Responsibility and Environmental Management*, *26*(6), 1222–1234. DOI: 10.1002/csr.1743

Bhattacharyya, S., & Jha, S. (2020). Explicating micro foundations of corporate social responsibility: A moderated-mediation study of customer, investor and employee roles. *International Journal of Ethics and Systems*, *36*(4), 619–640. DOI: 10.1108/IJOES-05-2020-0073

Biran, D., Zack, M., & Briotta, R. (2013). Competitive intelligence and information quality. *ACM Journal of Data and Information Quality*, *4*(3), 1–20. DOI: 10.1145/2458517.2458520

Cavallo, A., Sanasi, S., Ghezzi, A., & Rangone, A. (2020). Competitive intelligence and strategy formulation: Connecting the dots. *Competitiveness Review*, *31*(2), 250–275. DOI: 10.1108/CR-01-2020-0009

Chakrabarty, S. (2020). Value creation in industrial clusters: The strategic nature of relationships with stakeholders and the policy environment. *Journal of Strategy and Management*, *13*(4), 535–550. DOI: 10.1108/JSMA-04-2020-0084

Chang, Y., & Yoo, J. (2023). When csr matters: The moderating effect of industrial growth rate on the relationship between csr and firm performance. *Sustainability (Basel), 15*(18), 13677. DOI: 10.3390/su151813677

Chaudhuri, A., Datta, P., Fernandes, K., & Xiong, Y. (2021). Optimal pricing strategies for manufacturing-as-a service platforms to ensure business sustainability. *International Journal of Production Economics, 234*, 108065. DOI: 10.1016/j.ijpe.2021.108065

Chernev, A., & Blair, S. (2015). Doing well by doing good: The benevolent halo of corporate social responsibility. *The Journal of Consumer Research, 41*(6), 1412–1425. DOI: 10.1086/680089

Choi, D., Chung, C., & Young, J. (2019). An economic analysis of corporate social responsibility in korea. *Sustainability (Basel), 11*(9), 2676. DOI: 10.3390/su11092676

Chung, C., Jung, S., & Young, J. (2018). Do CSR activities increase firm value? evidence from the Korean market. *Sustainability (Basel), 10*(9), 3164. DOI: 10.3390/su10093164

Cioffi, R., Travaglioni, M., Piscitelli, G., Petrillo, A., & Felice, F. (2020). Artificial intelligence and machine learning applications in smart production: Progress, trends, and directions. *Sustainability (Basel), 12*(2), 492. DOI: 10.3390/su12020492

D'Amato, A., & Falivena, C. (2019). Corporate social responsibility and firm value: Do firm size and age matter? empirical evidence from European listed companies. *Corporate Social Responsibility and Environmental Management, 27*(2), 909–924. DOI: 10.1002/csr.1855

Darnall, N., Henriques, I., & Sadorsky, P. (2010). Adopting a proactive environmental strategy: The influence of stakeholders and firm size. *Journal of Management Studies, 47*(6), 1072–1094. DOI: 10.1111/j.1467-6486.2009.00873.x

Deitiana, T. (2015). The determinant of CSR disclosure of the mining industry listed in the Indonesia Stock Exchange. *Asian Business Review, 5*(3), 141–148. DOI: 10.18034/abr.v5i3.66

Dela, E., Ye, J., & Berhe, H. (2024). The impact of corporate social responsibility on financial performance in highly polluted Indonesian industries: Mediating role of industry competitiveness. *SAGE Open*, *14*(4). Advance online publication. DOI: 10.1177/21582440241259479

Dmytriyev, S., Freeman, R., & Hörisch, J. (2021). The relationship between stakeholder theory and corporate social responsibility: Differences, similarities, and implications for social issues in management. *Journal of Management Studies*, *58*(6), 1441–1470. DOI: 10.1111/joms.12684

ElAlfy, A., Palaschuk, N., El-Bassiouny, D., Wilson, J., & Weber, O. (2020). Scoping the evolution of corporate social responsibility (CSR) research in the Sustainable Development Goals (SDGS) era. *Sustainability (Basel)*, *12*(14), 5544. DOI: 10.3390/su12145544

Faoziyah, S. (2022). Corporate social responsibility to reduce community rejection of a company existence: Analysis of business ethics perspective. *Journal of Scientech Research and Development*, *4*(1), 162–175. DOI: 10.56670/jsrd.v4i1.119

Feng, P., & Ngai, C. (2020). Doing more on the corporate sustainability front: A longitudinal analysis of CSR reporting of global fashion companies. *Sustainability (Basel)*, *12*(6), 2477. DOI: 10.3390/su12062477

Fernández-Kranz, D., & Santaló, J. (2010). when necessity becomes a virtue: The effect of product market competition on corporate social responsibility. *Journal of Economics & Management Strategy*, *19*(2), 453–487. DOI: 10.1111/j.1530-9134.2010.00258.x

Frishammar, J., Lichtenthaler, U., & Rundquist, J. (2012). Identifying technology commercialization opportunities: The importance of integrating product development knowledge. *Journal of Product Innovation Management*, *29*(4), 573–589. DOI: 10.1111/j.1540-5885.2012.00926.x

Frynas, J., & Yamahaki, C. (2016). Corporate social responsibility: Review and roadmap of theoretical perspectives. *Business Ethics (Oxford, England)*, *25*(3), 258–285. DOI: 10.1111/beer.12115

Geissdoerfer, M., Savaget, P., Bocken, N., & Hultink, E. (2017). The circular economy – a new sustainability paradigm? *Journal of Cleaner Production, 143*, 757–768. DOI: 10.1016/j.jclepro.2016.12.048

Giannoni, C., Alarcón, L., & Vera, S. (2017). Diagnosis of sustainable business strategies implemented by Chilean construction companies. *Sustainability (Basel), 10*(1), 82. DOI: 10.3390/su10010082

Glavas, A. (2016). Corporate social responsibility and employee engagement: Enabling employees to employ more of their whole selves at work. *Frontiers in Psychology, 7*. Advance online publication. DOI: 10.3389/fpsyg.2016.00796 PMID: 27303352

Grant, O. (2024). The influence of corporate social responsibility on supplier relationship management in e-commerce. https://doi.org/DOI: 10.20944/preprints202407.1079.v1

Grumbach, J. (2015). Polluting industries as climate protagonists: Cap and trade and the problem of business preferences. *Business and Politics, 17*(4), 633–659. DOI: 10.1515/bap-2015-0012

Guo, H. (2020). The evolution of strategic social responsibility of Chinese enterprises and the design of a decision support system. Destech Transactions on Social Science Education and Human Science, (ecemi). https://doi.org/DOI: 10.12783/dtssehs/ecemi2020/34702

Hörisch, J., Freeman, R., & Schaltegger, S. (2014). Applying stakeholder theory in sustainability management. *Organization & Environment, 27*(4), 328–346. DOI: 10.1177/1086026614535786

Ilić, M., Ranković, M., Dobrilović, M., Bucea-Manea- oni , R., Mihoreanu, L., Ghe a, M., & Simion, V. (2022). Challenging novelties within the circular economy concept under the digital transformation of society. *Sustainability (Basel), 14*(2), 702. DOI: 10.3390/su14020702

Impact of marketing intelligence on effectiveness of decision making: an Empirical study. (2023). *Journal of Informatics Education and Research*. https://doi.org/DOI: 10.52783/jier.v3i1.64

Ismaeel, B., Alkhawaldeh, B., & Alafi, K. (2023). The role of marketing intelligence in improving the efficiency of the organization: An empirical study on Jordanian hypermarkets. *Journal of Intelligence Studies in Business*, *13*(2), 32–42. DOI: 10.37380/jisib.v13i2.1082

Jaén, J., Guijarro, A., & Lema, D. (2021). The impact of corporate social responsibility on innovation in small and medium-sized enterprises: The mediating role of debt terms and human capital. *Corporate Social Responsibility and Environmental Management*, *28*(4), 1200–1215. DOI: 10.1002/csr.2125

Jia, X. (2019). Corporate social responsibility activities and firm performance: The moderating role of strategic emphasis and industry competition. *Corporate Social Responsibility and Environmental Management*, *27*(1), 65–73. DOI: 10.1002/csr.1774

Jiang, B. (2022). How consumers' response on CSR affects brand competitiveness in the fast fashion industry——case study of Zara (Inditex) and H&m. *Academic Journal of Business & Management*, *4*(1). Advance online publication. DOI: 10.25236/AJBM.2022.040117

Joo, J., Eom, M., & Shin, M. (2017). Finding the missing link between corporate social responsibility and firm competitiveness through social capital: A business ecosystem perspective. *Sustainability (Basel)*, *9*(5), 707. DOI: 10.3390/su9050707

Kai-xing, W. & Sun, Q. (2021). Corporate social responsibility and cash holdings.. https://doi.org/DOI: 10.2991/assehr.k.211209.152

Kan, L., & Xiang, H. (2023). Corporate social responsibility, advertising competition and consumer welfare: A research on the model of oligopoly competition theory. *American Journal of Industrial and Business Management*, *13*(03), 140–153. DOI: 10.4236/ajibm.2023.133010

Kang, Y., & Chiu, C. (2016). How corporate social responsibility indicators influence organization identification? the perspective of labor relations. *Ibusiness*, *08*(04), 61–69. DOI: 10.4236/ib.2016.84007

Kartikasary, M., Wijanarko, H., Tihar, A., & Zaldin, A. (2023). The effect of financial distress and firm size on carbon emission disclosure. E3S Web of Conferences, 426, 02093. https://doi.org/DOI: 10.1051/e3sconf/202342602093

Khương, M., & Nguyen, A. (2022). The impact of corporate social responsibility performance on competitive advantage and business success. *International Journal of Asian Business and Information Management*, *12*(3), 1–15. DOI: 10.4018/IJABIM.294095

Khương, M., Nguyen, A., & Nguyen, T. (2021). Implementation of corporate social responsibility strategy to enhance firm reputation and competitive advantage. *Journal of Competitiveness*, *13*(4), 96–114. DOI: 10.7441/joc.2021.04.06

Kim, B., Quaquebeke, N., Chang, Y., & Kim, T. (2024). When and how corporate social responsibility promotes innovation: A multi-level moderated mediation model. *Corporate Social Responsibility and Environmental Management*, *32*(1), 1325–1345. DOI: 10.1002/csr.2984

Kurniawan, I., & Arief, N. (2023). Creating shared value in an upstream oil and gas company and the community: A case study of CSR implementation in PT Pertamina EP Tarakan field. *European Journal of Business Management and Research*, *8*(4), 282–292. DOI: 10.24018/ejbmr.2023.8.4.2091

Kwon, K., & Lee, J. (2021). Corporate social responsibility advertising in social media: A content analysis of the fashion industry's CSR advertising on Instagram. *Corporate Communications*, *26*(4), 700–715. DOI: 10.1108/CCIJ-01-2021-0016

Lailiyah, N. (2021). *Media relations and corporate reputations in the corporate social responsibility (CSR) activities of PT*. Indonesia Power Semarang Up Generation., DOI: 10.4108/eai.9-10-2020.2304798

Latif, A., Hadi, N., & Khurshid, J. (2020). Does CSR add value to service innovation performance via HRM? A conceptual framework and future research agenda. Global Management Sciences Review, V(III), 73-83. https://doi.org/DOI: 10.31703/gmsr.2020(V-III).08

Lazarenko, Y., Garafonova, O., Marhasova, V., & Grigashkina, S. (2021). Gaining a competitive advantage through sustainability strategy: managerial applications for the mining sector. E3S Web of Conferences, 278, 03036. https://doi.org/DOI: 10.1051/e3sconf/202127803036

Li, J., Qin, X., & Lin, Y. (2024). Strategy, corporate social responsibility and investment efficiency: The role of substitute and complement. *Business & Society*, *64*(4), 757–803. DOI: 10.1177/00076503241254544

Li, K., Khalili, N., & Cheng, W. (2019). Corporate social responsibility practices in China: Trends, context, and impact on company performance. *Sustainability (Basel)*, *11*(2), 354. DOI: 10.3390/su11020354

Lies, J. (2019). Marketing intelligence and big data: Digital marketing techniques on their way to becoming social engineering techniques in marketing. *International Journal of Interactive Multimedia and Artificial Intelligence*, *5*(5), 134. DOI: 10.9781/ijimai.2019.05.002

Liu, Y., & Xu, H. (2022). Strategic corporate social responsibility with spillover effect in innovation. *Nankai Business Review International*, *13*(2), 318–339. DOI: 10.1108/NBRI-04-2021-0025

Lu, J., Ren, L., Yao, S., Qiao, J., Mikalauskienė, A., & Štreimikis, J. (2020). Exploring the relationship between corporate social responsibility and firm competitiveness. *Ekonomska Istrazivanja*, *33*(1), 1621–1646. DOI: 10.1080/1331677X.2020.1761419

Mas, F., Tucker, W., Massaro, M., & Bagnoli, C. (2021). Corporate social responsibility in the retail business: A case study. *Corporate Social Responsibility and Environmental Management*, *29*(1), 223–232. DOI: 10.1002/csr.2198

Mattera, M., González, F., Ruiz-Morales, C., & Gava, L. (2021). Facing a global crisis - how sustainable business models helped firms overcome COVID-19. *Corporate Governance (Bradford)*, *21*(6), 1100–1116. DOI: 10.1108/CG-07-2020-0309

Mohammadalian, S., Nazemi, E., & Tarokh, M. (2013). Propose a conceptual model of adaptive competitive intelligence (aci). *International Journal of Business Intelligence Research, 4*(4), 22–32. DOI: 10.4018/ijbir.2013100102

Muhandi, A. (2024). Corporate social responsibility practices and stakeholder perceptions: A cross-cultural analysis in Kenya. *International Journal of Leadership and Governance, 4*(2), 49–60. DOI: 10.47604/ijlg.2695

Muntean, M. (2018). Business intelligence issues for sustainability projects. *Sustainability (Basel), 10*(2), 335. DOI: 10.3390/su10020335

Nasri, W. (2011). Competitive intelligence in Tunisian companies. *Journal of Enterprise Information Management, 24*(1), 53–67. DOI: 10.1108/17410391111097429

Nawangsari, L., & Sutawidjaya, A. (2021). How can SMES achieve sustainable business? *Business and Entrepreneurial Review (Ber), 21*(1), 153–170. DOI: 10.25105/ber.v21i1.9271

Nenzhelele, T. (2016). Competitive intelligence practice challenges in the South African property sector. *Problems and Perspectives in Management, 14*(2), 298–305. DOI: 10.21511/ppm.14(2-2).2016.05

Nixon, M., & Thato, M. (2016). Linking business intelligence to a knowledge-based sustainable competitive advantage in organizations. *African Journal of Business Management, 10*(19), 459–468. DOI: 10.5897/AJBM2016.8059

Obonyo, M., & Kilika, J. (2020). Competitive intelligence and corresponding outcome in a strategic management process: A review of literature. *Journal of Economics and Business, 3*(4). Advance online publication. DOI: 10.31014/aior.1992.03.04.313

Omale, S. A., Yusuf, S. O., Oyenuga, M. O., Ikemefuna, M., Ojo, S. S., & Momodu, I. D. (2024). Organizational Learning in the Post-COVID-19 Era: A Prerequisite for Stakeholder Satisfactions. Twist 19(3), 265-272 https://twistjournal.net/twist/article/view/339

Oyedele, M. O., Marcus, G. O., & Ahungwa, A. I. (2023). Do Consumers Care About Green Marketing Practices? Insight From A Developing Nation. *Budapest International Research and Critics Institute Journal(BIRCIJournal)* 6(3), (1424-1436) https://bircu-journal.com/index.php/birci/article/view/7665

Oyedele, O. M. (2025). Digital Circular Economy: Driving Sustainable Innovation Through Stakeholder Synergy. In Singh, R., & Kumar, V. (Eds.), *Sustainable Innovations and Digital Circular Economy*. Springer., DOI: 10.1007/978-981-96-1064-8_4

Oyenuga, M. O., Ahungwa, A. I., & Onoja, E. (2021). Effect of Brand Equity on consumer behaviour among students of Veritas University, Nigeria: A Study of Apple Smartphones. *Marketing and Branding Research, 8*, 48–64. DOI: 10.33844/mbr.2021.60329

Oyenuga, M. O., & Fredrick, E. (2023). Managing Product Features and Customer Satisfaction via Product Development, Product Branding, and Product Packaging: Evidence from CWAY Table Water. *Marketing and Branding Research*, *10*(1), 28–44. DOI: 10.32038/mbr.2023.10.01.03

Oyetunde, T. O., Oyenuga, M. O., & Adoga, G. J. (2023). Green Management Practices and Organisational Efficiency in Higher Institutions. *Budapest International Research and Critics in Linguistics and Education (BirLE). Journal*, *6*(3), 276–290. https://bircu-journal.com/index.php/birle/article/view/7716

Padgett, R., & Moura-Leite, R. (2012). Innovation with high social benefits and corporate financial performance. *Journal of Technology Management & Innovation*, *7*(4), 59–69. DOI: 10.4067/S0718-27242012000400005

Palilingan, V. & Batmetan, J. (2019). Competitive intelligence framework for increasing competitiveness in vocational high school management.. https://doi.org/DOI: 10.2991/ictvet-18.2019.52

Pan, X., Sinha, P., & Chen, X. (2020). Corporate social responsibility and eco-innovation: The triple bottom line perspective. *Corporate Social Responsibility and Environmental Management*, *28*(1), 214–228. DOI: 10.1002/csr.2043

Rayed, C. (2019). Using business intelligence solutions for forecasting in marketing researches. International Journal of Informatics and Communication Technology (Ij-Ict), 8(2), 102. https://doi.org/DOI: 10.11591/ijict.v8i2.pp102-110

Rith, R., & Spinelli, R. (2024). Examining the x factor of corporate social responsibility in professional football clubs: An integrative literature review. *Corporate Social Responsibility and Environmental Management*, *31*(4), 3487–3501. DOI: 10.1002/csr.2750

Sambharya, R. (2024). Are discrete dimensions of corporate social responsibility disclosures global, regional or hybrid? *Cross Cultural & Strategic Management*, *31*(4), 725–747. DOI: 10.1108/CCSM-03-2024-0066

Sarjana, S. & Khayati, N. (2016). CSR strategy in industrial city to achieve competitive advantage. https://doi.org/DOI: 10.2991/gcbme-16.2016.152

Srivastava, M., Franklin, A., & Martinette, L. (2013). Building a sustainable competitive advantage. *Journal of Technology Management & Innovation*, *8*(2), 7–8. DOI: 10.4067/S0718-27242013000200004

Stoyanova, T., & Angelova, M. (2018). From sustainable to transient competitive advantage. *International Conference Knowledge-Based Organization*, 24(2), 134-139. https://doi.org/DOI: 10.1515/kbo-2018-0078

Szegedi, K., Németh, T., & Körtvési, D. (2023). Employer branding in the fashion industry: CSR actions by fashion SMES. *Sustainability (Basel)*, *15*(3), 1827. DOI: 10.3390/su15031827

Tarnovskaya, V. (2023). Sustainability as the source of competitive advantage. how sustainable is it?., 75-89. https://doi.org/DOI: 10.1108/S1876-066X20230000037005

Taylor, J., Vithayathil, J., & Yim, D. (2018). Are corporate social responsibility (CSR) initiatives such as sustainable development and environmental policies value enhancing or window dressing? *Corporate Social Responsibility and Environmental Management*, *25*(5), 971–980. DOI: 10.1002/csr.1513

Tinonetsana, F. & Musariwa, P. (2024). Integration of sustainability marketing into business strategies: challenges during adoption. International Journal of Research in Business and Social Science (2147-4478), 13(2), 23-30. https://doi.org/DOI: 10.20525/ijrbs.v13i2.3011

Trivellas, P., Rafailidis, A., Polychroniou, P., & Dekoulou, P. (2019). Corporate social responsibility (CSR) and its internal consequences on job performance. *International Journal of Quality and Service Sciences*, *11*(2), 265–282. DOI: 10.1108/IJQSS-12-2017-0117

Tu n, L. (2013). Competitive intelligence and other levers of brand performance. *Journal of Strategic Marketing*, *21*(3), 217–239. DOI: 10.1080/0965254X.2013.765501

Vázquez, B., & Fornés, G. (2015). Corporate social responsibility in emerging markets: Case studies of Spanish MNCS in Latin America. *European Business Review*, *27*(2), 214–230. DOI: 10.1108/EBR-03-2013-0053

Vorozheykina, T., Muravitskaya, N., Lukyanenko, G., Antonova, O., Lyalkova, E., & Basova, M. (2019). Technologies of corporate social responsibility in accounting and statistics. *International Journal of Recent Technology and Engineering*, *8*(2), 3871–3876. DOI: 10.35940/ijrte.B3075.078219

Waithaka, P. (2021). Key vulnerabilities and the competitive advantage among commercial banks in Kenya. *Journal of Contemporary Research in Social Sciences*, *3*(4), 114–124. DOI: 10.33094/26410249.2021.34.114.124

Wang, J., Tian, Y., Wang, Y., Yang, J., Wang, X., Wang, S., & Kwan, O. (2023). A framework and operational procedures for metaverses-based industrial foundation models. *IEEE Transactions on Systems, Man, and Cybernetics. Systems*, *53*(4), 2037–2046. DOI: 10.1109/TSMC.2022.3226755

Wang, Z. (2021). Business analysis on sustainable competitive advantages. E3S Web of Conferences, 235, 03009. https://doi.org/DOI: 10.1051/e3sconf/202123503009

Xia, T., Luo, X., Liao, Y., & Liu, W. (2018). Corporate governance, corporate social responsibility and corporate performance study.. https://doi.org/DOI: 10.2991/sshr-17.2018.10

Yadav, M., & Sinha, N. (2021). Investigating the impact of corporate social responsibility on competitive performance: An empirical study based on panel data analysis. *Fiib Business Review*, *11*(2), 165–173. DOI: 10.1177/23197145211015443

Yang, L., Ngai, C., & Lu, W. (2020). Changing trends of corporate social responsibility reporting in the world-leading airlines. *PLoS One*, *15*(6), e0234258. DOI: 10.1371/journal.pone.0234258 PMID: 32511253

Yin, Y., Zhang, Z., Da, K., & Wen, X. (2023). Sustainable influence mechanism of technological innovation diffusion on intelligent transformation of manufacturing enterprises based on competitive advantage and value chain can regulate mediation effect analysis. *Polish Journal of Environmental Studies*, *33*(2), 1429–1441. DOI: 10.15244/pjoes/173439

Yousfi, O., Elkateb, M., & Omri, A. (2023). Perspective chapter: Rethinking CSR strategies in the era of COVID-19.. https://doi.org/DOI: 10.5772/intechopen.106248

Yu, H., Kuo, L., & Kao, M. (2017). The relationship between CSR disclosure and competitive advantage. *Sustainability Accounting Management and Policy Journal*, *8*(5), 547–570. DOI: 10.1108/SAMPJ-11-2016-0086

Yu, S., & Liang, W. (2020). Exploring the determinants of strategic corporate social responsibility: An empirical examination. *Sustainability (Basel)*, *12*(6), 2368. DOI: 10.3390/su12062368

Zhao, L. & Du, J. (2017). Certification of environmental corporate social responsibility activities in a differentiated duopoly market. Mathematical Problems in Engineering, 2017(1). https://doi.org/DOI: 10.1155/2017/2597159

Chapter 4
Designing a Convenient Performance Metric Model to Support Quick Decisions for SMEs Using the 7-SF Methodology

Subhashini Durai
LEAD College of Management, India

Geetha Manoharan
https://orcid.org/0000-0002-8644-8871
SR University, India

ABSTRACT

Workforce effectiveness measures quality, utilization, and performance, which affect productivity. Performance evaluation is needed for organizational decision-making. Technology-driven businesses use new instructional methods. KPIs and appropriate performance measures for workforce effectiveness metrics must be linked since they impact performance management. HR decisions and procedures benefit from metrics and data. The project's main goal is a realistic 7SF Performance Metric

DOI: 10.4018/979-8-3373-2690-0.ch004

Model. From an open-approach technique, a flexible 7-step conceptual framework for assessing workforce effectiveness utilizing HR metrics and performance indicators was created. In today's competitive workplace, HR managers want predictive analytics. To improve performance management, the chapter will identify relevant HR metrics from literature databases to measure workforce effectiveness linked to appropriate performance measures in an organization. Academics, organizations, practitioners, researchers, and students will be interested.

INTRODUCTION

Performance management is a crucial aspect inside businesses of varying scales, encompassing small, medium, and large enterprises (Jaichandran, R., et al., 2023). The process involves the collection, analysis, and presentation of data related to the performance of an individual, group, organization, system, or component (Manoharan & Rajoli, 2024). The significance of individual performance metrics is paramount, as it form the basis for team achievement, organizational effectiveness, and economic outcomes. Presently, there exists an emerging inclination inside firms to investigate innovative methodologies to maximize the efficacy of their human capital and augment overall operational effectiveness. Workforce effectiveness is a quantitative measure employed to evaluate the quality of work, utilization of employees (Manoharan, G., & Ashtikar, S. P. 2022), and levels of performance, all of which exert a substantial impact on the overall productivity of an organization (Sangeetha, M., et al., 2024). The assessment of workforce performance (Gopinathan, R., & Manoharan, G. 2022; Melanie Lourens., et al., 2022) is of significant importance in providing valuable insights for organizational decision-making processes.

To accomplish this goal, organizations utilize new techniques to deliver training to their employees within a highly advanced and technologically-driven work setting (Krishnan, S. G., & Manoharan, G. 2022). The human capital of a company is widely recognized as a valuable resource (Deviprasad, S., et al., 2023), and its performance (Rachana J., et al., 2022) may be assessed using metrics that align with the objectives of the enterprise.

The establishment of a relationship between the key performance indicators of workforce effectiveness metrics and the relevant performance measures (Manoharan G., et al., 2023; Selvaraj et al., 2024) is crucial due to the significant impact these metrics have on the overall performance management system.

Hence, this exercise boosts the measure of strategic performance and hence contributes to the organizational decision-making process. In a nutshell, the HRM managers who deal with assessing the performance of workforce performance across businesses from different industries (Manoharan, G., et al., 2024) have to be capable enough to apply metrics and analytics for better running their business so that others may take an action on the basis of their advice. The utilization of HR metrics (Durai, S., et al., 2022) and analytics enhances the decision-making capabilities of HR managers, while also playing a significant role in the entire decision-making process of the business.

OBJECTIVES OF THE STUDY

The primary aim of this research is to develop a practical Performance Metric Model utilizing the 7SF technique. Therefore, an endeavor was undertaken to construct a conceptual framework for assessing workforce effectiveness using HR metrics, which is connected to performance indicators derived from an open-approach methodology encapsulated within a versatile 7-step framework. This technique has the potential to increase managers' understanding of workforce effectiveness measurements and their connection to suitable performance measurement. The aforementioned factors contribute to the establishment of an effective business environment, enhanced quality control measures, efficient cost management, and the formulation of the company's overarching strategy. This tool serves as a convenient instrument for assessing performance and making evidence-based decisions to improve business profitability.

CONTRIBUTIONS OF THE STUDY

Academics, organizations, practitioners, researchers, and students will all find something of interest in this paper because of its primary goal: to find appropriate HR metrics in literature databases that measure the effectiveness of a company's workforce about appropriate performance measures, which in turn contribute to an efficient performance management system in that company. According to M. Ashok Sathe et al. (2024), HR managers in today's competitive work climate have made Predictive Analysis their ultimate goal when it comes to metrics and analytics. Human resource managers, according to proponents of evidence-based management (Ramachandran, K. K., et al., 2022), should not depend just on their own subjective opinions and theoretical frameworks when making choices; instead, they should use data gathered from organizational systems as empirical proof.

Ayres (2007) states that the best way to get data for decision-making is to organize an internal operational experiment. One way to make sense of a dynamic business climate is to model workforce performance using HR indicators. The company's competitive edge grows as a result of these changes, which boost sales, alter product demand, inspire new product development, etc.

LITERATURE REVIEW

Workforce Effectiveness

Workforce effectiveness is a critical area of study within organizational behavior and human resource management, focusing on how employee performance, engagement, and development contribute to organizational success. This literature review synthesizes key themes and findings related to workforce effectiveness, highlighting the factors that influence it and the implications for practice. Workforce effectiveness encompasses the ability of an organization's employees to meet objectives efficiently and productively. Other definitions emphasize the engagement, fit, and overall support towards organizational goals (Kahn, 1990; Saks, 2006).

Many studies link employee engagement with workforce effectiveness. Engaged employees are productive and committed to their jobs, according to Harter et al. (2002) and Saks (2006). Engagement is affected by job satisfaction, organizational culture, and leadership styles (Bakker & Demerouti, 2008). Effective performance management systems, including regular feedback and clear goal-setting, contribute greatly to workforce effectiveness. The studies emphasize that individual performance should be aligned with the objectives of the organization (Aguinis, 2009). The importance of training and developing investment in the improvement of the effectiveness of an organization's workforce cannot be exaggerated. Better performance and greater employee retention result from it due to continual learning (Noe, 2017; Salas et al., 2012).

It makes application of HR analytics, thereby providing an organization with analysis and forecasting of workforce data so that it can give some informed decisions on talent management. The applied-use method improves the understanding of factors that influence workforce effectiveness. There have been discussions in the area of KPI measures of workforce effectiveness. Indicators such as the rate of turnover, the levels of productivity, and employee satisfaction scores reflect performance.

The determining factor for organizational culture effectiveness is its influence on an organization's workforce. Performance and engagement levels among its employees will significantly be elevated in an inclusive, varied, and teamwork-based environment (Schein, 2010; McKinsey, 2015). Still, there are other factors facing the organization concerning workforce effectiveness. They range from fear of change to weakly designed training activities and substandard leadership. The major steps in these challenges towards workforce effectiveness will need to be eliminated or improved as well.

PERFORMANCE MEASUREMENT

Performance measurement is the process by which efficiency and effectiveness may be quantified in action, and is therefore, an important management function in any organization in terms of measuring performance. The rationale of performance measurement is always to make judgments about existing performance with a view to informing future courses of action. It measures productivity, the effectiveness of employees or teams generally and an organization's general performance as a whole. This is a literature review that synthesized major themes and findings for performance measurement in relation to its definition, framework, and metrics and problems. Other definitions emphasize the alignment of organizational activities with strategic objectives and the feedback for improvement (Neely et al., 2002; Parmenter, 2015). It involves financial and non-financial measures and is a component of performance management systems.

The Balanced Scorecard by Kaplan and Norton (1992) is one of the most widely used frameworks for performance measurement. In fact, it requires an approach that is multidimensional in nature, involving a financial, customer, internal process, and learning and growth perspective that gives a picture of the organization's performance. Performance Prism, developed by Neely et al. (2002), is still further extended from the basic framework by including stakeholder satisfaction as a prime aspect. The approach underlines the balance of needs of all stakeholders: customers, employees, and shareholders.

KPIs are those particular measures defined to evaluate performance against the strategic objectives. The extant literature highlighted the consideration of choosing relevant and action-oriented KPIs consistent with the organizational goals (Aguinis, 2009; Parmenter, 2015). Best KPIs should:

- Specific and measurable
- Aligned with strategic objectives
- Communicated clearly to stakeholders

Performance measurement incorporates both quantitative and qualitative data. Quantitative measures, such as sales figures or productivity rates, provide an objective view, whereas qualitative measures, such as employee satisfaction surveys, are a more subjective measure of performance (Bititci et al., 2012). The advent of data analytics and business intelligence transformed the face of performance measurement to now enable the efficient gathering and analysis of vast volumes of data (Bersin, 2014). Real-time performance monitoring becomes easy with the technologies; there is also an increase in the decision-making ability.

Challenges in Performance Measurement

Despite its importance, performance measurement faces several challenges:

- Inconsistent or poor-quality data can undermine the effectiveness of performance measurement efforts (Kellen, 2003).
- Employees and managers may resist new measurement systems due to fear of accountability or lack of understanding (Kotter, 1996).
- An excessive focus on metrics can lead to tunnel vision, where organizations prioritize short-term results over long-term sustainability (Marr, 2012).

Performance measurement is one of the most important functions in an organization, giving the necessary insights into efficiency and effectiveness. The literature points out different frameworks, the importance of choosing appropriate KPIs, and the challenges of implementation. As organizations evolve, further research and adaptation of performance measurement practices will be required to ensure relevance and effectiveness in achieving strategic objectives.

HR METRICS

HR metrics are quantitative measurements used to appraise the impact of HR practices on performance. The literature review outlines key themes and findings of HR metrics, including definition, types, challenges facing implementation, and future areas of focus. HR metrics are data points that can be used to give insight into various aspects of human resource management. They are imperative in measuring the effectiveness of HR processes and their roles in the achievement of strategic business objectives (Boudreau & Ramstad, 2007). It will allow organizations to take decisions based on facts as HR practices are aligned to organizational performance as a whole.

Types of HR Metrics

- Operational Metrics: It deals with the operational aspects of HR processes. Main examples include:
- Time to Fill: The average time taken to fill a position, indicating the efficiency of the recruitment process.
- Cost per Hire: The total cost associated with hiring new employees, providing insights into recruitment expenditures (Phillips & Gully, 2015).

Employee Engagement Metrics: Metrics related to employee engagement assess workforce sentiment and commitment. General measures include employee satisfaction surveys and engagement scores, which are associated with organizational performance and retention (Harter et al., 2002).

Performance Metrics: Performance metrics measure the productivity and effectiveness of employees. Performance appraisal scores, accomplishment of KPIs, and overall team performance metrics are some examples (Aguinis, 2009).

Retention Metrics: Retention metrics allow organizations to understand workforce stability and the effectiveness of their retention strategies through turnover rates and employee tenure (Griffeth et al., 2000).

Implementation of HR Metrics

Effective HR metrics must base their effectiveness on robust data collection and analysis processes. This can be achieved by making use of the data produced from HR information systems and data analytics in the collection and interpretation of workforce data accurately (Bersin, 2014). In order to be effective, HR metrics must align themselves with the overall goals of an organization. According to research, proper metrics ought to reflect the strategic aim of an organization (Becker & Huselid, 2006).

Challenges in Utilizing HR Metrics

Despite its importance, performance measurement has the following challenges:

- Despite the advantages of HR metrics, several challenges often prevent their effective use: Inaccurate or inconsistent data can raise questions about the reliability of metrics (Kellen, 2003).
- Employees and management may resist new measurement systems because of accountability and transparency concerns (Kotter, 1996).
- An excessive focus on metrics can lead to short-term thinking, potentially neglecting long-term development and engagement (Marr, 2012).

The Role of Technology in HR Metrics

The increasing adoption of technology in HR has transformed how metrics are collected and analyzed. Advanced analytics and artificial intelligence (AI) enable organizations to derive deeper insights from workforce data, predicting trends and enhancing decision-making capabilities (Bersin, 2014).

HR metrics are essential for evaluating the effectiveness of human resource practices and their alignment with organizational goals. The literature highlights various types of metrics, the importance of data quality, and the challenges faced in their implementation. As organizations increasingly embrace technology, the future of HR metrics lies in leveraging advanced analytics to drive strategic HR initiatives.

The firm is facing a need for an enhanced performance management system due to the escalating competitiveness and evolving work environment.

Performance management is widely recognized as a crucial determinant of organizational success. Historically, the evaluation of performance has been conducted through the utilization of financial ratios. Subsequently, the concept of time-based measurement introduced by Stalk (1988) gained prominence in academic discourse. Additionally, the works of Goldratt and Cox (1992) explored the utilization of efficiency, activities, input, inventory, and money as key factors in organizational analysis (M. B. Alazzam, et al., 2024). The performance pyramid, as described by Wedman and Graham (1998), was employed to find areas for improvement in performance. The utilization of an activity-based costing system was also employed for performance measurement (Manoharan G., et al., 2022). The Balanced Scorecard, initially introduced by Kaplan and Norton in 1992, evolved as a more effective and easily applicable methodology.

The categorization of performance metrics into five core types is outlined in the Performance-Based Management Handbook of 2001. The individuals under consideration are: The concept of "Input Measures" pertains to the evaluation of the human and capital resources utilized in the process of generating outputs. The phrase "Process Measures" is utilized to evaluate the actions related to the manufacturing of goods or provision of services. The phrase "Output Measures" pertains to the metrics utilized for assessing the product or service provided by a firm and its distribution to customers. The term "Outcomes Measures" is utilized to evaluate the expected, intended, or achieved outcomes that influence the overall effectiveness of an organization. The term "Impact Measures" is used to measure direct or indirect effects of varying outcomes on the organizational goal. In this study, the concept of measures serves as a tool for measurement of the effectiveness of worker performance.

Worker performance achievement is something that a business has to be acknowledged by all stakeholders. Moreover, performance feedback should be provided for the company, according to Mento et al. (1987). In line with this, according to Humble (1987), the four main variables can be applied to measure the workforce effectiveness of an organization. The dimensions covered are quantity, quality, time, and cost. Other measures of workforce performance also include job-specific competence at a specified level (Campbell et al, 1990) and interpersonal proficiency by Lance et al, (1992). According to Maxham et al. (2008), in-role performance should be accompanied by an examination of an employee's extra-role behavior towards customers and the business so that a perfect evaluation of the general performance of the employee can be achieved. Mael et al. (2010) have suggested that, for a general assessment of employee performance, criteria include employee support, service, citizenship behavior, and management behavior.

Kaplan and Norton, 1996, presented balanced scorecard as an integrated approach that considers development of suitable performance measures from various significant perspectives including customer satisfaction Motwani et al., 2024, process efficiency Shameem et al., 2023, staff growth, and financial performance Manoharan G., et al., 2023. The HR scorecard, conceptualized by Becker, Huselid, and Ulrich (2001), is regarded as a conceptual model that drives the need for alignment between HR practices and business strategy and organizational results. Organisations have increasingly adopted the systematic and standardized reporting process of various HR metrics mainly because of the significant progress in computer-mediated communication infrastructures and better access to data through integrated human resource information systems (HRIS) (Manoharan, G., et al., 2023). According to Cascio, 1987, many organizations measure and analyze HR plans and operations; according to others, including Fitz-enz and Davidson, 2002. In addition, they develop HR metrics for employee assistance and work-life programs, according to Cascio, 2000, among others, Manoharan G., et al., 2023.

Various authors have developed different measures, and the Society for Human Resource Management (SHRM, 2010; Manoharan, G., et al., 2023; Raj, R., et al., 2024) has recognized several metrics that firms can use to measure the performance of their workforce. The model by Hollmann (2002) can be used to measure absenteeism, while the method proposed by Cascio (2000) can be used to measure turnover. Battagello et al. (2016) have proposed in their study the methodology, known as the 7-SF approach. Characterized by a clustering procedure and open, this approach can be very flexible and can be used in numerous applications. The perspective here is values-centered. Often, the instrument is used as a benchmark in numerous research studies.

The process has seven sequential steps through which a comprehensive framework can be developed.

The component utilized for evaluating HR Metrics, Workforce Effectiveness, and Performance Measurement, using components drawn from a variety of writers' ideas. Here is a list:

Workforce Effectiveness

According to Stephen J. DeGroot in his book "Workforce Effectiveness: A Practical Guide", 2013, Workforce Effectiveness is often defined as the degree to which an organization's workforce can achieve its goals and objectives efficiently and productively. It involves factors such as employee engagement, skills utilization, and alignment of workforce activities with organizational strategies. In this book, DeGroot discusses various elements that contribute to workforce effectiveness, including talent management, leadership, and performance measurement.

Humble's suggestion, which includes quantity, quality, time, and cost, is taken into consideration for the study because the objective is to use HR metrics for measuring the various determinants of workforce performance. Although other authors suggest a variety of important dimensions to measure the effectiveness of the workforce, Humble's suggestion is the particular one that is taken into consideration. First, the elements that contribute to the effectiveness of the workforce are identified, and then, after that, they are categorized into key performance indicators that are in line with the goals of both the business and the person.

Workforce Effectiveness refers to the ability of an organization's employees to achieve desired outcomes efficiently and productively. It encompasses various dimensions, including:

- The level of commitment and enthusiasm employees have toward their work and the organization.
- Ensuring that employees' skills and competencies are aligned with their roles and organizational needs.
- Implementing systems for setting clear goals, providing regular feedback, and measuring employee performance against those goals.
- Offering opportunities for continuous learning and skill enhancement to improve individual and team performance.

- Fostering a positive work environment that encourages collaboration, innovation, and employee well-being.
- Utilizing HR metrics and analytics to inform strategies and interventions that enhance workforce productivity.

Ultimately, workforce effectiveness is critical for achieving organizational goals and sustaining competitive advantage. Organizations that prioritize these elements are better positioned to adapt to changes, improve employee satisfaction, and drive overall success.

Performance Measurement

According to Robert D. Austin in his book "Measuring and Managing Performance in Organizations", 1996, Performance Measurement refers to the process of evaluating the efficiency and effectiveness of actions within an organization. It refers to the use of metrics for determining the degree to which organizational goals and objectives are being met, hence, for informed decision-making and improvements. Austin investigates different frameworks and methodologies for performance measurement, elaborating on how organizations can better track and analyze performance data to drive improvement, in this book.

According to Parmenter, David in his book " Key Performance Indicators: Developing, Implementing, and Using Winning KPIs", 2015, work focuses on practical designing and utilization of KPIs for effective measuring performance in organizations. Relevant to the effectiveness of work force is its place inside the organizational performance management system. According to the Performance-Based Management Handbook, which was published in 2001, performance metrics fall into five broad categories. Among these available measurements, input measures, process measures, output measures, outcome measures, and impact measures are found. Indicators are one of the methods through which effectiveness of the workforce performance is determined. This study bases its discussion on indicators.

Performance Measurement: A systematic approach to the measurement of effectiveness and efficiency of performance relative to organizational objectives and achievement of goals. It quantifies, based on various indicators or metrics, this aspect of the performance for:

- Ensuring that performance measures are directly linked to the organization's strategic objectives.
- Identifying relevant metrics that provide insights into critical areas, such as productivity, quality, and customer satisfaction.
- Gathering quantitative and qualitative data to evaluate performance over time and identify trends.
- Implementing processes for regular feedback and communication among teams to foster continuous improvement.
- Comparing performance metrics against industry standards or competitors to gauge effectiveness and identify best practices.

Using performance data to inform decision-making, drive improvement initiatives, and allocate resources effectively. With an effective performance measurement structure in place, organizations could boost their accountability, drive more strategic initiatives, and subsequently better their overall performance in being competitive.

HR Metrics

According to Jac Fitz-enz in his book "The New HR Analytics: Predicting the Economic Value of Your Company's Human Capital Investments", 2010, HR metrics are quantified measures designed to measure how effectively and efficiently human resources are practiced within an organization. In this regard, metrics allow the organization to gauge performance through employee performance, recruitment, retention, among other related HR activities so that strategic decisions can be made in the process of development of strategy. In this book, Fitz-enz has discussed many of the HR metrics and analytics that provide insights into how organizations can utilize these metrics in improving their HR functions and overall organizational performance.

In "HR Metrics: How to Measure and Improve HR Performance", 2015, Bersin indicates that Josh provides an overview of types of HR metrics organizations ought to consider and how one can apply them to make the most out of a successful business. The relevance of the effectiveness of the workforce remains in its position within the organizational performance management system. According to the Performance-Based Management Handbook, published in 2001, performance metrics fall into five major categories. Among these categories are input measures, process measures, output measures, outcome measures, and impact measures. Indicators are selected in this research for measuring the workforce's performance.

HR Metrics are quantifiable measures to gauge the effectiveness and efficiency of human resource management practices of an organization. These metrics will enable HR professionals and their leaders to analyze the performance of their workforce and make decisions. Some key aspects are as follows:

1. Recruitment Metrics: Track time-to-fill, cost to hire, and source-of-hire effectiveness in terms of hiring.
2. Retention Metrics: Track turnover rates, employee tenure, and departures to better understand the causes of retention failures.
3. Engagement Metrics: Measurement of employee engagement and satisfaction is conducted by asking surveys and feedback tools.
4. Performance Metrics: Employee performance will be measured through performance appraisals, productivity measures, and achievement of KPIs.
5. Training and Development Metrics: Analyze the effectiveness of training programs, including participation rates, skill improvements, and training ROI.
6. Diversity Metrics: Monitor the diversity of the workforce and assess the effectiveness of inclusion initiatives.
7. Workforce Planning Metrics: Forecast future HR needs and assess the alignment of workforce skills with organizational goals.

By leveraging HR metrics, organizations can gain insights into workforce dynamics, enhance decision-making, improve employee engagement and performance, and ultimately drive organizational success.

Figure 1. Conceptual framework for linking workforce effectiveness metrics with the performance management measures

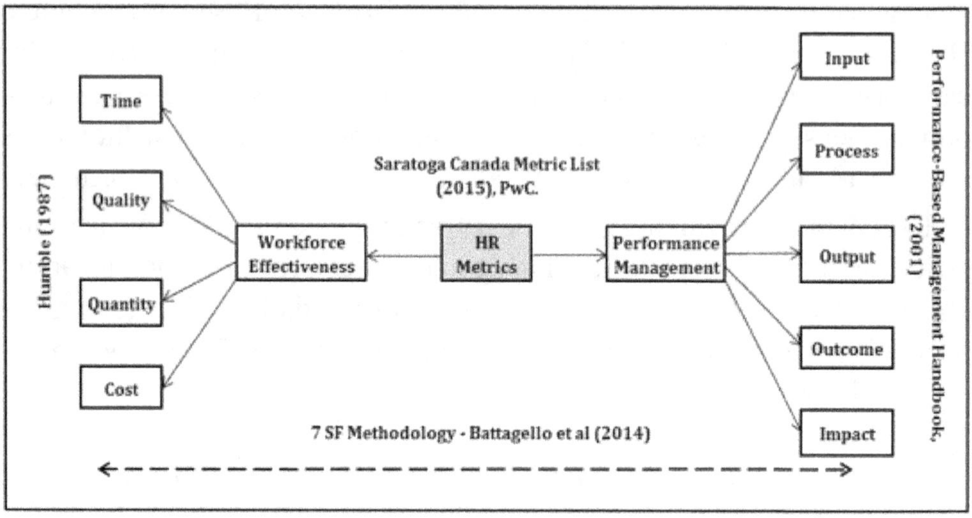

Source: Author's Constructs (2017)

RESEARCH METHODOLOGY

The HR metrics that were identified from the literature that helps to measure various determinants of workforce effectiveness such as "Cost," "Quality," "Quantity," and "Time" are linked with the appropriate performance measures (Input, Output, Process, Outcome, and Impact) by utilizing the 7-Step Framework, which is a clustering tool that is open to the public. As a benchmarking tool, it is utilized in a variety of research projects.

Seven separate steps are included in the process, and through these processes, an open framework can be constructed. Identifying a value creation area, also known as "Deliverable Values," is the first step that the researcher takes in the process of doing the research. In the second phase, which is referred to as the "V-Domain," the detected values are clustered according to different core research domains that are relevant to the investigation. The components that are referred to as "V-Components1 and V-Components2" are populated with quantifiable features that contribute to the development of deliverable values during the third and fourth steps of the process. The introduction and computation of "Appropriate HR Metrics" constitutes the fifth step in the process. The Human Resources Metrics are essential indicators that shed light on the results of the deliverable values by providing clarification. In the end, the performance measurements are connected to the derived set of HR measurements, which is described in a variety of scholarly sources, by means of an analysis of the impact and functioning of these measures.

In conclusion, a model that is resembling a leaf has been derived from the value domain tree, and the findings have been effectively communicated to both readers and practitioners in a manner that is succinct. The current research makes use of Key Result Areas (KRAs), Key Performance Indicators (KPIs), and performance metrics in order to evaluate the efficiency of the workforce by utilizing a variety of performance measures. In order to improve the efficiency of the presentation of the study, the 7SF technique is utilized.

RESEARCH FINDINGS

The 7-Step Framework is a set of open-access clustering tools that consists of seven primary phases to cluster the output of workforce effectiveness metrics with performance measurement. Each stage has been broken down into its component parts below.

Step 1: "Deliverable Value"

It is essential for businesses that want to improve their overall effectiveness to have a primary emphasis on the efficiency of their personnel. Because of this, an improvement in the efficacy of the workforce leads to an improvement in the overall effectiveness of the overall organization. For the sake of this investigation, determining the efficiency of the workforce has become the primary objective, and it is presumed that this will be the deliverable value in the initial stage.

Step 2 to 4: Identification of "V- Domains", "V-Component 1" and "V-Component 2"

When it comes to determining the effectiveness of the workforce, there are a lot of literatures that provide an explanation of the significant factors that contribute to it. However, to determine the suitable factors that measure the effectiveness of the workforce in the organization, a number of different literatures are surveyed, and this process ultimately results in the identification of a set of determinants that evaluate the workforce's effectiveness. Time, quality, cost, and quantity are the four factors that are considered to be V-Domains, and according to the description provided by Humble (1987), the factors that determine the efficacy of the workforce are classified into these four categories.

V-Components 1 and V-Components 2 are figured out for each of the V-Domains in the succeeding stage of the process. In accordance with the Cost Accounting Standard 1 (CAS-1) that was developed by the Institute of Cost and Management Accountants (ICMA), direct costs are defined as expenses that can be easily traced to a particular product, cost unit, cost center, or individual activity. When we talk about indirect costs, we are referring to expenses that are difficult to assign to a particular product or that are considered to be economically impracticable to assign. The term "shared costs" is another name for "common costs," which consists of costs that are typically encountered in several commodities. For the purpose of this investigation, which aims to determine the most important performance area that is associated with the determinant of "Cost," the idea is initially divided into two unique components, which are referred to as "Direct Cost" and "Indirect Cost." It is possible for individual, departmental, or organizational elements to have a role in making the determination of whether costs are direct or indirect. Therefore, the determinant known as "Cost" is broken down into quantifiable parts, and the HR metrics are determined for each of these units.

Both "Historical" and "Predetermined" are categorizations that can be used to the determinant "Time." Specifically, historical data refers to the actual data that has been recorded during the course of the time period that is being considered for analysis. Predetermined factors are statistics that are computed in advance by management in order to establish standards or estimations with which actual performance is compared. These factors are used to benchmark actual performance. The primary purpose is to determine the degree to which actual performance differs from the standards or estimations that have been established by the organization in that particular functional or operational area.

Regarding the determinant 'Quantity' or 'Volume,' it is possible to categorize it as either 'Fixed' or 'Variable' for the time of accounting that has been specified. A performance is said to have a fixed character if it is measured in a consistent manner over the course of a period of time, regardless of whether the period is short run or long run. Whether it is for a temporary or permanent purpose, it is essential to determine the nature of the situation. The term "variable nature" refers to any performance that has a tendency to change in quantity over the course of a certain time period based on the amount of activity that is taking place. The identification of the performance variance in activities that are directly related with production and that are in the supporting areas for production is an important step that must be taken.

The determinant of 'Quality' can be classified into two categories, namely 'Controllable' and 'Uncontrollable', according to the quality feature that it possesses. Controllable factors are influenced by the organization's policy maker, who has the ability to exercise influence. Belkaoni asserts that all characteristics of a variable nature that are associated with direct costs and over a longer length of time are controllable in nature. Non-controllable elements are those that are fixed by nature and relate to indirect costs for a shorter time of measurement. These factors are not impacted by any level of management and are not subject to any kind of influence.

Step 5: Identification of "KPI" or "HR Metrics"

The Saratoga Canada Metrics list from 2015 contains the appropriate metrics for monitoring workforce effectiveness, which are taken from the list. There is a collection of thirty-five (35) indicators that have been identified as being pertinent to the four V-Domains that determine the effectiveness of the workforce. Thirty-five (35) measures for measuring the efficacy of the workforce have been identified. Seven (7) metrics have been identified to assess the 'Cost' element, seven (7) metrics have been identified to measure the 'Quantity' factor, eleven (11) metrics have been identified to measure the 'Quality' component, and ten (10) metrics have been identified to measure the 'Time' factor.

Step 6: "Categories" of Performance Measurement:

There are five primary categories that are used to classify the performance measures. Input Measures, Process Measures, Output Measures, Outcome Measures, and Impact Measures are the several categories that can be used to differentiate the aforementioned measurements. In accordance with the fundamental qualities and goals that are intended for these measures, they are once again connected to the pertinent metrics that pertain to human resources that were discussed in the stage before this one. Once more, attention is taken to determine the nature of each and every performance measure, and then it is linked with the metrics that are most relevant. The purpose of this stage is to provide a clear conceptualization of the set of metrics that are taken into consideration as components of each of the performance measures. In other words, it suggests that in order to evaluate a specific performance measure, the right set of metrics needs to be calculated. The structure that contains all of the stages together with the necessary function is referred to as a value domain tree, and it is shown in table 1 below.

Figure 2. Value Domain Tree showing the seven steps of 7SF Methodology

Step 1 DELIVERABLE VALUES	Step 2 V-DOMAIN	Step 3 V-COMPONENT 1	Step 4 V-COMPONENT 2	Step 5 KPI	Step 6 CATAGORIES	Step 7 PERFORMANCE
WORKFORCE EFFECTIVENESS	COST	DIRECT	INDIVIDUAL	HR METRICS	INPUT MEASURES	PERFORMANCE MANAGEMENT SYSTEM
		INDIRECT	DEPARTMENT ORGANISATION		PROCESS MEASURES	
	TIME	HISTORICAL	ACTUAL			
		PRE-DETERMINED	STANDARD /ESTIMATES		OUTPUT MEASURES	
	QUANTITY	FIXED	SHORT RUN LONGRUN		OUTCOME MEASURES	
		VARIABLE	DIRECT			
	QUALITY	CONTROLLABLE	INDIRECT INDIVIDUAL DEPARTMENT		IMPACT MEASURES	
		UN-CONTROLLABLE	ORGANISATION			

Source: Author's Constructs (2017)

Step 7: "Performance Measurements"

In the context of performance management systems, the efficacy of the workforce is an essential component. It is impossible to avoid the duty of identifying the many metrics that are utilized in the process of analyzing the comprehensive performance measurement of the workforce functioning inside an organization. Within the framework of the 7SF approach, a comprehensive collection of measurements is presented in the form of a leaf-like paradigm. Additionally, it suggests two different reporting formats to display the results. These forms are the top-down side format and the bottom-up side model.

Reporting Formats:

Top-Down side Format

When considering the 'Cost' of workforce effectiveness as a single factor, the top-down side structure is shown in Figure 3, which explains. This format provides an explanation of the flow sequence that begins with the determination of the component of workforce effectiveness, which is cost and continues with the division of that factor into several key performance areas and indicators. Following that, it has been connected with the HR metrics that have been derived from the literature search database. Last but not least, these measurements are once more connected to the proper measures of the performance management system. The concluding presentation of this report is designed to resemble a leaf-like model, which enables the readers to easily and swiftly comprehend the connection between the variety of characteristics that comprise the framework.

Figure 3. Top-Down side Reporting format: Metrics measuring the cost factor of workforce effectiveness linked with PMS measures using 7SF Methodology.

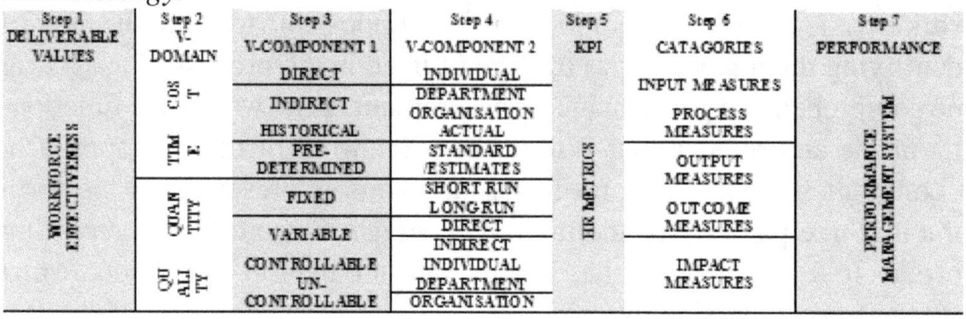

Source: Author's Constructs (2017)

Bottom-up side Format

Using the PMS input measure as an example, this bottom-up side format is explained in Figure 4, which may be found here. Five different kinds of measures are included in a performance management system. These are input, process, output, outcome, and impact measures. Each statistic is examined with the assistance of a collection of human resource metrics that have been derived from the relevant literature. As an illustration, the input measure is analyzed with the assistance of ten (10) HR metrics, which of course are associated with a variety of aspects that contribute to the effectiveness of the workforce. This assists in identifying metrics that are deemed to be input measurements, which are again related with various elements such as the cost, quality, quantity, and time of workforce effectiveness. Consequently, this style makes it easier for the reader to comprehend, from the point of view of the PMS, the collection of workforce effectiveness metrics that are used to analyze various measures of performance levels.

Figure 4. Bottom-Up side Reporting Format: Metrics to evaluate Input Measures of PMS measurement linked with factors of Workforce Effectiveness using 7SF Methodology.

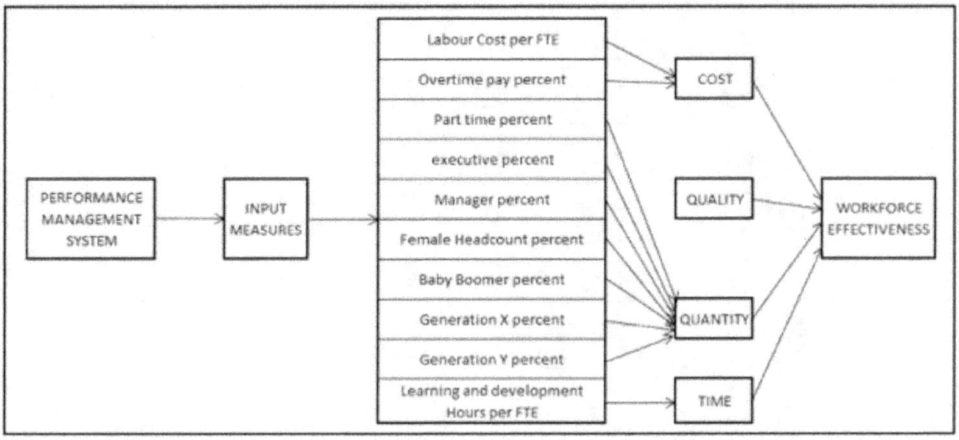

Source: Author's Constructs (2017)

The overall output of the workforce effectiveness metrics linked with performance measures are given below in Figure 5.

Figure 5. Workforce effectiveness Metrics linked with PMS measures using 7SF Methodology.

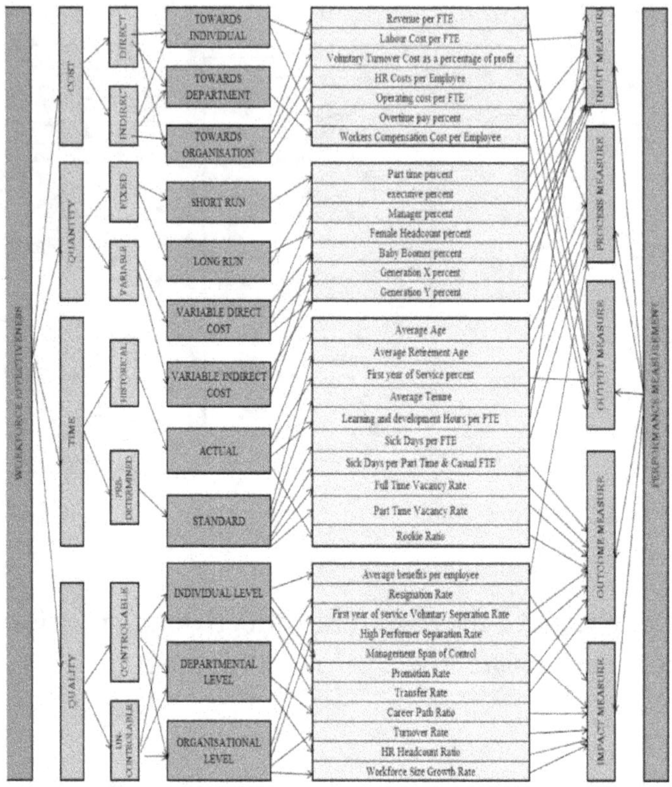

Source: Author's Constructs (2017)

RECOMMENDATIONS

Recommendations in Increasing Workforce Effectiveness

- Increasing workforce effectiveness involves a strategic approach that combines several best practices. Here are some solutions and recommendations:
- Encourage a culture where employees feel comfortable sharing their ideas and concerns.

- Use engagement surveys to gather feedback and understand employee sentiments.
- Use SMART (Specific, Measurable, Achievable, Relevant, Time-bound) criteria for goal-setting.
- Establish a routine for performance reviews and ongoing feedback to ensure alignment and growth.
- Offer workshops, online courses, and mentorship programs to develop employees' skills.
- Organize events that strengthen team relationships and improve morale.
- Tailor training to individual career goals and competencies.
- Promote a diverse workforce and foster an inclusive environment where everyone feels valued.
- Offer options such as remote work, flexible hours, or compressed workweeks.
- Employ data-driven tools to analyze workforce metrics, identify trends, and make informed decisions.
- Create recognition programs that celebrate employee achievements, both big and small.
- Implement project management and communication platforms to improve collaboration among teams.
- Continuously review workforce effectiveness initiatives to gauge success and make necessary adjustments Consider financial rewards or benefits for achieving specific targets.
- Involve employees in decision-making processes to improve buy-in and motivation.
- Provide resources for mental health, physical wellness, and stress management.
- Compare your metrics with industry standards to identify areas for improvement.
- Regularly assess processes to eliminate inefficiencies and reduce redundancy.

RECOMMENDATIONS IN IMPROVING PERFORMANCE MEASUREMENT

Improving performance measurement within an organization involves establishing clear, actionable metrics and fostering a culture of continuous improvement. Here are some solutions and recommendations to enhance performance measurement:

- Ensure that all performance metrics are directly tied to the organization's overall goals and objectives.
- Encourage regular feedback between managers and employees rather than relying solely on annual reviews.
- Ensure goals are Specific, Measurable, Achievable, Relevant, and Time-bound.
- Leverage data to forecast future performance trends and identify areas for improvement.
- Focus on metrics that provide insights into performance and are relevant to specific roles or departments.
- Share performance data with teams to promote accountability and collaboration.
- Recognize and reward individuals and teams who meet or exceed performance metrics to motivate others.
- Use technology to collect, analyze, and visualize data related to employee performance and productivity.
- Continuously assess and update KPIs to ensure they remain aligned with changing business objectives.
- Look for patterns over time to understand performance dynamics and identify areas needing attention.
- Train employees and managers on how to interpret performance metrics and utilize them for improvement.
- Share success stories and high performance to inspire the workforce.
- Incorporate feedback from peers, subordinates, and supervisors for a well-rounded view of performance.
- Empower employees to take ownership of their performance metrics and outcomes.

- Compare performance against industry standards or competitors to gauge effectiveness.
- Regularly ask for employee feedback on existing performance measures and make adjustments based on their insights.
- Be adaptable to changing the strategy and metrics due to business needs or employee feedback that is constantly evolving.
- Provide goal-setting and performance monitoring training.
- Employment participation should be encouraged by setting performance measures so as to have buy-in and relevance.
- Schedule regular reviews of performance measurement practice to make sure they are adequate and relevant.

RECOMMENDATIONS IN USING HR METRICS

Using HR metrics effectively can greatly enhance workforce management and decision-making in an organization. Here are some strategies and recommendations for leveraging HR metrics:

- Ensure that HR metrics support the broader organizational goals. For example, if a company aims to improve customer service, focus on metrics related to employee training and satisfaction.
- Measure turnover rates, employee tenure, and reasons for leaving to understand retention challenges.
- Track time to fill, cost per hire, and source of hire to evaluate recruitment effectiveness.
- Develop dashboards that display key HR metrics in relation to business objectives for easier tracking and reporting.
- Use employee satisfaction scores and engagement survey results to assess workforce morale.
- Use tools like Tableau or Power BI to create visual representations of HR data for clearer insights.
- Implement systems that allow for real-time tracking and analysis of HR metrics.
- Establish a routine to review key HR metrics regularly, allowing for timely adjustments and interventions.

- Review metrics over time to determine whether there are patterns or anomalies that require attention.
- Use clear, concise reports to share insights from HR metrics with stakeholders.
- Engage employees in discussions about what metrics are important to them and how they are measured.
- Compare your HR metrics regularly against industry benchmarks to gauge performance and identify areas for improvement.
- Educate managers on interpreting HR metrics and using them to inform decision-making.
- Share the success stories behind data-driven decisions.
- Share the value of tracking particular HR metrics and how this helps benefit employees and the organization at large.
- Develop proactive strategies in case of predictions such as succession planning or recruitment drives at specific levels.
- Involvement in industry groups or forums for best-practice sharing and metrics.
- Detect problems early with the help of metrics, such as rising turnover rates or engagement scores.
- Develop an action plan based on data analysis to address the specific problems; for example, targeted training programs may be used to enhance the engagement.
- Agree to refine metrics and approaches as needed based on what is learned through the analysis and employee feedback.
- Use historical data to predict future trends about recruitment, retention, and performance.

FUTURE RESEARCH DIRECTIONS

These should include directions for future research work on workforce effectiveness, performance measurement, and HR metrics. The suggestions should be able to open further avenues for understanding, improving, and applying their contents in organizational contexts as well.

- Explore the impact of employee well-being initiatives on the overall effectiveness of the workforce and develop metrics that incorporate well-being into performance measurement.
- Explore how AI can predict employee performance, turnover, and engagement using historical data.
- Explore how flexible work arrangements influence employee performance and retention and identify best practices for flexible work arrangements.
- Explore how diversity teams impact organizational performance and identify metrics that effectively capture diversity-related outcomes.
- Data collection and analytics automation in order to enhance the precision of performance measurement.
- Methodologies that can be developed to measure the inclusivity of organizational cultures and their connections with workforce effectiveness.
- Explore strategies that can measure and enhance employee engagement in remote teams.
- Research how new metrics for virtual collaboration and productivity can be developed into performance measurement in remote and hybrid work settings.
- Investigation of real-time performance metrics and their effectiveness in driving agile decision-making within the HR function.
- Study on how performance measurement can be integrated across departments toward enhancing overall organizational effectiveness.
- Conduct studies comparing regions or industries on practices of performance measurement.
- Study the effects of continuous feedback systems on employee performance and engagement.
- Examine the development of shared metrics that promote collaboration between HR and functions such as finance and operations.
- How do the effects of a continuous learning culture build workforce effectiveness and performance?
- Assess the comparative effectiveness of various types of training on employee performance; develop measures for the assessment of return on investment by training

- Examine how a culture of organizations influences how HR metrics are interpreted or used in alternative geographic or cultural contexts.
- Longitudinal research is conducted to isolate long-run effects of any HR interventions on workforce effectiveness and measurement of performance.
- Research how aspects of the employee experience-be it onboarding, or career development, or maybe the workplace environment-can actually be measured and related back to overall performance.
- Investigate how relevancy and effectiveness of human resource metrics change over time with changing workforce dynamics
- Research employee journey mapping as one tool for understanding and making improvements in workforce effectiveness.

IMPLICATIONS

Measuring workforce performance at regular intervals has several important implications for organizations:

- Regular performance measurement helps ensure that individual and team efforts are aligned with organizational goals, facilitating better strategic execution.
- Frequent assessments allow for timely feedback, enabling employees to understand their strengths and areas for development. This encourages a culture of continuous improvement.
- Regular performance evaluations promote accountability among employees, encouraging them to take ownership of their work and meet expectations consistently.
- Regular data collection gives managers a clearer picture of workforce performance, enabling data-driven decisions regarding promotions, training, and resource allocation.
- Organizations that measure performance regularly can adapt more quickly to changes in the business environment or shifts in workforce dynamics.

- Ongoing performance measurement facilitates benchmarking against industry standards and the identification of best practices within the organization.
- Routine evaluations can identify performance issues or trends early, allowing organizations to address problems before they escalate.
- Understanding workforce performance trends enables better resource allocation, ensuring that talent is effectively utilized to meet organizational needs.
- Regular evaluations help identify specific training and development needs, allowing for more targeted and effective learning initiatives.
- Consistent feedback mechanisms can increase employee engagement, as individuals feel valued and recognized for their contributions.

CONCLUSION

A literature database will be used to compile a collection of workforce effectiveness indicators that are associated with approved performance measures. The purpose of this research is to establish such relationships. The objective is to provide evidence that these metrics serve as drivers and provide assistance to human resource practitioners in implementing and monitoring the effectiveness of their workforces inside their respective businesses. When it comes to management, decision-making procedures frequently place a high priority on the utilization of data that is conveniently accessible. Accounting systems are generally responsible for providing a substantial amount of the information that is utilized in these processes. In most cases, the department of human resources (HR) is in possession of qualitative data rather than quantitative data, which presents difficulties when it comes to utilizing this data appropriately for decision-making purposes. Unfortunately, during the process of making decisions as a whole, management frequently fails to take into account these qualitative considerations. On the other hand, human resource metrics place a larger emphasis on quantification and may be easily calculated using a variety of indicators such as head count, ratios, and formulas, which frequently serve as substitutes for financial accounts (Bhavya, K. R., et al., 2023). There is a widespread consensus that managerial decisions are arrived at after giving serious attention to the costs and advantages that are connected with each available alternative. Therefore, if the Human Resource Information Systems (HRIS) just provide information about expenses, then the value of such information is poor for the management of the organization when it comes to making decisions based on it. The purpose of this research is to develop a comprehensive set of metrics that can be applied to the evaluation of the efficiency of the workforce. Consequently, this leads to the establishment of an effective performance management system that enables management to make decisions that are informed and based on empirical data.

REFERENCES

Aguinis, H. (2009). *Performance management* (2nd ed.). Pearson Prentice Hall.

Austin, R. D. (1996). *Measuring and managing performance in organizations*. Dorset House Publishing.

Ayres, I. (2007). *Super crunchers: Why thinking-by-numbers is the new way to be smart*. Bantam Books.

Bakker, A. B., & Demerouti, E. (2008). Towards a model of work engagement. *Career Development International, 13*(3), 209–223. DOI: 10.1108/13620430810870476

Battagello, F. M., Cricelli, L., & Grimaldi, M. (2016). Benchmarking strategic resources and business performance via an open framework. *International Journal of Productivity and Performance Management, 65*(3), 324–350. DOI: 10.1108/IJPPM-08-2014-0129

Becker, B. E., & Huselid, M. A. (2006). Strategic human resources management: Theory and practice. In *The handbook of human resource management* (pp. 3–26). Blackwell Publishing.

Becker, B. E., Huselid, M. A., & Ulrich, D. (2001). *The HR scorecard: Linking people, strategy, and performance*. Harvard Business School Press.

Bersin, J. (2014). Big data in human resources: The future of HR analytics. *Deloitte University Press*. https://www2.deloitte.com/us/en/insights/deloitte-review/issue-14/dr14-big-data-in-human-resources.html

Bhavya, K. R., Dharmaraj, A., Pareek, P., Sathe, M. A., Tiwari, M., & Manoharan, G. (2023). Application of soft computing techniques for predictive analytics in financial markets. In *2023 6th International Conference on Contemporary Computing and Informatics (IC3I)* (pp. 1756–1760). IEEE. DOI: 10.1109/IC3I59117.2023.10397684

Bititci, U. S., Carrie, A. S., & McDevitt, L. (2012). Dynamic performance measurement systems. *International Journal of Production Economics, 139*(1), 238–248. DOI: 10.1108/01443570010321676

Boudreau, J. W., & Ramstad, P. M. (2007). *Beyond HR: The new science of human capital*. Harvard Business Review Press.

Campbell, J. P., McHenry, J. J., & Wise, L. L. (1990). Modeling job performance in a population of jobs. *Personnel Psychology, 43*(2), 313–333. DOI: 10.1111/j.1744-6570.1990.tb01561.x

Canada, P. (2015). *PwC Saratoga human capital effectiveness survey (HCES) - 2015 PwC Saratoga Canada metric list*. PwC Canada.

Cascio, W. F. (1987). *Costing human resources: The financial impact of behavior in organizations* (2nd ed.). Kent Publishing.

Cascio, W. F. (2000). *Costing human resources: The financial impact of behavior in organizations* (4th ed.). Kent Publishing.

DeGroot, S. J. (2013). *Workforce effectiveness: A practical guide*. Self-published.

Durai, S., Krishnaveni, K., & Manoharan, G. (2022a). Designing entrepreneurial performance metric (EPM) framework for entrepreneurs owning small and medium manufacturing units (SME) in Coimbatore. In *AIP Conference Proceedings* (Vol. 2418, No. 1). AIP Publishing. DOI: 10.1063/5.0081941

Durai, S., Krishnaveni, K., & Manoharan, G. (2022b). Leveraging HR metrics for effective recruitment & selection process in IT industries in Chennai and Coimbatore, Tamil Nadu. In *AIP Conference Proceedings* (Vol. 2418, No. 1). AIP Publishing. DOI: 10.4018/979-8-3693-1343-5.ch010

Durai, S., Krishnaveni, K., & Manoharan, G. (2022c). Metric based performance management of employees: A case study of MSME unit in Coimbatore, Tamil Nadu. In *AIP Conference Proceedings* (Vol. 2418, No. 1). AIP Publishing. DOI: 10.1063/5.0081943

Fitz-enz, J. (2010). *The new HR analytics: Predicting the economic value of your company's human capital investments*. AMACOM.

Fitz-enz, J., & Davidson, B. (2002). *How to measure human resources management* (3rd ed.). McGraw-Hill.

Gopinathan, R., & Manoharan, G. (2022). Work-life balance practices and organizational performance for achieving superior performance. In *The changing role of human resource management in the global competitive environment* (pp. 217–230). Book Rivers.

Griffeth, R. W., Hom, P. W., & Gaertner, S. (2000). A meta-analysis of antecedents and correlates of employee turnover: Update, moderator tests, and research implications for the next millennium. *Journal of Management, 26*(3), 463–488. DOI: 10.1177/014920630002600305

Harter, J. K., Schmidt, F. L., & Hayes, T. L. (2002). Business-unit-level relationship between employee satisfaction, employee engagement, and business outcomes: A meta-analysis. *The Journal of Applied Psychology, 87*(2), 268–279. https://psycnet.apa.org/doi/10.1037/0021-9010.87.2.268. DOI: 10.1037/0021-9010.87.2.268 PMID: 12002955

Hollmann, R. W. (2002). Absenteeism: Analyzing work absences (SHRM White Paper). Society for Human Resource Management.

Jaichandran, R., Krishna, S. H., Madhavi, G. M., Mohammed, S., Raj, K. B., & Manoharan, G. (2023). Fuzzy evaluation method on the financing efficiency of small and medium-sized enterprises. In *2023 International Conference on Artificial Intelligence and Knowledge Discovery in Concurrent Engineering (ICECONF)* (pp. 1–7). IEEE. DOI: 10.1109/ICECONF57129.2023.10083731

Kahn, W. A. (1990). Psychological conditions of personal engagement and disengagement at work. *Academy of Management Journal, 33*(4), 692–724. DOI: 10.2307/256287

Kaplan, R. S., & Norton, D. P. (1992). The balanced scorecard: Measures that drive performance. *Harvard Business Review, 70*(1), 71–79. PMID: 10119714

Kaplan, R. S., & Norton, D. P. (1996). *The balanced scorecard: Translating strategy into action.* Harvard Business School Press.

Kellen, V. (2003). Measuring performance: The key to achieving better results. *International Journal of Productivity and Performance Management, 52*(2), 179–194. DOI: 10.1108/17410400310469192

Kotter, J. P. (1996). *Leading change*. Harvard Business Review Press.

Krishnan, S. G., & Manoharan, G. (2022). An investigation in analysing the key aspects of high-performance work practice for enhancing productivity in the organisation. In *The changing role of human resource management in the global competitive environment* (pp. 31–44). Book Rivers.

Mael, F. A., O'Shea, P. G., Smith, M. A., Burling, A. S., Carman, K. L., Haas, A., & Rogers, K. S. (2010). Development of a model and measure of process-oriented quality of care for substance abuse treatment. *The Journal of Behavioral Health Services & Research, 37*(1), 4–24. DOI: 10.1007/s11414-009-9180-4 PMID: 19462245

Manoharan, G., Ashtikar, S. P., Durai, S., & Selvaraj, F. J. (2022). Work-Life Balance Perceptions of Women in the IT and ITeS Sectors in Kerala: A Research Study. *European Journal of Molecular and Clinical Medicine, 9*(7), 4764+. https://link.gale.com/apps/doc/A737509380/AONE?u=anon~92871157&sid=googleScholar&xid=0e0a5afe

Manoharan, G., Ashtikar, S. P., Durai, S., & Selvaraj, F. J. (2022). Work-Life Balance Perceptions of Women in the IT and ITeS Sectors in Kerala: A Research Study. *European Journal of Molecular and Clinical Medicine, 9*(7), 4764+. https://link.gale.com/apps/doc/A737509380/AONE?u=anon~e39eb447&sid=googleScholar&xid=70aae9af

Manoharan, G., Durai, S., & Rajesh, G. A. (2022). Identifying performance indicators and metrics for performance measurement of the workforce is the need of the hour: A case of a retail garment store in Coimbatore. In *AIP Conference Proceedings* (Vol. 2418, No. 1). AIP Publishing. DOI: 10.1063/5.0081821

Manoharan, G., Durai, S., Rajesh, G. A., & Ashtikar, S. P. (2023a). Credit and risk analysis in the financial and banking sectors: An investigation. In *Artificial intelligence for capital markets* (pp. 57–72). Chapman and Hall/CRC., DOI: 10.1201/9781003327745-5

Manoharan, G., Durai, S., Rajesh, G. A., Razak, A., Rao, C. B., & Ashtikar, S. P. (2023b). A study on the perceptions of officials on their duties and responsibilities at various levels of the organizational structure in order to accomplish artificial intelligence-based smart city implementation. In *Artificial intelligence and machine learning in smart city planning* (pp. 1–10). Elsevier., DOI: 10.1016/B978-0-323-99503-0.00007-7

Manoharan, G., Durai, S., Rajesh, G. A., Razak, A., Rao, C. B., & Ashtikar, S. P. (2023c). An investigation into the effectiveness of smart city projects by identifying the framework for measuring performance. In *Artificial intelligence and machine learning in smart city planning* (pp. 71–84). Elsevier., DOI: 10.1016/B978-0-323-99503-0.00004-1

Manoharan, G., Jalaja, V., Sathe, M. A., Lourens, M., & Suresh, K. (2023). Machine learning and data privacy in human resource management. In *2023 4th International Conference on Computation, Automation and Knowledge Management (ICCAKM)* (pp. 1–6). IEEE. DOI: 10.1109/ICCAKM58659.2023.10449576

Manoharan, G., & Rajoli, S. B. (2024). Leveraging technology for enhancing performance appraisal. In Rajapakshe, W. (Ed.), *Employee performance management for improved workplace motivation* (pp. 289–310). IGI Global., DOI: 10.4018/979-8-3693-4387-6.ch012

Manoharan, G., Razak, A., Rajchandar, K., Nithya, G., Durai, S., & Ashtikar, S. P. (2024). Digital learning for professional development in varied fields of service sectors: Embracing technological advancements. In *Embracing technological advancements for lifelong learning* (pp. 111–137). IGI Global., DOI: 10.4018/979-8-3693-1410-4.ch006

Marr, B. (2012). *Key performance indicators: The 75+ measures every manager needs to know*. Pearson.

McKinsey & Company. (2015). *Why diversity matters*. https://www.mckinsey.com/business-functions/people-and-organizational-performance/our-insights/why-diversity-matters

Motwani, B., Haryani, S., Manoharan, G., & Razak, A. (2024). Impact of workforce emotional intelligence on patient satisfaction: A sentiment analysis approach using supervised machine algorithms. In Rajapakshe, W. (Ed.), *Employee performance management for improved workplace motivation* (pp. 263–288). IGI Global., DOI: 10.4018/979-8-3693-4387-6.ch011

Neely, A., Adams, C., & Crowe, P. (2002). *The performance prism: The scorecard for measuring and managing business success*. Cambridge University Press.

Noe, R. A. (2017). *Employee training and development* (7th ed.). McGraw-Hill Education.

Parmenter, D. (2015). *Key performance indicators: Developing, implementing, and using winning KPIs* (3rd ed.). Wiley. DOI: 10.1002/9781119019855

Phillips, J. J., & Gully, S. M. (2015). *Strategic staffing* (3rd ed.). Pearson.

Ramachandran, K. K., Mary, S. S. C., Painoli, A. K., Satyala, H., Singh, B., & Manoharan, G. (2022). Assessing the full impact of technological advances on business management techniques. *The British Journal of Administrative Management, 58*(Special Issue 06). https://tbjam.org/vol58-special-issue-06

Saks, A. M. (2006). Antecedents and consequences of employee engagement. *Journal of Managerial Psychology, 21*(7), 600–619. DOI: 10.1108/02683940610690169

Sangeetha, M., Gupta, R., Reddy, K. S., Nanda, S. K., Mannar, B. R., Manoharan, G., & Liudmyla, I. (2024). Detailed investigation of digital transformational strategies to enhance business productivity. In *Proceedings of recent advances in management and engineering* (pp. 45–51). CRC Press. DOI: 10.1201/9781003532026-8

Schein, E. H. (2010). *Organizational culture and leadership* (4th ed.). Jossey-Bass.

Selvaraj, F. J., Singh, R., Manoharan, G., Razak, A., Kukreja, J., & Ashtikar, S. P. (2024). Evaluation of customer loyalty and customer relationship management in mobile communication lesson from new normal. In *2024 3rd International Conference on Computational Modelling, Simulation and Optimization (ICCMSO)* (pp. 216–221). IEEE. DOI: 10.1109/ICCMSO61761.2024.00052

Shameem, A., Ramachandran, K. K., Sharma, A., Singh, R., Selvaraj, F. J., & Manoharan, G. (2023). The rising importance of AI in boosting the efficiency of online advertising in developing countries. In *2023 3rd International Conference on Advance Computing and Innovative Technologies in Engineering (ICACITE)* (pp. 1762–1766). IEEE. DOI: 10.1109/ICACITE57410.2023.10182754

Chapter 5
Ethical Leadership Effect on Competitive Intelligence by Mediation of Digital Platforms in Horn of Africa

Shashi Kant
https://orcid.org/0000-0003-4722-5736
Bule Hora University, Ethiopia

Wako Jio
https://orcid.org/0009-0003-6192-459X
Bule Hora University, Ethiopia

Zerihun Kinde Alemu
https://orcid.org/0000-0002-8546-2882
Ethiopian Civil Service University, Ethiopia

Gebre Sorsa Takaro
https://orcid.org/0000-0003-0846-2894
Ethiopian Civil Service University, Ethiopia

DOI: 10.4018/979-8-3373-2690-0.ch005

ABSTRACT

This article aims to explore the association among leaders ethics and the influence use of platforms founded on digital technologies in nurtures intelligence to compete within corporates. It addresses the challenge of bring into ethical leadership practices with technological advancements to improve competitive policymaking. The study employs quantitative surveys to gather data from various industries regarding leadership styles and technology exploitation. Key outcomes manifest that leaders ethics worthy influences the adoption of digital tools, which in turn augments intelligence to compete capabilities. Corporates with a strong ethical ethos are more likely to leverage data influence in their competitive processes. The outcomes depict that nurturing leader's ethics is fundamental for corporates seeking to improve their intelligence to compete. Future directions assimilate investigating the specific traits of leader's ethics and the influence of emerging technologies on policymaking practices. Recommendations emphasize the need for training programs and approaches of leadership.

INTRODUCTION

In contemporary quickly changing global marketplace, leaders' ethics have emerged as a critical effect on intelligence to compete, especially in the context of platforms that utilize digital technology (Joseph et al., 2024). The Horn of Africa, an area distinguished by its unique socioeconomic dynamics and problems, provides a compelling case study for understanding the interaction of these aspects (Kant & Adula, 2025). While corporations increasingly rely on digital technologies for intelligence to compete, the role of leaders' ethics becomes critical within negotiating the difficulties of evidence the leadership team, stakeholder involvement, and competitive policies (Komolafe et al., 2024). The concept of leaders ethics can be traced back to foundational theories in leadership studies, emphasizing the implication of integrity, transparency, and accountability (Tadesse et al., 2024). Leader's ethics are tasked with not only steering their corporates towards success but also ensuring that their practices bring into line with honest and communal customs (Kant et al., 2025). In the background of intelligence to compete, leader's ethics nurtures a ethos of trust and collaboration, nurtures the excellence and reliability of evidence gathered through platforms founded on digital technologies (.Elifneh et al., 2024). Empirical literature underscores the positive correlation among leader's ethics and corporate growth, highlighting how ethical considerations shape competitive approaches and market positioning (Jio et al., 2025).

Despite the recognized prominence of leader's ethics, practical challenges persist in the Horn of Africa. Issues such as corruption, lack of regulatory frameworks, and inadequate digital infrastructure impede the influence implementation of leader's ethics principles (Kant et al., 2025). Also, the digital divide exacerbates these challenges, limiting access to evidence and hindering the potential for intelligence to compete among corporates in the region. Existing literature reveals worth gaps regarding how leaders ethics specifically mediates the association among intelligence to compete and platforms founded on digital technologies in this background (Jio et al., 2024).

This chapter aims to address these research gaps by providing a comprehensive analysis of the function of leaders ethics in nurtures intelligence to compete through platforms founded on digital technologies in the Horn of Africa. By exploring the interplay among these variables, the study will offer insights into influence leadership practices and their implications for corporate success. Also, it will identify practical approaches for policymakers and corporate leaders to augment leaders ethics and leverage platforms founded on digital technologies for improved intelligence to compete. The central research question guiding this investigation is: ***"How does leaders ethics influence intelligence to compete through the mediation of platforms founded on digital technologies in the Horn of Africa?'*** The matter is important not only in terms of educational discussion, but also for practitioners attempting to navigate the intricacies of the current corporate world. By delving into this subject, the chapter will contribute to an improved awareness of the dynamics at work and provide meaningful recommendations for future study and policy initiatives. Finally, the investigation aims to uncover routes towards cultivating ethical leaders, developing competitive intelligence, and supporting environmentally conscious growth in the Horn of Africa.

BACKGROUND OF STUDY

In the past few years, leaders' ethics have emerged as a vital aspect in navigating the intricacies of intelligence to compete, particularly in the context of emerging platforms based on digital technology (Maluleka & Chummun, 2024). The leaders' ethics, defined by the concepts of honesty, fairness, as well as accountability, serves as a foundation for corporations, affecting operational procedures along with competitive decisions. nevertheless implementing leaders' ethics throughout this region involves significant challenges, frequently originating from historical, political, as well as economic difficulties (Adeola, 2024). The previously Ethiopian telecoms sector is a renowned case study that illustrates these problems. Ethiopia's telecom sector became competitive to feed the first time in 2019, allowing private players to participate and diversify offerings (Kebede et al., 2024). But the legacy past state control and corruption has prompted ethical issues about openness in economic activities. While leaders' ethics might contribute to a healthier competitive atmosphere by promoting fair procedures and ingenuity, instances of nepotism including a lack of responsibility hampered the formation of a level playing field. Companies entering the sector experienced challenges while earning stakeholder trust, since the expectation of unethical behaviour continued. This narrative highlights the paramount necessity for leaders to reinstate trust and improve intelligence in order to succeed in a fast changing market (Kant et al., 2025).

In a comparable manner Somalia's rehabilitation from decades of violence provides another powerful evidence. The country has experienced an increase in wireless banking and digital platforms, spurred by the demand for financial inclusion (Joseph et al., 2024). Also, the lack of strong governing structures and ethical standards has hampered potential expansion. In accordance to research, corporations operating in Somalia frequently face corruption and a lack of transparency, which have a direct impact on their intelligence and competitive efforts (Demissie et al., 2024). For example, organizations attempting to benefit from platforms based on digital technology to feed market analysis typically have difficulties in acquiring genuine information owing to prevalent illegal acts. This not only jeopardizes their fiercely competitive judgments, but additionally feeds a cycle of distrust among customers and investors (Komolafe et al., 2024). Likewise, Djibouti's competitive position as a logistics center emphasizes the need of leadership ethics in cultivating international collaborations. Though the government has made efforts to attract international investment, charges of corruption and a lack of accountability have caused fear amid potential investors. The leaders' ethical divide has resulted within wasted possibilities for nurturing intellect to compete through joint initiatives, impeding economic progress. Successful partnerships operate on honesty and confidence, and without executives who prioritize rules of conduct, corporations may not be inclined to join completely, restricting their access to vital market knowledge (Maluleka & Chummun, 2024).

Several case studies highlight the significant issues of adopting leaders' ethics across the Horn of Africa. They stress the negative effects of corruption, a lack of transparency, and insufficient regulatory settings upon intelligence competition initiatives. The region's distinct sociopolitical situation needs a specialized approach that leader ethics, one that not only tackles these problems nevertheless leverages the possibilities of modern technology-based platforms to reinforce an ethos of honesty and responsibility. through studying these processes, the research hopes offering practical insights that leaders and policymakers, highlighting their significance of ethical frameworks that can adapt to the intricacies that define the Horn of Africa's commercial environment.

STATEMENT OF PROBLEM

The Horn of Africa stands at a crossroads where the potential for economic growth and development is undermined by persistent challenges related to leaders ethics and its influence on intelligence to compete (Joseph et al., 2024). The perfect situation envisions an area in which corporations use leaders' ethics to increase confidence, openness, and collaboration, eventually nurturing their intellect and competing through digitally based platforms (Kant et al., 2025). Nevertheless, the reality is far different, as various studies and empirical data indicate a disturbing picture marked by corruption, a lack public accountability, excessive influence government (Jio et al., 2025). This distinction raises serious concerns surrounding the feasibility of leadership ethics as a transformational force in the area (Adeola, 2024). Evidence from various studies depicts that while leaders ethics is associated with improved corporate growth globally, its application in the Horn of Africa remains ambiguous. Inconclusive outcomes emerge from existing literature, which often fails to establish a clear causal association among leaders ethics and intelligence to compete (Demissie et al., 2024). Some studies highlight positive outcomes in specific backgrounds, while others report minimal influence, leading to a fragmented understanding of how these concepts interact in the region. This inconsistency underscores worth theoretical gaps, particularly in the frameworks that define leader's ethics and its operationalization within the unique socio-economic backgrounds of the Horn of Africa (Maluleka & Chummun, 2024).

Knowledge gaps are also evident in the limited research specifically addressing the mediation of platforms founded on digital technologies in the association among leaders ethics and intelligence to compete. While digital transformation is reshaping business practices worldwide, there is a dearth of localized studies that explore how digital tools can either facilitate or hinder the leaders ethics framework in this background . (Demissie et al., 2024). Also, background gaps arise from the diverse cultural, political, and economic realities across the Horn of Africa, which are often overlooked in broader leadership studies. This oversight hampers the applicability of global theories to local situations, limiting the influenceness of proposed solution (Duressa & Kidane, 2024). Real-world problems exacerbate the situation even further. Corporates across the Horn of Africa frequently encounter structural difficulties, such as insufficient laws and regulations as well as a lack of resources, which impede the application of ethical standards (Adeola, 2024).. The pervasive culture of lawlessness and the growing acceptance of unethical behavior provide significant challenges over leaders seeking to effect change. Precisely a result, even well-intentioned attempts might fail, repeating cycles of mistrust and bureaucracy (Komolafe et al., 2024).

This study aims to address these gaps by providing a comprehensive analysis of how leaders ethics can be influence integrated into intelligence to compete practices through the mediation of platforms founded on digital technologies in the Horn of Africa. By synthesizing existing literature, conducting empirical research, and offering localized case studies, the study will contribute to a deeper understanding of the dynamics at play. Also, it will propose actionable recommendations for policymakers and corporate leaders, guiding them in nurturing leaders ethics practices that resonate with the region's unique challenges. Ultimately, this research aspires to illuminate pathways for future studies and practical interventions, ensuring that leaders ethics develops a cornerstone of intelligence to compete in the Horn of Africa.

THEORETICAL FRAMEWORK

Transformational Leadership Theory: James MacGregor Burns founded Transformational Leadership Theory, that was later modified through Bernard Bass, and it stresses leaders' capacity to inspire and motivate followers to reach above and beyond their own accord self-interests for the greater good (Ferede et al., 2024). According to this notion, transformative leaders exhibit actions that encourage a culture of trust, cooperation, and innovation. In the Horn of Africa, where leaders' ethics are critical to feed negotiating complicated sociopolitical contexts, transformational leadership can enable corporations to establish moral policies that supplement intellect to compete. Leaders that exemplify transformational skills may inspire their teams to emphasize ethical issues, fostering a climate of integrity that is in keeping with the needs within the quickly evolving digital world (Joseph et al., 2024).

Ethical Leadership Theory: Leaders ethics Theory focuses specifically on the behaviors and values of leaders that promote ethical conduct within corporates. This theory posits that leaders ethics not only model ethical behavior but also create an corporate ethos that prioritizes honest principles. In the Horn of Africa, where corruption and unethical practices are prevalent, Leaders ethics Theory is particularly pertinent. It serves as the main theoretical lens for this study, guiding the exploration of how leaders ethics can mediate the association among intelligence to compete and platforms founded on digital technologies (Adeola, 2024).

Stakeholder Theory: Stakeholder Theory, created by R. Edward Freeman, holds that corporations should consider the needs of all stakeholders, not just shareholders, while making decisions (Kant & Adula,

2025). This theory highlights the importance of ethical concerns in stakeholder relationships and shows how corporations can secure long-term success by meeting the requirements of many stakeholders. For the Horn of Africa, whereby multiple stakeholder interests frequently collide, this theory emphasizes the critical role of leaders' ethics in managing these organizations. Leaders may increase cognition by prioritizing stakeholder involvement including ethical issues (Komolafe et al., 2024).

Technology Assimilate Model (TAM): The Technology Assimilate Model, developed by Fred Davis, seeks to manifest how operators come to assimilate and use technology. It posits that perceived ease of use and perceived usefulness are critical factors influencing technology adoption. In the background of platforms founded on digital technologies in the Horn of Africa, TAM can be instrumental in understanding how leaders ethics influences the assimilate and exploitation of technology for intelligence to compete. Leader's ethics can augment perceptions of technology by endorsing its benefits and ensuring that it is implemented in a manner that respects ethical standards. This bring into prominence among leaders ethics and technology assimilate is fundamental for nurturing an corporate ethos that encirclements digital transformation (Maluleka & Chummun, 2024).

While each of these theories subsidizes valuable insights, "*Ethical Leadership Theory*" serves as the primary lens for this study. It directly addresses the ethical dimensions of leadership and their implications for intelligence to compete within the unique socio-economic background of the Horn of Africa. By focusing on leaders ethics, this study aims to provide a comprehensive understanding of how leaders can influence navigate the complexities of the region, nurturing ethical practices that augment intelligence to compete through platforms founded on digital technologies. This theoretical framework will guide the research, ensuring that the outcomes are grounded in relevant leadership concepts that resonate with the challenges faced by corporates in the Horn of Africa.

DEFINITION AND ORIGIN OF CONCEPTS

Ethical Leadership: Leaders' ethics promote the health and happiness of their followers. They appear to be function models, driving their companies to excellent achievements while upholding high ethical standards. The notion regarding management ethics has its origins in ancient philosophical traditions, such as Aristotle's teachings on virtue ethics. Nevertheless acquired significant momentum in the late decade of the century, notably in the realms of corporate behavior and management inquiry. Scholars such as John Ciulla and Linda Treviño have provided significant contributions to the creation of management ethics frameworks, with an emphasis on ethical policymaking (Jio et al., 2025).

Digital Platforms: Platforms built around digital technologies are online environments that allow the exchange using evidence, commodities, or services between operators, usually via the use of technology. These platforms can take numerous forms, including social media, e-commerce websites, and collaboration tools that allow operators to communicate and engage with one another (Joseph et al., 2024). Platforms built on digital technologies play an important role towards fostering connectedness, allowing corporations to reach a larger audience and engage with stakeholders with more power. This concept of digital platforms originated with the emergence of the internet as well as technical breakthroughs in the late twentieth century. In the beginning, platforms were primarily concerned with e-commerce and evidence sharing. Also, with the introduction of networking websites and mobile applications, the range of platforms constructed using digital technology has grown (Adeola, 2024).

EMPIRICAL LITERATURE REVIEW

Ethical Leadership and competetive Intelligence

Leaders ethics plays a pivotal function in shaping intelligence to compete within corporates, particularly in environments marked by uncertainty and complexity. Leaders who embody ethical principles create a ethos of trust and transparency, which is essential for nurturing open communication and collaboration among team members (Duressa & Kidane, 2024). This trust encourages employees to share insights and evidence more freely, nurtures the organization's collective intelligence. When team members feel secure in their functions and confident that their contributions are valued, they are more likely to engage in proactive evidence-gathering and analysis, which are critical components of influence intelligence to compete (Maluleka & Chummun, 2024). Also, leaders ethics helps corporates bring into line their intelligence to compete practices with honest and communal values. Leaders ethics prioritize integrity in their policymaking processes, ensuring that the evidence gathered and analyzed adheres to legal and ethical standards. This bring into prominence not only mitigates risks associated with unethical behavior, such as data manipulation or privacy violations, but also augments the credibility of the intelligence produced. Stakeholders, including customers and business partners, are more likely to trust an organization that demonstrates a commitment to ethical practices, thereby strengthening the organization's reputation and competitive position in the market (Komolafe et al., 2024).

As well, leader's ethics influences the way corporates approach competitor analysis and market research. In the background of the Horn of Africa, where challenges such as corruption and lack of regulatory frameworks are prevalent, the function of leader's ethics develops even more critical (Joseph et al., 2024). Leader's ethics can navigate these complexities by establishing robust frameworks for intelligence to compete that emphasize ethical behavior and accountability. By doing so, they can drive their corporates toward innovative solutions while maintaining a commitment to ethical practices. Ultimately, the synergistic association among leaders ethics and intelligence to compete creates an environment where corporates can thrive, nurturing resilience and adaptability in an progressively competitive landscape (Demissie et al., 2024).

Ethical Leadership and Digital Platforms

Ethics in leadership impacts how to use and influence of digital technology-based platforms within corporations? Leaders that uphold ethical values set the tone regarding how technology is used in their organizations, affecting the culture around digital activities (Duressa & Kidane, 2024). Leaders who prioritize openness, honesty, accountability, and integrity encourage their staff to implement digital technologies responsibly, ensuring that these platforms are exploited in ways that align with the organization's values (Tadesse et al., 2024). Such ethical approach fosters a climate of trust in which workers are encouraged to interact with digital technology-based platforms without being concerned about their contributions being misused or exploited (Adeola, 2024). In addition, leaders' ethics play an important role in defining the rules and norms that regulate the usage using digital platforms. Leaders that prioritize ethics are more inclined to push for rules that safeguard user privacy, enhance security of information, and maintain regulatory compliance (Ferede et al., 2024). This determination not only protects the organization's image, but it also increases user trust in the platforms built on digital technology. When workers including external stakeholders believe that the business emphasizes moral problems, they are more likely to actively participate in these spaces, resulting in improved cooperation, knowledge exchange, including innovation (Kant & Adula, 2025).

Furthermore, ethical leadership determines how corporations handle the digital shift. Leaders that hold ethical beliefs are more likely to address the more general societal ramifications of technology adoption, such as concerns regarding fairness and access. This approach pushes corporations towards developing platforms based on digital technologies that are inclusive and accessible to a wide range of user groups, hence increasing their impact on society. Leaders can promote increased participation while increasing a sense of community within the environment of technology by ensuring that digital projects take into consideration the expectations and opinions of many stakeholders (Jio et al., 2025). In the background of the Horn of Africa, where platforms founded on digital technologies are progressively vital for economic development, the function of leaders ethics is particularly pronounced. Leaders ethics can guide corporates in navigating the complexities of digital transformation amid challenges such as inadequate infrastructure and regulatory uncertainty. By endorsing ethical practices in the adoption and use of platforms founded on digital technologies, these leaders can help build a foundation of trust and credibility that is essential for nurturing long-term success (Komolafe et al., 2024).

Digital Platforms and competitive Intelligence

Platforms developed using digital technologies have drastically altered the terrain of intelligence competition by giving corporations unparalleled knowledge of facts and tools that help them make competitive policy decisions (Maluleka & Chummun, 2024). These networks make it easier to acquire, analyze, and disseminate knowledge about market trends, competitor activity, and consumer buying habits, allowing businesses to make more informed decisions. Companies may use digital technology to monitor real-time shifts in the market, permitting them to adapt quickly to unforeseen developments and preserve a competitive advantage (Jio et al., 2024). A couple of the key advantages of platforms built on technological advances is their capacity to consolidate massive volumes of data from various places. With the incorporation of analytics technologies, businesses can handle and analyze data more effectively than ever before (Joseph et al., 2024). For example, messaging platforms and online review sites provide significant knowledge into client feelings and preferences, which are critical for organizations to compete. Corporates may spot developing patterns along with shifts in customer behavior by evaluating the information in question, allowing them to alter their methods proactively and with more effect (Komolafe et al., 2024).

Furthermore, interfaces built on digital technology improve cooperation and information exchange within corporations. Teams may use online applications and collaborative software to communicate insights and intelligence across departments, breaking down the barriers that usually impede evidence flow (Duressa & Kidane, 2024). This collaborative setting fosters innovation whereas also allowing corporations to collect multiple ideas, resulting in more complete competitive analysis. The ability to leverage shared understanding improves an organization's ability to predict fluctuations in the market and competitor moves, thereby boosting its adversarial stance (Adeola, 2024). Fortunately the effectiveness of platforms based on digital technologies and cultivating intelligence to compete is dependent on their ethical use. To preserve confidence between customers and stakeholders, corporations must guarantee sure their data collection processes follow privacy legislation and ethical requirements (Demissie et al., 2024). As organizations traverse the complexity of digital transformation, including ethical concerns into the usage of venues based on digital technologies will be critical for realizing all that they can accomplish and maintaining a sustainable competitive edge. Finally, the collaboration of platforms which utilize computer technology as well as intelligence to compete provides a revolutionary possibility for enterprises to prosper in an increasing competitive global context (Kant & Adula, 2025).

Ethical Leadership, Competitive Intelligence Mediation of Digital Platforms

The amalgamation of leaders' ethics, competitive intelligence, and infrastructure built on digital technology is a vital nexus for corporations looking for success in today's complicated business climate. Leaders' ethics have an enormous effect on how corporations use platforms built around digital technology to acquire and analyze intelligence to compete (Duressa & Kidane, 2024). Leaders that promote ethical behaviors contribute to a culture about openness and trust, which is critical for harnessing digital technologies' consequence. This trust allows workers to interact openly through digital technology-based platforms, exchanging ideas and focusing using data-driven policymaking processes which supplement knowledge to provide competitive advantage (Jio et al., 2025). Platforms built on digital technologies are critical instruments for collecting and distributing data regarding market trends, rival activity, and customer behavior. Whenever leaders in ethics advocate for the ethical use of digital platforms, they create norms to protect data privacy, integrity, as well as regulatory compliance (Ferede et al., 2024). By embracing a moral structure regarding digital engagement, leaders may improve the quality of evidence acquired and assessed. This ethical posture not only reduces the potential risks of data misuse, but it also increases the credibility given to the intelligence provided, since stakeholders are more inclined to accept data information has been collected and managed properly (Maluleka & Chummun, 2024).

Leaders ethics often prioritize inclusivity, encouraging team members from various departments to contribute their insights and data. As platforms founded on digital technologies facilitate collaboration and knowledge-sharing, this collective intelligence develops a rich resource for competitive analysis. The synergy among leader's ethics and the collaborative capabilities of platforms founded on digital technologies allows corporates to develop more comprehensive and actionable intelligence to compete approaches (Jio et al., 2024). In the background of the Horn of Africa, where corporates face unique challenges related to governance and transparency, the function of leaders ethics develops even more pronounced. Leaders who embody ethical principles can influence guide their corporates in navigating the complexities of digital transformation (Demissie et al., 2024). By nurturing an ethical ethos around platforms founded on digital technologies, these leaders can augment the organization's ability to gather and analyze intelligence to compete responsibly and influence. This approach not only leads to improved competitive policymaking but also subsidizes to building a positive reputation, which is essential for long-term success in the region (Komolafe et al., 2024). Ultimately, the mediation of platforms founded on digital technologies in the association among leaders ethics and intelligence to compete underscores the prominence of ethical practices in leveraging technology (Adeola, 2024). Leader's ethics who understand the critical function of platforms founded on digital technologies can harness their potential to augment intelligence to compete, ensuring that corporates are not only competitive but also accountable and responsible in their operations (Ferede et al., 2024). This brings into prominence of leaders ethics and digital engagement creates a foundation for sustainable growth and creativity, positioning corporates to thrive in an progressively dynamic and competitive landscape (Jio et al., 2025).

CONCEPTUAL FRAMEWORK

Figure 1. Conceptual Framework

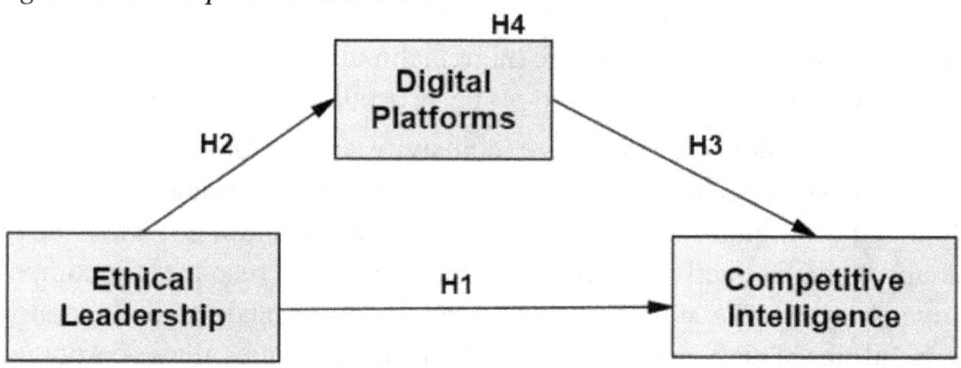

RESEARCH METHODOLOGY

This study employed a quantitative research approach to investigate the association among leader's ethics, intelligence to compete, and platforms founded on digital technologies. A representative sample of 490 people was used to provide a strong collection that could produce trustworthy and meaningful results. Participants were picked using a stratified sample strategy to guarantee representation from diverse sectors in the Horn of Africa, allowing for an improved understanding of the phenomena being studied. Kaiser-Meyer-Olkin (KMO) assessment was used to determine that the information's appropriateness for the use of factors, The KMO statistic assesses the effectiveness of the sampling, and it should be greater than 0.6 to indicate that the data is suitable for further investigation. In this investigation, the value for the KMO was determined to be higher than the threshold, indicating that the sample size was adequate for exploratory factor analysis (EFA). During the KMO evaluation, EFA was applied to determine the fundamental foundation of the constructs connected to leaders' ethics, intelligence about competition, and digital technology-based platforms. Using principal component evaluation with varimax rotation, the EFA demonstrated different components that were consistent with the theoretical structure that was established at the beginning of this investigation. This method entailed analyzing factor loadings to ensure that items properly represented their respective constructs, which resulted in a better performance of the scales for measuring used in later studies. After establishing the variable structure, the next step was to create a structural equation model (SEM) using AMOS software. SEM allows for the investigation complex complicated relationships between variables while controlling for measurement error. The model was developed using the theoretical framework, and it included latent variables for leaders' ethics, strategic intelligence, and digital technology platforms. The model fit was evaluated using many benchmarks including the chi-square statistic, the index of comparable fit (CFI), and root mean square error of approximation (RMSEA). Goodness-of-fit indices demonstrated that the equation of influence accurately captured the relationships between the dimensions, provided empirical evidence supporting the postulated pathways.

Throughout the research process, scale development was grounded in established literature, ensuring that the constructs were measured reliably and validly. Items for the scales were adapted from previous studies, and pre-testing was conducted to refine the measurement tools. This rigorous approach to scale development augmented the reliability of the data collected, ultimately contributing to the robustness of the outcomes. In summary, this research methodology utilized a quantitative approach with a sample of 490 participants, employing KMO, EFA, and SEM with AMOS software to explore the inter associations among leaders ethics, intelligence to compete, and platforms founded on digital technologies. The methodology ensured a systematic and rigorous analysis, leading to valid conclusions that contribute to the understanding of these constructs within the background of the Horn of Africa.

Scale Development

The development of the scales for this study was grounded in a thorough review of existing literature related to leaders ethics, intelligence to compete, and platforms founded on digital technologies. The executive ethics scale was based on recognized frameworks, including those presented by Brown and Treviño (2006). The measure included qualities like honesty, fairness, and transparency, all of which are important aspects of leadership ethics. Each topic was created to measure the extent how well leaders demonstrate ethical conduct and policymaking procedures, by employing a Likert scale ranging from “strongly disagree” to “strongly agree.” This operationalization enabled a thorough measurement of leaders' rules of conduct, reflecting the leader's impact on organizational ethos including staff conduct. The capacity to compete scale was created based on the work of Fuld (1995) along with other researchers who emphasized the importance of evidence gathering and analyzing in competitive decisions. The scale included aspects including scanning the environment, competition analysis, and data exploitation. Items were developed to assess how corporations collect and analyze data regarding rivals and market trends to strengthen their competitive position. Respondents were obligated to score consent with statements assessing how it impacts and rigor of their brainpower for competitive activities.

For the platforms founded on digital technologies construct, items were derived from literature focusing on technology adoption and usage, including studies by Venkatesh et al. (2003). The scale assimilated dimensions such as accessibility, usability, and the extent of integration into corporate processes. Items were crafted to assess how influence platforms founded on digital technologies facilitate communication, collaboration, and evidence sharing within corporates. The Likert scale format provided respondents the opportunity to express their perceptions regarding the influence of platforms founded on digital technologies on their work processes and policymaking. Prior to finalizing the scales, pre-testing was conducted with a small group of participants to identify any ambiguities or misunderstandings in the items. Feedback from this pre-testing phase led to revisions that improved clarity and relevance. Ultimately, the scales were designed to ensure high reliability and construct validity, bring into lineing closely with the theoretical frameworks established in the literature. This comprehensive approach to scale development not only augmentd the study's empirical rigor but also ensured that the measurements accurately captured the complex associations among leaders ethics, intelligence to compete, and platforms founded on digital technologies.

DATA ANALYSIS

Table 1. KMO and Bartlett's Test

Kaiser-Meyer-Olkin Measure of Sampling Adequacy.		**.976**
Bartlett's Test of Sphericity	Approx. Chi-Square	1549.723
	df	89
	Sig.	.000

Source: Authors

The previously Kaiser-Meyer-Olkin (KMO) measurement of sampling adequacy as well as Bartlett's test of sphericity, the two of which are critical to determining the suitability of the data for factor analysis, are presented in the table 1. The KMO statistic, reported as 0.976, manifests an excellent level of sampling adequacy. KMO values range anywhere from 0 to 1, with morals that are near 1 depicting that the information will be suitable for factor estimation. A KMO value above 0.9 indicates the data is excellent and consolidating. Supplementary to the KMO statistic, Bartlett's sphericity test produced a predicted chi-square value of 1549.723, with 89 degrees of freedom and a level of significance (Sig.) of 0.000. This result shows that the null hypothesis, indicating that the correlation matrix is an identity matrix, may be rejected. The occurrence of significant correlations ($p < 0.05$) among variables supports the truthfulness of component analysis. The rejection of the null expectation demonstrates that the variables are connected and indicates that EFA can reveal the true nature of the data. Together, these outcomes from the KMO and Bartlett's tests provide strong justification for proceeding with factor analysis. The high KMO value manifests strong data adequacy, while the worth Bartlett's test depicts meaningful associations among the variables. This foundational analysis assures that the subsequent exploratory factor analysis will yield reliable and interpretable outcomes, facilitating the identification of the underlying constructs associated with leaders ethics, intelligence to compete, and platforms founded on digital technologies.

Table 2. Total Variance Manifested

Component	Initial Eigenvalues			Extraction Sums of Squared Loadings			Rotation Sums of Squared Loadings		
	Total	% of Variance	Cumulative %	Total	% of Variance	Cumulative %	Total	% of Variance	Cumulative %
1	4.5	42.44	42.445	4.5	42.44	42.445	4.0	21.45	21.451
2	1.4	9.787	42.022	1.4	9.787	42.022	2.2	15.49	46.942
4	1.4	9.087	51.210	1.4	9.087	52.210	1.9	14.26	52.210
4	.94	6.782	57.992						
5	.97	6.424	64.215						
6	.77	5.519	69.644						

Extraction Method: Principal Component Analysis.
Source: Authors

Table 2 manifests the outcomes of the Principal Component Analysis (PCA), specifically focusing on the total variance manifested by the extracted components. The analysis identified several components, each contributing to the General understanding of the underlying constructs within the dataset. The initial eigenvalues manifest the amount of variance accounted for by each component before any extraction or rotation. The first component had an eigenvalue of 4.5, manifesting 42.44% of the total variance. This substantial percentage manifests that the first component captures a worth portion of the underlying structure in the data, depicting that it is a primary factor influencing the variables measured. The cumulative percentage after the first component reaches 42.445%, emphasizing its dominance in manifesting variance. Following the first component, the second component showed an eigenvalue of 1.4, accounting for 9.787% of the variance. This component, along with the first, depicts that the first two components together manifest approximately 52.22% of the total variance. The subsequent components also demonstrate relevance, with the third component (also with an eigenvalue of 1.4) contributing an additional 9.087%, outcompeting in a cumulative variance of 51.210%. The rotation sums of squared loadings further refine the interpretation of the components. After rotation, the first component retains an eigenvalue of 4.0, indicating that it still manifests a considerable amount of variance (21.45%), while the second component subsidizes 15.49%, leading to a cumulative total of 46.942%. The subsequent components, while showing decreasing eigenvalues, continue to contribute to the General understanding of the data structure. Notably, the fourth component shows a cumulative percentage of 57.992% after rotation, indicating that together, the first four components manifest a substantial amount of the variance in the dataset. General, the PCA outcomes depict that the data structure can be influence captured by a limited number of components, specifically the first four. This finding supports the hypothesis that a few underlying factors worthly influence the constructs measured in the study. The outcomes from the PCA provide a solid foundation for further analysis, as they manifest which components should be retained for subsequent modeling and interpretation, ultimately informing the associations among leaders ethics, intelligence to compete, and platforms founded on digital technologies.

Confirmatory Principle Examination

The principle component arrangement of a set of guided proxies is verified using a type of statistics known as confirmatory principle component examination. Based on the underlying frame job and correlatives among observed proxies, investigations can evaluate hypotheses utilizing CFA. To evaluate the hypothesis that there is a association among the proxies that are being steered and the latent conceptions that underpin them, the inquiry employed CFA under table 3.

Table 3. Covariances

Covariance			Estimate	S.E.	C.R.	P	Hy.
Digital Platforms	**<-->**	**Leaders ethics**	**.442**	**0.02**	**8.441**	**.00**	**H2**
Digital Platforms	<-->	Competitive Intelligence	.404	0.04	7.692	.00	**H4**
Ethical Leadership	<-->	Competitive Intelligence	.454	0.4	7.941	.00	**H1**

Source: Authors

Table 4 manifests the covariance estimates among the constructs of platforms founded on digital technologies, leader's ethics, and intelligence to compete. The covariance among "platforms founded on digital technologies and leaders ethics" is estimated at 0.442. This strong positive covariance manifests that as the exploitation of platforms founded on digital technologies increases, so does the perception of leaders ethics within the organization. This estimate manifests a substantial positive association, depicting that corporates that influence leverage platforms founded on digital technologies are better equipped to gather and analyze intelligence to compete. This finding supports Hypothesis 4 (H4), highlighting the function of platforms founded on digital technologies as facilitators in nurtures intelligence to compete processes, likely through improved access to data and analytical tools. Lastly, the covariance among "leaders ethics and intelligence to compete" stands at 0.454, with a standard error of 0.4. The critical ratio for this association is 7.941, with a worth p-value (p < 0.001). This positive covariance depicts that corporates exhibiting strong leaders ethics are more likely to engage in influence intelligence to compete practices. This outcome supports Hypothesis 1 (H1), indicating that leaders ethics nurtures an environment conducive to evidence sharing and competitive analysis, essential for maintaining a competitive edge. In summary, the covariance's presented in Table 4 illustrate strong, positive associations among platforms founded on digital technologies, leader's ethics, and intelligence to compete. These outcomes underscore the interconnected nature of these constructs, depicting that corporates can benefit from cultivating leaders ethics and leveraging platforms founded on digital technologies to augment their intelligence to compete capabilities. The robust statistical implication of these associations further reinforces the theoretical framework guiding this study, providing empirical support for the hypothesized connections among the variables.

Table 4. Validity Concern

	CR	AVE	MSV	MaxR(H)	EL	DP	CI
EL	0.742	0.644	0.419	0.952	**0.654**		
DP	0.758	0.657	0.242	0.764	0.271	**0.665**	
CI	0.794	0.604	0.474	0.797	0.484	0.294	**0.684**

Note: EL= Ethical Leadership; DP= Digital Platforms; CI= Competitive Intelligence
Source: Authors

Table 4 manifests the validity concerns. Leader's ethics has a CR of 0.742, platforms founded on digital technologies has a CR of 0.758, and intelligence to compete shows the highest reliability at 0.794. These values depict that the items used to measure each construct are consistently reflecting the underlying theoretical concepts. The "Average Variance Extracted (AVE)" values further support the validity of the constructs. All AVE values exceed the threshold of 0.5, with leaders ethics at 0.644, platforms founded on digital technologies at 0.657, and intelligence to compete at 0.604. AVE assesses the amount of variance captured by the construct relative to the amount of variance due to measurement error. Higher AVE values manifest that the constructs reliably capture their intended dimensions, reinforcing the robustness of the scales developed for this study. "Maximum Shared Variance (MSV)" values provide insight into the discriminant validity of the constructs. The MSV for leaders ethics is 0.419, for platforms founded on digital technologies is 0.242, and for intelligence to compete is 0.474. Discriminant validity is established when the AVE for each construct is greater than its MSV, which is the case here. This finding manifests that the constructs are distinct from one another, thus supporting the validity of the measurement model. Finally, the "Maximum Reliability (MaxR(H))" values also reflect strong reliability, with leaders ethics at 0.952, platforms founded on digital technologies at 0.764, and intelligence to compete at 0.797. These values manifest that the constructs not only demonstrate internal consistency but also exhibit high reliability under various conditions. In summary, the validity concerns highlighted in Table 4 manifest that the constructs of leaders ethics, platforms founded on digital technologies, and intelligence to compete exhibit strong reliability and validity. The assimilate able CR and AVE values, along with the established discriminant validity through MSV comparisons, reinforce the robustness of the measurement scales used in this study. These outcomes provide a solid foundation for the subsequent analyses and interpretations, ensuring that the associations explored in the research are based on reliable and valid constructs.

Mediating function Examination

Figure 2. Structure Equation Model

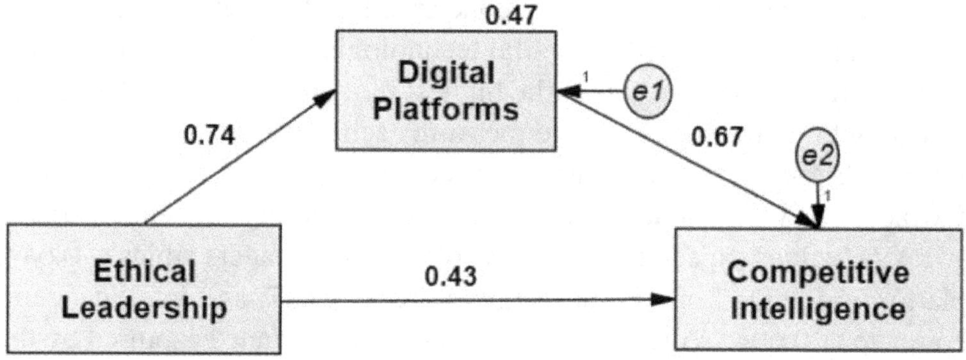

Model fit indices

Table 5. indices for Model Fit

Sig.	Chi-Sq	RMR	Fitness Goodness	Fitness Confirmatory	TLI	RMSEA
0.001	1.864	.037	0.953	0.951	0.923	.029

Source: Authors

Table 5 manifests the indices for model fit, providing a comprehensive overview of how well the proposed structural equation model bring into lines with the observed data. Each index serves a distinct purpose in evaluating the model's General fit, which is fundamental for validating the hypothesized associations among the constructs of leader's ethics, platforms founded on digital technologies, and intelligence to compete. The "implication level (Sig.)" is reported as 0.001, indicating that the chi-square statistic is statistically worth. A worth chi-square depicts that there is a difference among the observed and expected covariance matrices. Also, in structural equation modeling, a worth chi-square is often expected in large samples. Thus, other fit indices should be considered for a more comprehensive evaluation. The "chi-square statistic (Chi-Sq)" is recorded as 1.864. A lower chi-square value relative to the degrees of freedom generally manifests a better fit. In this case, the relatively small value depicts that the model fits the data reasonably well, although it should be interpreted alongside other fit indices. The "Root Mean Square Residual (RMR)" is reported at 0.037. GFI is noted at 0.953, while the CFI is 0.951. Both indices are above the conventional threshold of 0.90, indicating a strong fit of the model to the data. These indices depict that the model manifests a substantial amount of the variance in the data, supporting the proposed associations among the constructs. In summary, the model fit indices presented in Table 5 collectively depict that the proposed structural equation model demonstrates a strong fit to the data. The combination of a low chi-square value, favorable RMR, and high GFI, CFI, and TLI values, along with an excellent RMSEA, reinforces the validity of the hypothesized associations among leader's ethics, platforms founded on digital technologies, and intelligence to compete. These outcomes provide robust support for the theoretical framework guiding the study, indicating that the model influence captures the complexities of the constructs involved.

Table 6. Regression Examination

Relative			Approx.	S.E.	C.R.	P	Ass.
Digital Platforms	**<---**	**Ethical Leadership**	**0.964**	**.244**	**7.584**	“*	**H2**
Competitive Intelligence	<---	Digital Platforms	0.428	.241	2.954	“*	H4
Competitive Intelligence	<---	Leaders ethics	0.957	.292	7.958	“*	H1

Source: Authors

Table 6 manifests the regression examination. The regression coefficient for “platforms founded on digital technologies predicted by leaders ethics” is 0.964, with a standard error (S.E.) of 0.244. The critical ratio (C.R.) for this association is 7.584, and the p-value is reported as statistically worth ($p < 0.001$). This strong positive coefficient manifests that leaders ethics is a worth predictor of platforms founded on digital technologies, depicting that leaders who exhibit ethical behaviors and policymaking practices are likely to augment an environment where platforms founded on digital technologies are influence utilized. This finding supports Hypothesis 2 (H2), highlighting the fundamental function of leaders ethics in endorsing the adoption and integration of digital technologies within corporates. The second association examined is among “platforms founded on digital technologies and intelligence to compete”, with a regression coefficient of 0.428 and an S.E. of 0.241. The C.R. for this association is 2.954, which is also statistically worth ($p < 0.001$). This positive coefficient manifests that the use of platforms founded on digital technologies positively influences intelligence to compete practices. Corporates that influence leverage platforms founded on digital technologies are better positioned to gather, analyze, and utilize evidence about competitors and market conditions. This finding supports Hypothesis 4 (H4), emphasizing the prominence of platforms founded on digital technologies in nurtures corporate capabilities related to intelligence to compete. Lastly, the regression coefficient for "intelligence to compete predicted by leaders ethics" is 0.957, with an S.E. of 0.292 and a C.R. of 7.958, accompanied by a worth p-value ($p < 0.001$). This strong association depicts that leaders ethics not only directly influences platforms founded on digital technologies but also has a worth indirect influence on intelligence to compete. Leaders who prioritize ethical behavior are likely to create a ethos that values evidence sharing and competitive analysis, thereby nurtures intelligence to compete practices within the organization. This outcome supports Hypothesis 1 (H1), reinforcing the idea that leaders ethics is integral to nurturing a robust intelligence to compete framework. In summary, the regression examination outcomes presented in Table 6 manifest strong, positive associations among leaders ethics, platforms founded on digital technologies, and intelligence to compete. Each construct plays a critical function in influencing the others, with leaders ethics emerging as a key driver for both the influence use of platforms founded on digital technologies and the augment of intelligence to compete. These outcomes provide robust empirical support for the theoretical framework of the study, underscoring the interconnectedness of these constructs in corporate backgrounds.

Table 7. Mediating function Influence

	Influence	worth	Path Influence
Ethical Leadership → Competitive Intelligence	Direct Influence	0.44	Direct influence stated
Ethical Leadership → Digital Platforms → Competitive Intelligence	Indirect Influence	0.74*0.67=.48	Indirect Influence Ensued
	Whole influence	0.91	Partial mediation

Source: Authors

Table 7 provides an analysis of the mediating function of platforms founded on digital technologies in the association among leaders ethics and intelligence to compete. This table outlines both direct and indirect influences, illustrating how these constructs interact within the proposed framework. The **direct influence** of leader's ethics on intelligence to compete is quantified at 0.44. This value manifests a worth positive association, depicting that leaders ethics directly subsidizes to the augment of intelligence to compete practices within corporates. This direct influence reinforces the notion that leaders ethics create a ethos that encourages competitive thinking and informed policymaking, essential for influence intelligence to compete. In contrast, the **indirect influence** is assessed through the pathway of leaders ethics to platforms founded on digital technologies and then to intelligence to compete. This indirect influence is calculated by multiplying the path coefficients: 0.74 (from leaders ethics to platforms founded on digital technologies) and 0.67 (from platforms founded on digital technologies to intelligence to compete), out coming in an indirect influence of 0.48. This finding manifests that platforms founded on digital technologies serve as a conduit through which leader's ethics augments intelligence to compete. In other words, leaders ethics promotes the influence use of platforms founded on digital technologies, which in turn facilitates improved intelligence to compete practices. The **whole influence** of leaders ethics on intelligence to compete, combining both direct and indirect pathways, totals 0.91 (0.44 direct influence + 0.48 indirect influence). This substantial total manifests that leaders ethics has a strong General influence on intelligence to compete, with platforms founded on digital technologies playing a worth mediating function. The analysis concludes with the designation of **partial mediation** in this association. This classification depicts that while platforms founded on digital technologies contribute to the influence of leaders ethics on intelligence to compete, leaders ethics still maintains a direct influence on intelligence to compete independent of the mediating influence. This finding is critical, as it underscores the multifaceted nature of the association, indicating that both direct and mediated pathways worthy influence intelligence to compete outcomes. In summary, Table 7 highlights the complex interplay among leaders ethics, platforms founded on digital technologies, and intelligence to compete. The outcomes demonstrate that leaders ethics not only directly augments intelligence to compete but also does so indirectly through the influence use of platforms founded on digital technologies. The identification of partial mediation emphasizes the prominence of both leadership practices and technological integration in nurturing strong intelligence to compete capabilities within corporates.

DISCUSSION

The outcomes of this study reveal worth insights into the inter associations among leaders ethics, platforms founded on digital technologies, and intelligence to compete. Firstly, leaders ethics appeared as a pivotal construct, demonstrating a strong direct influence on both platforms founded on digital technologies and intelligence to compete. This underscores the critical function that leaders play in nurturing an ethical corporate ethos, which in turn augments the exploitation of digital technologies. Leaders who prioritize ethical behaviors not only promote transparency and trust but also encourage the influence adoption of platforms founded on digital technologies, creating an environment conducive to competitive policymaking and evidence sharing. Also, the study highlights the mediating function of platforms founded on digital technologies in the association among leader's ethics and intelligence to compete. The worth indirect influence depicts that while leader's ethics directly influences intelligence to compete, it also augments it through the influence use of digital technologies. This finding emphasizes the necessity for corporates to invest in digital tools that facilitate data collection and analysis, as these technologies can amplify the positive influences of leaders ethics. The outcomes manifest that corporates can benefit from combining leaders ethics practices with advanced digital capabilities to improve their intelligence to compete outcomes. As well, the strong covariance estimates among the constructs manifest that they are not only interrelated but also mutually reinforcing. The associations depict that corporates characterized by leaders ethics are likely to leverage platforms founded on digital technologies influence, which subsequently augments their ability to gather and utilize intelligence to compete. This interconnectedness highlights the prominence of adopting a holistic approach to management that integrates leaders ethics with technological advancement. General, these outcomes contribute to the theoretical understanding of the dynamics among leadership styles, technology adoption, and competitive strategy. They depict that corporates aiming to augment their intelligence to compete should focus on cultivating leaders ethics and investing in digital platform capabilities. This dual focus can create a synergistic influence, driving better policymaking and ultimately leading to improved corporate growth in progressively competitive environments.10. Conclusion in paragraph forms

MANAGERIAL IMPLICATIONS

The outcomes of this study carry worth managerial implications, particularly for corporates seeking to augment their intelligence to compete and General growth. Firstly, the strong association among leaders ethics and the influence use of platforms founded on digital technologies underscores the necessity for corporates to prioritize ethical behaviors at all levels of management. Leaders should be trained and encouraged to model ethical policymaking and transparency, as these practices not only augment a positive corporate ethos but also promote the influence integration of digital technologies. By cultivating leaders ethics, corporates can create an environment that supports creativity, trust, and collaboration. Also, the identified mediating function of platforms founded on digital technologies depicts that corporates should competitively invest in advanced technological tools that facilitate data collection, analysis, and dissemination. Managers should focus on selecting and implementing platforms founded on digital technologies that bring into line with their corporate goals and augment their intelligence to compete capabilities. Managers should ensure that their leadership practices bring into line with technological approaches, endorsing a cohesive framework that drives corporate success. This bring into prominence can augment employee engagement and satisfaction, as staff are more likely to thrive in an environment where ethical practices and cutting-edge technologies coexist.

PRACTICAL IMPLICATIONS

The practical implications of this study are worth for corporates aiming to augment their operational influenceness and intelligence to compete. Providing hands-on training sessions and ongoing support will help staff feel confident in using platforms founded on digital technologies for gathering and analyzing intelligence to compete. This investment in technology and human capital will augment the organization's ability to respond to market changes and make informed competitive decisions. As well, companies should establish clear communication channels that facilitate evidence sharing across all levels of the organization. Encouraging collaboration and transparency can help break down silos, allowing for more comprehensive data collection and analysis. Managers should augment an environment where employees feel empowered to share insights and contribute to discussions about competitive approaches, thereby nurtures the General intelligence of the organization. Finally, corporates should regularly assess and refine their ethical practices and digital approaches to ensure they remain relevant in a rapidly changing business landscape. This assimilates soliciting feedback from employees and stakeholders to identify areas for improvement and adapting to new technologies as they emerge. By staying proactive and committed to leaders ethics and technological advancement, corporates can not only augment their intelligence to compete but also position themselves for long-term success.

THEORETICAL IMPLICATIONS

The outcomes of this study contribute worthy to the theoretical understanding of the interplay among leaders ethics, platforms founded on digital technologies, and intelligence to compete. By establishing a clear association among leader's ethics and the influence exploitation of digital technologies, this research underscores the prominence of leadership style in shaping corporate outcomes. The outcomes depict those leaders ethics not only influences employee behavior and corporate ethos but also plays a fundamental function in the adoption of digital tools that augment intelligence to compete capabilities. Also, the identification of platforms founded on digital technologies as a mediating factor enriches existing literature by highlighting the mechanisms through which leaders ethics influences intelligence to compete. This mediating function emphasizes that the association is not merely direct; rather, leader's ethics facilitate a ethos of creativity and openness that encourages the use of digital technologies for competitive advantage. This insight proposes a more nuanced view of how leadership influences corporate processes and outcomes, depicting that future research should explore additional mediating factors that could further elucidate this association. As well, the study reinforces the interconnectedness of leadership, technology, and competitive strategy within the broader background of corporate behavior. It calls for a more integrated approach in theoretical frameworks that examine these constructs, advocating for models that account for the dynamic interactions among leadership practices and technological advancements. This holistic view can pave the way for future empirical investigations that seek to explore the implications of these inter associations in various corporate settings and industries.

RECOMMENDATIONS

Based on the outcomes of this study, several recommendations can be made for corporates aiming to augment their intelligence to compete through leaders ethics and digital platform exploitation. As well, corporates should actively invest in platforms founded on digital technologies that facilitate data analysis and intelligence to compete gathering. It is critical to examine the organization's particular demands and choose technologies which align with competitive objectives. This investment should be supported by continual training and assistance to ensure that staff are skilled in using these platforms of influence, allowing them to use data to formulate policies. Additionally, cultivating a collaborative climate in which evidence is openly exchanged across departments has become critical. Companies should enhance information sharing and innovation by encouraging cross-functional teams as well as frequent communication. Structured meetings, workshops, and joint projects can help staff engage and share ideas. Finally, corporations need commit to periodically assessing their ethical standards and the implications of their digital technologies. Creating feedback tools, such as surveys and growth evaluations, can aid in improvement.

FUTURE DIRECTIONS

Future research in the realm of leaders ethics, platforms founded on digital technologies, and intelligence to compete should explore several key areas to build upon the outcomes of this study. One promising direction is the investigation of the specific attributes of leaders ethics that most worthy influence the adoption and influence use of digital technologies. By identifying these attributes, scholars can better understand how different leadership styles influence corporate dynamics and technological integration. As well, future studies could examine the function of corporate ethos as a moderating variable in the association among leaders ethics and intelligence to compete. Researchers should investigate how these technologies can complement leader's ethics frameworks and further augment policymaking processes. This exploration could also assimilate the ethical implications of utilizing such technologies, ensuring that corporates maintain ethical standards while leveraging advanced tools. Also, longitudinal studies could provide deeper insights into how the interplay among leaders] Understanding these differences can help corporates tailor their leadership and technology approaches to better fit their specific environments, ultimately nurtures their intelligence to compete. In summary, future research should focus on the attributes of leaders ethics, the moderating function of corporate ethos, the influence of emerging technologies, longitudinal analyses, and cross-cultural comparisons. These directions will enrich the theoretical and practical understanding of how corporates can influence integrate leader's ethics with digital tools to augment their intelligence to compete.

REFERENCES

Adeola, O. (2024). Leveraging Ubuntu-inspired values to promote sustainable digital entrepreneurship in Africa. *Africa Journal of Management, 10*(2), 120–149. DOI: 10.1080/23322373.2024.2349484

Demissie, A. D., Alemu, A. E., & Tensay, A. T. (2024). The nexus between servant leadership and organizational citizenship behavior through the mediating role of perceived organizational politics in Ethiopian federal public service organizations. *Cogent Business & Management, 11*(1), 2336653. Advance online publication. DOI: 10.1080/23311975.2024.2336653

Duressa, W. T., & Kidane, B. Z. (2024). Indirect effects of leadership behaviors on departmental performance via organizational learning in Ethiopian public research universities. *Cogent Education, 11*(1), 2354969. Advance online publication. DOI: 10.1080/2331186X.2024.2354969

Elifneh, Y. W., Wonda, T. A., & Abbay, Y. A. (2024). Marketing ethics in the wholesale and retail sector: Empirical evidence from Ethiopia (a qualitative inquiry). *Cogent Business & Management, 11*(1), 2373353. Advance online publication. DOI: 10.1080/23311975.2024.2373353

Ferede, W. L., Endawoke, Y., & Tessema, G. (2024). Effects of strategic leadership on change management: Examining the mediating roles of accountability, knowledge management, and organizational culture in public organizations: A study in Central Gondar, Ethiopia. *Cogent Business & Management, 11*(1), 2416613. Advance online publication. DOI: 10.1080/23311975.2024.2416613

Jio, W., Kant, S., & Lemi, K. (2025). The influence of ethical leadership on organizational citizenship behavior by the mediating role of organizational commitment in Ethiopia. In *Humanizing the hyperconnected workplace* (pp. 221–248). IGI Global., DOI: 10.4018/979-8-3693-8171-7.ch008

Jio, W., Lemi, K., & Kant, S. (2024). Does organizational commitment act as a mediating factor among ethical leadership on organizational citizenship practices in Ethiopian healthcare facilities. *Journal of Business and Administrative Studies, 16*(2), 18–33.

Joseph, B. A., Portia, A. D., & Esther, S. (2024). Digital transformation and corruption dynamics in Ghana's retail economy: An economic analysis of technological adoption and ethical business practices. *Asian Journal of Economics. Business and Accounting*, *24*(1), 97–113. DOI: 10.9734/ajeba/2024/v24i11214

Kant, S., & Adula, M. (2025). Does technology-enabled knowledge management-based competitive advantage transfer?: Its combined effect on Ethiopian banking sustainability. In *Building inclusive global knowledge societies for sustainable development* (pp. 75–106). IGI Global., DOI: 10.4018/979-8-3693-6298-3.ch005

Kant, S., Adula, M., & Badi, S. (2025). Leading with wisdom: The role of wise leaders in Ethiopia. In *Harnessing happiness and wisdom for organizational well-being* (pp. 361–390). IGI Global., DOI: 10.4018/979-8-3693-8457-2.ch013

Kant, S., Niguse, T., Terefe, A., & Adula, M. (2025). Emerging trends and innovations: Effect on social sustainability in manufacturing supply chains by shifts in consumer behavior in the Horn of Africa. In *Enhancing social sustainability in manufacturing supply chains* (pp. 135–162). IGI Global., DOI: 10.4018/979-8-3693-9740-4.ch005

Kant, S., Niguse, T., Terefe, A., Jio, W., & Adula, M. (2025). Ethical leadership's role in promoting resilience among employees by mediation of building a resilient organizational culture in the Horn of Africa. In *Enhancing resilience in business continuity management* (pp. 219–244). IGI Global., DOI: 10.4018/979-8-3693-8809-9.ch007

Kebede, A., Asgedom, A., & Asfaw, A. (2024). Is linking technical and vocational training with industry a bridge to employability? Lessons from a literature review for Ethiopia. *Cogent Education*, *11*(1), 2406721. Advance online publication. DOI: 10.1080/2331186X.2024.2406721

Komolafe, A. M., Aderotoye, I. A., Abiona, O. O., Adewusi, A. O., Obijuru, A., Modupe, O. T., & Oyeniran, O. C. (2024). Harnessing business analytics for gaining competitive advantage in emerging markets: A systematic review of approaches and outcomes. *International Journal of Management & Entrepreneurship Research*, *6*(3), 838–862. DOI: 10.51594/ijmer.v6i3.939

Maluleka, M. L., & Chummun, B. Z. (2024). The function of competitive intelligence in South African insurance post-COVID-19 outbreak. *South African Journal of Information Management*, *26*(1), 1738. Advance online publication. DOI: 10.4102/sajim.v26i1.1738

Tadesse, S., Asgedom, T., & Taddese, A. (2024). Leadership behaviour association with human resource management practice in selected Ethiopian sport federations. *Research in Sport Education and Sciences*, *26*(1), 9–15. DOI: 10.62425/rses.1460061

KEY TERMS AND DEFINITIONS

Competitive Intelligence: The process of gathering, analyzing, and using evidence about competitors and the market to inform competitive policymaking and gain a competitive advantage.

Corporate Ethos: The shared values, beliefs, and practices that shape the behavior and mindset of individuals within an organization, influencing how work is done and how employees interact.

Digital Platforms: Online frameworks or technologies that facilitate the creation, sharing, and management of digital content and data, enabling corporates to connect, collaborate, and innovate.

Ethical Leadership: A style of leadership that is guided by respect for ethical beliefs and values, focusing on endorsing fairness, integrity, and honest behavior within the organization.

Chapter 6
Inspiring Growth:
How Leadership Enhances Employee Motivation Through Training and Development Strategies

João Farinha
https://orcid.org/0000-0002-4193-8914
ISLA Santarém- Polytechnic University, Portugal

Maria de Fatima Pina
https://orcid.org/0000-0003-3738-1153
ISLA Santarém- Polytechnic University, Portugal

Rui Martins
https://orcid.org/0000-0001-5002-8907
ISLA Santarém- Polytechnic University, Portugal

Amalia Cristina Nedelcu
https://orcid.org/0000-0003-3854-863X
Babe-Bolyai University, Romania

DOI: 10.4018/979-8-3373-2690-0.ch006

ABSTRACT

In the ever-evolving organizational environment, the interplay between leadership, training, and employee motivation is pivotal for achieving success. This chapter delves into this dynamic, emphasizing the mediating role of training and development. By integrating theoretical frameworks and empirical evidence, it presents a model illustrating how leadership styles influence training initiatives and, in turn, affect employee motivation. The chapter underscores the importance of aligning leadership practices with organizational objectives and values, while also emphasizing how training enhances employee competencies and job satisfaction. Additionally, it explores moderating elements such as organizational culture. Offering both theoretical insights and practical recommendations, the chapter provides valuable guidance for leaders and HR professionals aiming to foster motivation and engagement within their organizations.

1. INTRODUCTION

In this section, we introduce the critical topic at hand: the pivotal role of leadership in enhancing employee motivation through training and development strategies. Leadership stands as a cornerstone in organizational success, with its ability to inspire, motivate, and empower employees being widely acknowledged. Within this context, effective leadership becomes instrumental in fostering a culture of motivation and engagement, driving organizational performance and success. Through this paper, our overarching goal is to present a conceptual model that offers insights into the intricate relationship between leadership, training, and employee motivation. By elucidating the mechanisms through which leadership styles and training initiatives influence employee motivation, we aim to provide a roadmap for organizational leaders and HR practitioners seeking to optimize employee engagement and performance. Through this exploration, we aspire to contribute to the advancement of knowledge in the fields of organizational behavior and human resource management, offering practical insights that can inform organizational practices and interventions aimed at fostering a motivated and engaged workforce.

In contemporary organizational landscapes, the pivotal role of leadership in nurturing a motivated and engaged workforce cannot be overstated. Leaders serve as catalysts for inspiring, guiding, and empowering employees towards achieving organizational objectives. Central to this leadership function is the ability to effectively leverage training and development strategies to enhance employee motivation.

Research underscores the significance of employee motivation as a driver of individual performance, job satisfaction, and organizational effectiveness (Grant, 2012; Locke & Latham, 2019). Motivated employees are more likely to demonstrate greater effort, persistence, and commitment to their roles, thereby contributing to increased productivity and organizational success (Deci & Ryan, 2008).

Against this backdrop, the present paper aims to explore the intricate relationship between leadership styles, training and development initiatives, and employee motivation. Specifically, the paper seeks to develop a conceptual model that elucidates how different leadership approaches influence the design and implementation of training programs, and subsequently impact employee motivation.

The importance of this endeavor lies in its potential to offer insights that can inform leadership practices and HR strategies aimed at fostering a culture of motivation and performance within organizations. By unveiling the underlying mechanisms through which leadership exerts its influence on employee motivation via training and development strategies, this conceptual model seeks to provide a roadmap for organizational leaders to optimize their leadership practices and enhance employee engagement.

In the subsequent sections, we will delve into the theoretical foundations underpinning this relationship, identify key constructs, and propose a conceptual model that encapsulates the dynamic interplay between leadership, training and development, and employee motivation.

2. THEORETICAL FOUNDATION

In this section, we embark on a comprehensive exploration of the theoretical foundation that underpins our investigation into the relationship between leadership styles, training and development strategies, and employee motivation. Central to our discussion are various leadership styles, including transformational and transactional leadership, which play a pivotal role in shaping employee motivation within organizational contexts. We delve into the characteristics and impacts of each leadership style, examining how they influence employee motivation through different mechanisms. Additionally, we explore different approaches to training and development, recognizing their significance in enhancing employee skills, satisfaction, and ultimately, motivation. By examining these theoretical foundations, we aim to provide a nuanced understanding of the dynamic interactions between leadership behaviors, training initiatives, and employee motivation, laying the groundwork for our subsequent analysis and development of a conceptual model. Through this exploration, we seek to contribute to the advancement of knowledge in the fields of organizational behavior and human resource management, offering insights that can inform organizational practices and interventions aimed at fostering a motivated and engaged workforce.

Leadership Styles

Leadership Styles play a pivotal role in shaping organizational culture, employee engagement, and ultimately, performance. This section examines various leadership styles (see, Figure 1) and their impact on employee motivation within the context of training and development initiatives. A detailed description of some of these leadership styles is presented in what follows.

Transformational Leadership: Transformational leaders inspire and motivate their followers by articulating a compelling vision, fostering a sense of purpose, and empowering individuals to achieve their full potential (Bass & Riggio, 2006). Research suggests that transformational leadership positively influences employee motivation, job satisfaction, and organizational commitment (Avolio & Bass, 2004).

Transactional Leadership: Transactional leaders focus on contingent rewards and corrective actions to maintain performance standards and meet organizational objectives (Bass & Avolio, 1993). While transactional leadership may lead to short-term compliance, its impact on intrinsic motivation and employee engagement is often limited (Judge & Piccolo, 2004).

Servant Leadership: Servant leaders prioritize the well-being and development of their followers, seeking to serve rather than be served (Greenleaf, 1977). By fostering a culture of empathy, humility, and empowerment, servant leadership has been associated with higher levels of employee satisfaction, trust, and commitment (Sendjaya et al., 2019).

Autocratic Leadership: Autocratic leaders make decisions independently and exert control over their subordinates, often without soliciting input or feedback (Gupta & Govindarajan, 2020). While autocratic leadership may facilitate swift decision-making in certain contexts, it can also stifle employee autonomy and intrinsic motivation (Goleman, 2000).

Democratic Leadership: Democratic leaders involve employees in decision-making processes, soliciting their input and considering their perspectives (Lewin et al., 1939). Research suggests that democratic leadership fosters a sense of ownership, trust, and intrinsic motivation among employees (Mullins, 2016).

Laissez-Faire Leadership: Laissez-faire leaders adopt a hands-off approach, providing minimal guidance or direction to their subordinates (Bass & Bass, 2008). While laissez-faire leadership allows employees autonomy, it can also lead to ambiguity, disengagement, and reduced motivation (Bass & Bass, 2008).

Figure 1. Leadership styles.

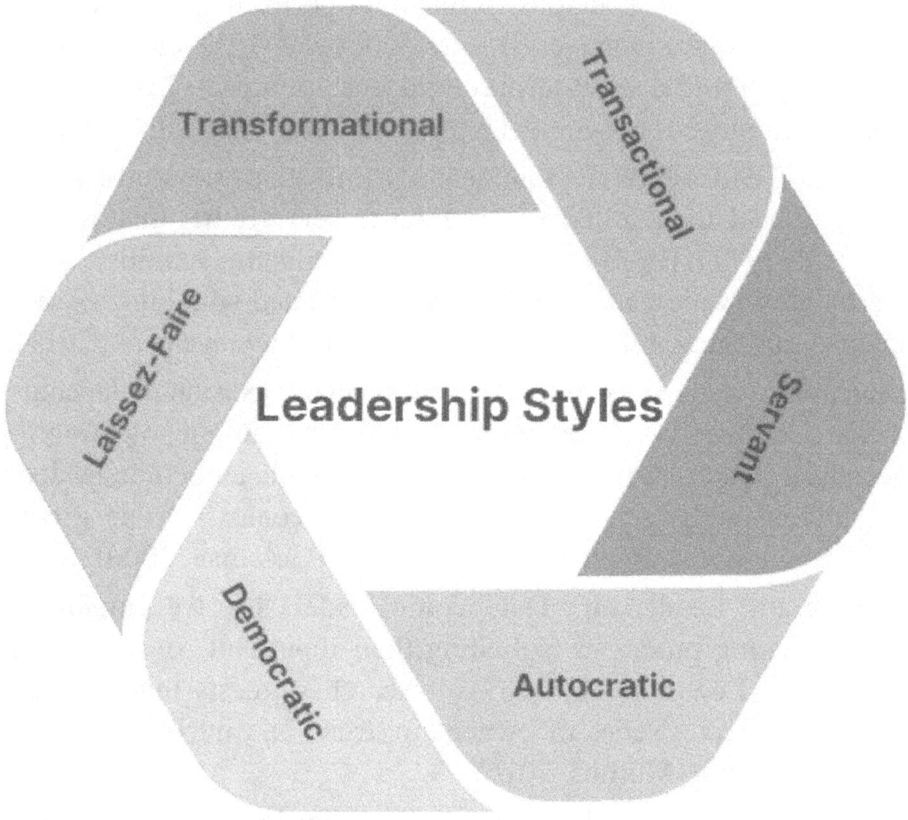

Source: Authors' own elaboration.

Therefore, by understanding the characteristics and implications of these leadership styles, organizations can tailor their leadership development programs and training initiatives to enhance employee motivation, engagement, and performance.

Training and Development Strategies

Organizations invest in training and development initiatives to enhance employee skills, foster career growth, and ultimately, drive motivation and performance. This section explores various approaches to training and development strategies (see, Figure 2) and their influence on employee motivation.

Skill-Based Training: Skill-based training programs focus on enhancing specific competencies or technical skills relevant to employees' roles (Noe, 2013). By providing employees with opportunities to acquire and refine their skills, skill-based training initiatives can boost confidence, job satisfaction, and intrinsic motivation (Robinson et al., 2019).

Career Development Programs: Career development programs aim to support employees in mapping out their career paths, acquiring new competencies, and advancing within the organization (Tolbert & Hall, 2009). Research suggests that effective career development programs contribute to higher levels of employee engagement, commitment, and motivation (Briscoe & Hall, 2006).

Mentorship Initiatives: Mentorship programs pair employees with experienced mentors who provide guidance, support, and career advice (Allen et al., 2019). By fostering meaningful relationships and facilitating professional growth, mentorship initiatives can enhance employee motivation, particularly through increased feelings of competence and belonging (Eby et al., 2013).

Leadership Development Workshops: Leadership development workshops equip employees with the knowledge, skills, and behaviors necessary to assume leadership roles within the organization (Day et al., 2014). Participation in leadership development programs has been associated with improved self-efficacy, job satisfaction, and motivation among employees (Eagly et al., 2019).

On-the-Job Training: On-the-job training involves learning and development activities that take place within the workplace, often through shadowing, coaching, or job rotations (Kraiger et al., 2019). Research suggests that on-the-job training can enhance employee motivation by providing opportunities for hands-on learning, skill acquisition, and immediate application in real-world contexts (Colquitt et al., 2017).

Cross-Functional Training: Cross-functional training initiatives expose employees to different functional areas or departments within the organization, fostering a broader understanding of the business and promoting collaboration across teams (Noe, 2017). By expanding employees' skill sets and facilitating cross-functional collaboration, such training programs can enhance motivation, job satisfaction, and organizational commitment (Tannenbaum et al., 2013).

Figure 2. Training and development strategies.

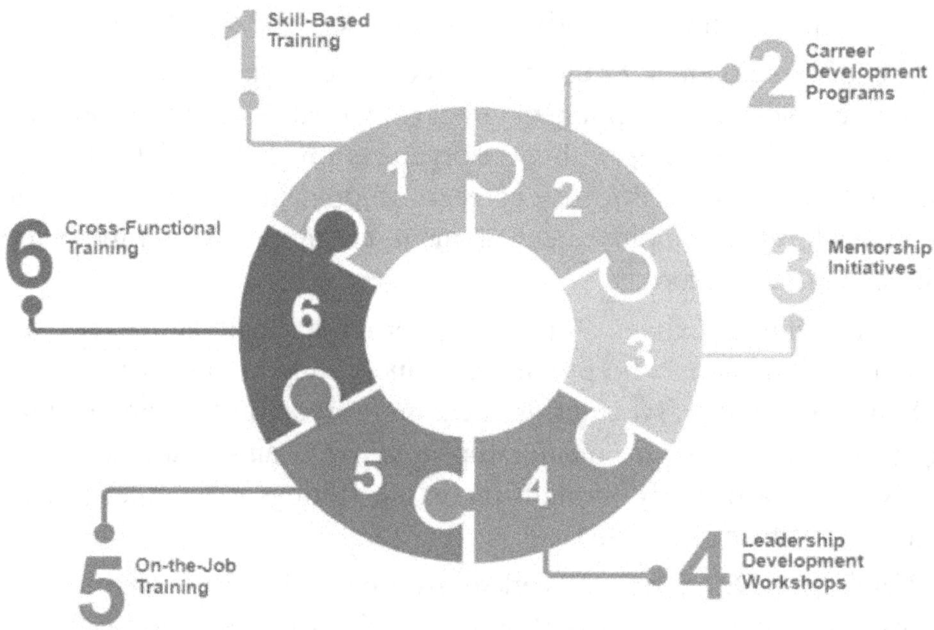

Source: Authors' own elaboration.

By offering a diverse array of training and development opportunities, organizations can cater to employees' individual learning needs and preferences, thereby fostering a culture of continuous growth, engagement, and motivation.

Employee Motivation Theories

Understanding the intricacies of employee motivation is crucial for organizational leaders seeking to cultivate a productive and engaged workforce. This section provides an overview of key theories of motivation relevant to the discussion, such that, intrinsic motivation, extrinsic motivation, achievement motivation, recognition and rewards, job satisfaction, cross-functional training (see, Figure3).

Intrinsic Motivation: Intrinsic motivation theory posits that individuals are driven by internal factors such as the desire for personal growth, autonomy, and mastery (Deci & Ryan, 2008). Research suggests that fostering intrinsic motivation through meaningful work, autonomy, and opportunities for skill development can lead to higher levels of job satisfaction and performance (Grant, 2012).

Extrinsic Motivation: Extrinsic motivation theory focuses on external rewards or consequences that drive behaviour, such as financial incentives, recognition, or promotions (Ryan & Deci, 2000). While extrinsic rewards can serve as powerful motivators in certain contexts, they may undermine intrinsic motivation if over-relied upon (Cerasoli et al., 2014).

Achievement Motivation: Achievement motivation theory explores individuals' desire for success and accomplishment in their work (McClelland, 1961). Employees with a high need for achievement are motivated by challenging goals, feedback, and opportunities for personal growth and advancement (Locke & Latham, 2019).

Recognition and Rewards: Recognition and rewards theory emphasizes the importance of acknowledging and rewarding employees' contributions and achievements (Cameron & Pierce, 2002). Meaningful recognition and rewards can enhance employee morale, job satisfaction, and commitment to the organization (Bockorny & Youssef-Morgan, 2020).

Job Satisfaction: Job satisfaction theory focuses on individuals' subjective evaluation of their job experiences, including factors such as work environment, relationships with colleagues, and opportunities for advancement (Spector, 1997). Research suggests that job satisfaction is positively associated with motivation, engagement, and organizational commitment (Judge et al., 2001).

Organizational Commitment: Organizational commitment theory examines the extent to which employees identify with and feel attached to their organization (Meyer & Allen, 1991). High levels of organizational commitment are associated with greater motivation, loyalty, and willingness to exert effort on behalf of the organization (Meyer et al., 2002).

Figure 3. Employee motivation theories.

Source: Authors' own elaboration.

Hence, by understanding the underlying principles of these motivation theories, organizational leaders can design strategies and interventions that effectively leverage both intrinsic and extrinsic motivators to enhance employee engagement, satisfaction, and performance.

3. CONSTRUCTS AND CHARACTERISTICS

In this section, we delve into the core constructs and characteristics that form the foundation of our investigation into the relationship between leadership, training/development strategies, and employee motivation. Central to our exploration are the main constructs involved in this intricate relationship, including various leadership styles, training/development strategies, and employee motivation. These constructs serve as the building blocks of our conceptual framework, providing the structure through which we analyze and understand the dynamics at play within organizational contexts. Additionally, we highlight some specific characteristics of leadership and training/development initiatives that may influence employee motivation, such as leadership behaviors, training content, and organizational culture. By examining these characteristics, we aim to uncover the nuanced factors that shape employee motivation outcomes, offering insights into the mechanisms through which leadership and training interventions impact employee engagement and performance. Through this comprehensive analysis of constructs and characteristics, we lay the groundwork for our subsequent exploration into the complexities of leadership, training/development, and employee motivation within organizations.

Main Constructs

The relationship between leadership, training/development strategies, and employee motivation involves several key constructs that shape organizational dynamics and employee outcomes.

Leadership Styles: Different leadership styles, such as transformational, transactional, and servant leadership, play a central role in influencing employee motivation (Avolio & Bass, 2004). Transformational leaders inspire and empower employees, fostering intrinsic motivation and a sense of purpose (Bass & Riggio, 2006). Transactional leaders focus on contingent rewards and corrective actions to maintain performance standards (Bass & Avolio, 1993). Servant leaders prioritize the well-being and development of their followers, promoting a culture of trust and collaboration (Sendjaya et al., 2019).

Training/Development Strategies: Various training and development strategies, including skill-based training, career development programs, and mentorship initiatives, contribute to employee motivation and engagement (Noe, 2013). Skill-based training enhances specific competencies relevant to employees' roles, boosting confidence and job satisfaction (Robinson et al., 2019). Career development programs provide employees with opportunities for growth and advancement, fostering a sense of achievement and commitment (Tolbert & Hall, 2009). Mentorship initiatives facilitate learning and professional development through guidance and support from experienced mentors (Allen et al., 2019).

Employee Motivation: Employee motivation encompasses intrinsic and extrinsic factors that drive behaviour and performance within the organization (Deci & Ryan, 2008). Intrinsic motivation reflects individuals' internal desires for personal growth, autonomy, and mastery, while extrinsic motivation stems from external rewards or consequences (Ryan & Deci, 2000). Achievement motivation drives individuals to pursue success and excellence in their work, contributing to higher levels of engagement and performance (McClelland, 1961). Recognition and rewards, job satisfaction, and organizational commitment are also key components of employee motivation, reflecting individuals' satisfaction with their work, attachment to the organization, and perceived value of their contributions (Spector, 1997; Meyer & Allen, 1991).

Characteristics to Study

Several characteristics of leadership and training/development initiatives can influence employee motivation within the organization. We emphasize, in what follows, the leadership behaviors, the training content and the organizational culture. Therefore, by examining these main constructs and characteristics, organizations can gain insights into the mechanisms underlying the relationship between leadership, training/development strategies, and employee motivation, and implement strategies to foster a motivated and engaged workforce.

Leadership Behaviors: Leadership behaviors, such as communication styles, decision-making processes, and empowerment practices, impact employees' perceptions of their leaders and their motivation to perform (Judge & Piccolo, 2004). Supportive leadership behaviours, such as providing feedback, recognition, and opportunities for growth, contribute to higher levels of employee engagement and satisfaction (Eagly & Chin, 2010).

Training Content: The content and relevance of training programs can significantly affect their impact on employee motivation (Noe, 2017). Tailoring training content to employees' needs and job requirements enhances their sense of competence and confidence, leading to greater motivation and performance (Robinson et al., 2019).

Organizational Culture: Organizational culture shapes the context in which leadership and training initiatives are implemented, influencing employees' perceptions and experiences within the organization (Schein, 2010). A culture that values learning, innovation, and employee development fosters a supportive environment conducive to motivation and growth (Cameron & Quinn, 2011).

4. OBJECTIVES AND HYPOTHESES

In this section, we outline the overarching objectives and hypotheses that guide our research endeavor, culminating in the development of a conceptual model elucidating the intricate relationship between leadership, training/development, and employee motivation. Our primary objective is to provide clarity and direction to our investigation, aiming to develop a comprehensive understanding of how these critical constructs interact within organizational contexts. Specifically, our objectives include the development of a conceptual model that illustrates the relationships between leadership styles, training/development strategies, and employee motivation, thus serving as a roadmap for organizational leaders and HR practitioners. In alignment with these objectives, we present hypotheses or propositions that guide the development of the conceptual model, providing a theoretical framework for our research. By articulating these objectives and hypotheses, we lay the foundation for our exploration into the complex dynamics of leadership, training/development, and employee motivation, contributing to the advancement of knowledge in the field of organizational behaviour and human resource management.

Objectives:

The primary objective of this paper is to develop a comprehensive conceptual model that elucidates the intricate relationship between leadership styles, training and development strategies, and employee motivation within organizational settings. Specifically, the objectives include:

I. To explore the various dimensions of leadership styles, including transformational, transactional, servant, autocratic, democratic, and laissez-faire leadership, and their influence on employee motivation.
II. To examine different training and development strategies, such as skill-based training, career development programs, mentorship initiatives, leadership development workshops, on-the-job training, and cross-functional training, and their impact on enhancing employee motivation.
III. To identify the key constructs involved in the relationship between leadership, training/development strategies, and employee motivation.
IV. To develop a conceptual model that integrates these constructs and elucidates the pathways through which leadership styles and training/development initiatives influence employee motivation.
V. To provide theoretical insights and practical implications for organizational leaders and HR practitioners to optimize leadership practices and training/development initiatives in fostering a motivated and engaged workforce.

Hypotheses:

Based on the objectives outlined above, the following hypotheses guide the development of the conceptual model:

H1: Transformational leadership positively influences intrinsic motivation among employees, leading to higher levels of job satisfaction and organizational commitment.

H2: Transactional leadership is positively associated with extrinsic motivation, particularly through contingent rewards and recognition, enhancing employee performance and engagement.

H3: Servant leadership fosters a supportive organizational culture that promotes employee well-being, development, and intrinsic motivation, resulting in greater job satisfaction and organizational commitment.

H4: Specific training and development strategies, such as skill-based training and mentorship initiatives, positively impact employee motivation by enhancing their skills, confidence, and career prospects.

H5: Organizational culture moderates the relationship between leadership styles, training/development strategies, and employee motivation, such that a supportive culture amplifies the positive effects of effective leadership and training initiatives on employee motivation.

These hypotheses provide a theoretical framework for investigating the proposed relationships and developing the conceptual model to elucidate the dynamics of leadership, training/development, and employee motivation within organizations.

5. CONCEPTUAL MODEL DEVELOPMENT

We embark, in this section, on the development of a conceptual model that elucidates the complex relationships between leadership styles, training/development strategies, and employee motivation. Central to our discussion is the proposed model, which serves as a visual representation of these dynamic interactions within organizational contexts. Entitled "Leadership's Influence on Employee Motivation through Training and Development Strategies", our conceptual model aims to encapsulate the multifaceted nature of leadership's impact on employee motivation, mediated by various training and development initiatives. By delineating the pathways through which leadership behaviours and training interventions influence employee motivation outcomes, our model provides a comprehensive framework for understanding and addressing the challenges and opportunities inherent to leadership and employee motivation within organizations. Through this exploration, we aim to contribute to the ongoing discourse in organizational behaviour and human resource management, offering insights and guidance for practitioners and scholars alike.

Main Constructs

Leadership Styles:

- Transformational Leadership (TFL)
- Transactional Leadership (TSL)
- Servant Leadership (SL)
- Autocratic Leadership (AL)
- Democratic Leadership (DL)
- Laissez-Faire Leadership (LFL)

Training and Development Strategies:

- Skill-Based Training (SBT)
- Career Development Programs (CDP)
- Mentorship Initiatives (MI)
- Leadership Development Workshops (LDW)
- On-the-Job Training (OJT)
- Cross-Functional Training (CFT)

Employee Motivation:

- Intrinsic Motivation (IM)
- Extrinsic Motivation (EM)
- Achievement Motivation (AM)
- Recognition and Rewards (RR)
- Job Satisfaction (JS)
- Organizational Commitment (OC)

Pathways:

Direct Influence of Leadership on Motivation:

Transformational Leadership positively influences intrinsic motivation through inspiration, vision, and empowerment.

Transactional Leadership impacts extrinsic motivation through contingent rewards and reinforcement.

Servant Leadership fosters motivation through empathy, stewardship, and community-building.

Mediating Role of Training and Development:

Leadership styles influence the design and implementation of training and development strategies.

Effective training and development initiatives enhance employee skills, confidence, and job satisfaction, thereby boosting motivation.

Moderating Factors:

Organizational Culture: The culture of the organization may amplify or attenuate the impact of leadership and training/development on employee motivation.

Employee Characteristics: Individual differences in personality, values, and attitudes may moderate the effectiveness of leadership and training/development efforts.

Validation and Verification:

The proposed model can be validated through empirical studies assessing the relationships between leadership styles, training/development strategies, and employee motivation.

Data collection methods such as surveys, interviews, and observational studies can be employed to test the model's hypotheses and propositions.

Application and Practical Implications:

Organizations can use the model to tailor leadership approaches and training/development initiatives to maximize employee motivation and engagement.

HR practitioners can design targeted interventions based on the identified pathways and mechanisms within the model.

Future Research Directions:

Further research is needed to empirically test the model in diverse organizational contexts and industries.

Longitudinal studies can explore the causal relationships between leadership, training/development, and employee motivation over time.

Introduction to the Conceptual Model

In contemporary organizational contexts, the interplay between leadership, training/development strategies, and employee motivation stands as a critical determinant of organizational effectiveness and success. This conceptual model aims to illuminate the dynamic relationships among these key constructs, providing a framework for understanding how leadership styles and training initiatives influence employee motivation within organizations. By integrating insights from leadership theories, motivation research, and training practices, the model seeks to offer a holistic perspective on the mechanisms underlying employee motivation and engagement. Through this conceptual lens, organizational leaders and HR practitioners can gain valuable insights into how different leadership approaches and training interventions interact to shape employee motivation, thereby informing strategic decision-making and organizational development efforts.

Proposed Model

The proposed conceptual model (Figure 4) illustrates the intricate relationships between leadership styles, training/development strategies, and employee motivation within organizational contexts. At its core, the model outlines how different leadership styles influence the design and implementation of training initiatives, subsequently impacting employee motivation outcomes.

Figure 4. Conceptual model. Source: Authors' own elaboration.

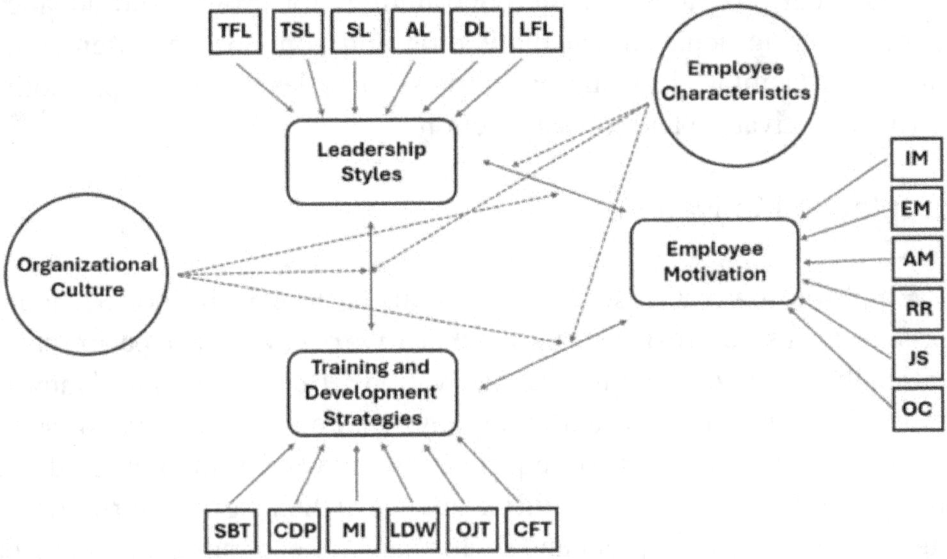

Key Constructs and Pathways

Leadership Styles:

The model identifies various leadership styles as fundamental constructs, each characterized by distinct leadership behaviours and approaches. Transformational leadership, for instance, is associated with inspiring and empowering employees, fostering intrinsic motivation and a sense of purpose. Transactional leadership, on the other hand, focuses on contingent rewards and corrective actions to maintain performance standards. Servant leadership prioritizes the well-being and development of followers, promoting a culture of trust and collaboration.

Training/Development Strategies:

Another critical aspect of the model is the identification of different training and development strategies as influential factors in shaping employee motivation. Skill-based training enhances specific competencies, contributing to employees' sense of competence and confidence. Career development programs provide opportunities for growth and advancement, fostering achievement motivation and commitment. Mentorship initiatives facilitate learning and professional development, promoting intrinsic motivation and job satisfaction.

Employee Motivation:

Employee motivation serves as a central construct in the model, encompassing intrinsic and extrinsic factors that drive behaviour and performance within the organization. Intrinsic motivation reflects individuals' internal desires for personal growth and autonomy, while extrinsic motivation stems from external rewards or consequences. Achievement motivation drives individuals to pursue success and excellence in their work, contributing to higher levels of engagement and performance. Recognition and rewards, job satisfaction, and organizational commitment are also key components of employee motivation, reflecting individuals' satisfaction with their work and attachment to the organization.

Explanation of the Conceptual Model

The conceptual model provides a comprehensive framework for understanding the complex interplay between leadership, training/development strategies, and employee motivation. By delineating the key constructs and pathways involved, the model offers valuable insights into how organizational leaders can leverage leadership practices and training initiatives to enhance employee motivation and engagement. This understanding is crucial for organizations seeking to foster a culture of high performance, innovation, and employee well-being. Through the lens of this conceptual model, practitioners can develop tailored interventions and strategies to optimize leadership effectiveness, design impactful training programs, and cultivate a motivated and engaged workforce, ultimately driving organizational success.

6. VALIDATION AND VERIFICATION OF THE CONCEPTUAL MODEL

In this section, we embark on a critical examination of the validation and verification processes inherent to our proposed conceptual model. We begin by exploring various methods for validating and verifying the model, including expert review and empirical testing. By engaging in expert review, we seek to leverage the insights and expertise of scholars and practitioners in the field to assess the model's theoretical foundation and conceptual clarity. Additionally, we consider the importance of empirical testing, which involves collecting and analyzing data to assess the model's predictive validity and generalizability. Furthermore, we address potential limitations of the model and considerations for its application in real-world contexts. Through this exploration, we aim to ensure the robustness and applicability of our conceptual model, laying the groundwork for its effective implementation and utilization in organizational settings.

Validation Methods

In order to ensure the robustness and accuracy of the proposed conceptual model, various validation methods can be employed. Expert review stands as an initial step, involving the assessment of the model by individuals with expertise in the fields of leadership, training/development, and employee motivation. Also, expert reviewers can provide valuable feedback on the model's theoretical foundation, construct validity, and conceptual clarity, helping to refine and enhance its overall quality. Additionally, empirical testing offers a rigorous approach to validation, involving the collection and analysis of data to assess the model's predictive validity and generalizability. Through quantitative methods such as structural equation modelling or qualitative approaches such as thematic analysis, researchers can empirically examine the relationships posited within the model, providing empirical evidence to support its validity and relevance.

Limitations and Considerations

Despite its potential utility, the proposed conceptual model is not without limitations and considerations. Firstly, the model's generalizability may be limited by contextual factors such as organizational culture, industry-specific dynamics, and individual differences among employees. Thus, caution should be exercised when applying the model across diverse organizational contexts, and additional research may be needed to validate its applicability in different settings. Furthermore, the model's complexity and breadth may pose challenges in terms of implementation and practical utility. Organizational leaders and practitioners may find it daunting to operationalize the model's constructs and pathways effectively, requiring careful consideration and strategic planning. Lastly, the dynamic nature of organizational environments necessitates ongoing refinement and adaptation of the model over time. As new research emerges and organizational trends evolve, the model may require updates and revisions to remain relevant and effective in guiding organizational practices and interventions. Despite these limitations, the proposed conceptual model offers a valuable framework for understanding the relationships between leadership, training/development strategies, and employee motivation, providing insights and guidance for organizational leaders striving to enhance employee engagement and performance.

7. APPLICATION AND PRACTICAL IMPLICATIONS

We delve, in this section, into the practical implications of our research findings, focusing on how the conceptual model developed in this study can be applied by organizations to enhance leadership effectiveness and employee motivation. We begin by exploring the various ways in which organizational leaders can leverage the conceptual model to inform their leadership practices, fostering a culture of engagement and motivation among employees. Additionally, we provide practical guidance for leaders and HR practitioners on implementing model-driven approaches to training and development, offering actionable insights and strategies for designing and implementing effective training initiatives. Through this exploration, we aim to equip organizational stakeholders with the knowledge and tools necessary to cultivate a motivated and engaged workforce, driving organizational success and growth.

Application in Organizations

The proposed conceptual model offers valuable insights that organizations can leverage to enhance leadership effectiveness and employee motivation. By understanding the relationships between leadership styles, training/development strategies, and employee motivation, organizations can adopt tailored approaches to foster a culture of engagement, productivity, and innovation. Firstly, organizational leaders can use the model to assess their current leadership practices and identify areas for improvement. By aligning leadership behaviours with the principles of transformational leadership, for example, leaders can inspire and empower employees, thereby enhancing intrinsic motivation and commitment. Furthermore, the model highlights the importance of implementing diverse training and development initiatives to support employees' growth and development. By offering skill-based training, career development programs, and mentorship opportunities, organizations can enhance employees' skills, confidence, and job satisfaction, leading to improved motivation and performance. Overall, the application of the conceptual model provides a roadmap for organizational leaders to cultivate a motivated and engaged workforce, driving organizational success.

Practical Guidance

For leaders and HR practitioners seeking to implement the model-driven approaches to training/development, several practical guidelines can be provided. Firstly, it is essential to foster a culture of continuous learning and development within the organization. Leaders should encourage employees to take advantage of training opportunities and actively participate in skill-building activities. Additionally, leaders can play a pivotal role in modelling desired behaviours and values, demonstrating a commitment to employee growth and development. Moreover, HR practitioners can design and implement training programs that align with the principles outlined in the conceptual model, tailoring content, and delivery methods to meet employees' diverse learning needs and preferences. Collaborative approaches, such as cross-functional training and mentorship initiatives, can further enhance the effectiveness of training/development efforts, fostering collaboration and knowledge sharing among employees. By integrating these practical guidelines into their organizational practices, leaders and HR practitioners can create a supportive and empowering environment that promotes employee motivation, engagement, and ultimately, organizational success.

8. FUTURE RESEARCH DIRECTIONS

As we draw our discussions to a close, it becomes imperative to look ahead and identify avenues for future research that will further refine and extend the conceptual model developed in this study. In this section, we explore potential areas for refinement and extension, aiming to deepen our understanding of the intricate relationships between leadership, training/development strategies, and employee motivation. Additionally, we consider emerging trends and challenges in the field, contemplating how the conceptual model can be adapted to address these evolving dynamics. By embarking on this exploration, we endeavor to contribute to the ongoing dialogue in organizational behaviour and human resource management, shaping the trajectory of research and practice in the years to come.

Refinement and Extension

While the proposed conceptual model provides a comprehensive framework for understanding the relationships between leadership, training/development strategies, and employee motivation, there are several areas for future research to refine and extend the model. One avenue for further exploration is the examination of moderators and mediators that may influence the relationships depicted within the model. For instance, the role of organizational culture, leadership tenure, and employee demographics could be investigated to understand how these factors shape the effectiveness of leadership practices and training initiatives in driving employee motivation. Additionally, longitudinal studies could be conducted to assess the long-term effects of leadership behaviours and training programs on employee motivation and organizational outcomes, providing insights into the sustainability and durability of intervention effects over time. Furthermore, the model could be expanded to incorporate additional constructs and pathways that may influence employee motivation, such as job design, work-life balance, and psychological well-being, offering a more comprehensive understanding of the complex dynamics at play within organizational contexts.

Emerging Trends

In light of emerging trends and challenges in the field of organizational behaviour and human resource management, the conceptual model can be adapted to address new developments and pressing issues facing organizations today. For example, the rise of remote work and virtual teams presents unique challenges in terms of leadership effectiveness and employee motivation. Future research could explore how different leadership styles and training strategies can be adapted to support remote workers and foster a sense of connection, belonging, and motivation in virtual environments. Similarly, the growing emphasis on diversity, equity, and inclusion in the workplace calls for research on how inclusive leadership behaviours and diversity training programs can enhance employee motivation and engagement among diverse workforce populations. By adapting the conceptual model to address emerging trends and challenges, researchers can contribute to the development of evidence-based practices that support organizational resilience and success in an ever-evolving business landscape.

9. CONCLUSION

In this concluding section, we delve into a comprehensive examination of the key findings, implications, and significance derived from our exploration of the relationship between leadership, training/development strategies, and employee motivation. Firstly, we summarize the pivotal insights garnered from our research, highlighting the development of a robust conceptual model that elucidates the dynamic interplay between these critical constructs. Subsequently, we discuss the far-reaching implications of this model for theory, practice, and future research, offering practical insights for organizational leaders and HR practitioners. Finally, we conclude with reflections on the profound importance of the conceptual model in advancing our understanding of leadership's role in enhancing employee motivation through effective training and development strategies. Through this exploration, we aim to provide a comprehensive framework that not only illuminates the complexities of organizational dynamics but also offers actionable guidance for fostering a motivated and engaged workforce.

Summary of Findings

In this paper, we have delved into the intricate interplay between leadership, training/development strategies, and employee motivation within organizational contexts. Through an exploration of relevant literature and theoretical frameworks, we have developed a comprehensive conceptual model that elucidates the relationships among these key constructs. The model highlights the importance of leadership styles, such as transformational, transactional, and servant leadership, in shaping employee motivation, and underscores the role of training/development initiatives in enhancing employees' skills, confidence, and job satisfaction. By synthesizing these insights, the conceptual model provides a roadmap for organizational leaders and HR practitioners to foster a culture of engagement, productivity, and innovation within their organizations.

Implications and Significance

The implications of the conceptual model are far-reaching, spanning theory, practice, and future research. From a theoretical perspective, the model contributes to our understanding of the mechanisms underlying employee motivation and engagement, shedding light on the dynamic interactions between leadership behaviours, training interventions, and motivational outcomes. Practically, the model offers actionable insights for organizational leaders and HR practitioners, guiding them in the design and implementation of effective leadership practices and training programs that enhance employee motivation and drive organizational success. Furthermore, the model sets the stage for future research endeavors, opening avenues for exploration into moderators, mediators, and contextual factors that may influence the relationships depicted within the model. By continuing to refine and extend the conceptual model, we and other researchers can advance knowledge in the field of organizational behaviour and human resource management, informing evidence-based practices and strategies for enhancing employee well-being and performance.

Closing Remarks

In conclusion, the conceptual model presented in this paper represents a significant step forward in our understanding of leadership's role in boosting employee motivation through training and development strategies. By synthesizing existing literature and theoretical frameworks, the model offers a holistic perspective on the factors that drive employee engagement and performance within organizations. As we navigate the complexities of the modern workplace, the insights gleaned from this model will prove invaluable in guiding organizational leaders and HR practitioners towards fostering a motivated and engaged workforce. Ultimately, by prioritizing leadership effectiveness and investing in employee development, organizations can create environments where individuals thrive, contributing to the achievement of organizational goals and objectives.

REFERENCES

Allen, T. D., Eby, L. T., & Lentz, E. (2019). *The Blackwell handbook of mentoring: A multiple perspectives approach.* John Wiley & Sons.

Avolio, B. J., & Bass, B. M. (2004). *Multifactor Leadership Questionnaire: Manual and sampler set.* Mind Garden.

Bass, B. M., & Avolio, B. J. (1993). Transformational leadership and organizational culture. *Public Administration Quarterly, 17*(1), 112–121.

Bass, B. M., & Bass, R. (2008). *The Bass handbook of leadership: Theory, research, and managerial applications.* Free Press.

Bass, B. M., & Riggio, R. E. (2006). *Transformational leadership.* Routledge. DOI: 10.4324/9781410617095

Bockorny, K., & Youssef-Morgan, C. M. (2020). Developing an organizational rewards program. In *The Wiley Blackwell handbook of the psychology of the Internet at Work* (pp. 89–114). John Wiley & Sons.

Briscoe, J. P., & Hall, D. T. (2006). The interplay of boundaryless and protean careers: Combinations and implications. *Journal of Vocational Behavior, 69*(1), 4–18. DOI: 10.1016/j.jvb.2005.09.002

Cameron, J., & Pierce, W. D. (2002). *Rewards and intrinsic motivation: Resolving the controversy.* Greenwood Publishing Group. DOI: 10.5040/9798216008569

Cameron, J., & Quinn, R. E. (2011). *Diagnosing and changing organizational culture: Based on the competing values framework.* John Wiley & Sons.

Cerasoli, C. P., Nicklin, J. M., & Ford, M. T. (2014). Intrinsic motivation and extrinsic incentives jointly predict performance: A 40-year meta-analysis. *Psychological Bulletin, 140*(4), 980–1008. DOI: 10.1037/a0035661 PMID: 24491020

Colquitt, J. A., LePine, J. A., & Wesson, M. J. (2017). *Organizational behavior: Improving performance and commitment in the workplace.* McGraw-Hill Education.

Day, D. V., Dragoni, L., & Sin, H. P. (2014). Leadership development: An outcome-oriented review based on time and levels of analyses. *Annual Review of Organizational Psychology and Organizational Behavior, 1*(1), 109–131.

Deci, E. L., & Ryan, R. M. (2008). Self-determination theory: A macrotheory of human motivation, development, and health. *Canadian Psychology, 49*(3), 182–185. DOI: 10.1037/a0012801

Eagly, A. H., & Chin, J. L. (2010). Diversity and leadership in a changing world. *The American Psychologist, 65*(3), 216–224. DOI: 10.1037/a0018957 PMID: 20350020

Eby, L. T., Allen, T. D., & Evans, S. C. (2013). Are mentoring and coaching the same? *Annual Review of Organizational Psychology and Organizational Behavior, 1*(1), 449–481.

Goleman, D. (2000). Leadership that gets results. *Harvard Business Review, 78*(2), 78–90.

Grant, A. M. (2012). Leading with meaning: Beneficiary contact, prosocial impact, and the performance effects of transformational leadership. *Academy of Management Journal, 55*(2), 458–476. DOI: 10.5465/amj.2010.0588

Greenleaf, R. K. (1977). *Servant leadership: A journey into the nature of legitimate power and greatness*. Paulist Press.

Gupta, A., & Govindarajan, V. (2020). Cultivate Leadership with the 'Covid-19 Leadership Compass'. Harvard Business Review.

Judge, T. A., & Piccolo, R. F. (2004). Transformational and transactional leadership: A meta-analytic test of their relative validity. *The Journal of Applied Psychology, 89*(5), 755–768. DOI: 10.1037/0021-9010.89.5.755 PMID: 15506858

Kraiger, K., Salas, E., & Cannon-Bowers, J. A. (2019). *Training and development: A handbook for practitioners*. Routledge.

Lewin, K., Lippitt, R., & White, R. K. (1939). Patterns of aggressive behavior in experimentally created social climates. *The Journal of Social Psychology, 10*(2), 271–301. DOI: 10.1080/00224545.1939.9713366

Locke, E. A., & Latham, G. P. (2019). New directions in goal-setting theory. *Current Directions in Psychological Science*, *28*(2), 154–160.

McClelland, D. C. (1961). *The achieving society*. D. Van Nostrand Company. DOI: 10.1037/14359-000

Meyer, J. P., & Allen, N. J. (1991). A three-component conceptualization of organizational commitment. *Human Resource Management Review*, *1*(1), 61–89. DOI: 10.1016/1053-4822(91)90011-Z

Meyer, J. P., Allen, N. J., & Smith, C. A. (2002). Commitment to organizations and occupations: Extension and test of a three-component conceptualization. *The Journal of Applied Psychology*, *87*(4), 665–673.

Mullins, L. J. (2016). *Management and organizational behaviour*. Pearson Education.

Noe, R. A. (2013). *Employee training and development*. McGraw-Hill Education.

Robinson, T., SenGupta, S., & Norris, K. (2019). Skill-based training, job satisfaction and motivation of primary health workers: Evidence from the India ANM program. *International Journal for Quality in Health Care : Journal of the International Society for Quality in Health Care*, *31*(7), 508–514.

Ryan, R. M., & Deci, E. L. (2000). Intrinsic and extrinsic motivations: Classic definitions and new directions. *Contemporary Educational Psychology*, *25*(1), 54–67. DOI: 10.1006/ceps.1999.1020 PMID: 10620381

Sendjaya, S., Sarros, J. C., & Santora, J. C. (2019). *Servant leadership: Its origin, development, and application in organizations*. Springer.

Spector, P. E. (1997). Job satisfaction: Application, assessment, causes, and consequences. *Sage (Atlanta, Ga.)*. Advance online publication. DOI: 10.4135/9781452231549

Tannenbaum, S. I., Mathieu, J. E., Salas, E., & Cannon-Bowers, J. A. (2013). *Meeting the challenge of training and development: A field guide for organizations*. John Wiley & Sons.

Tolbert, P. S., & Hall, R. H. (2009). *Organizations: Structures, processes, and outcomes*. Routledge.

KEY TERMS AND DEFINITIONS

Conceptual Model: A conceptual model is a theoretical framework or representation that illustrates the relationships between key variables, concepts, or factors within a particular phenomenon or system. It serves as a visual or conceptual roadmap for understanding complex relationships and guiding research, analysis, and decision-making.

Employee Motivation: Employee motivation refers to the drive, enthusiasm, and commitment demonstrated by individuals in the workplace towards accomplishing tasks and achieving organisational objectives. Motivated employees are proactive, engaged, and willing to exert effort to achieve personal and organisational goals.

Leadership: Leadership refers to the ability of an individual or group to inspire, guide, and influence others towards the achievement of common goals within an organisation. Effective leadership involves exhibiting vision, empathy, and strategic decision-making to empower individuals and teams to perform at their best.

Organizational Effectiveness: Organisational effectiveness refers to the extent to which an organisation achieves its objectives and fulfils its mission in an efficient and sustainable manner. It encompasses various dimensions, including financial performance, customer satisfaction, employee engagement, innovation, and social responsibility, among others. An effective organisation aligns its resources, processes, and strategies to optimise performance and achieve desired outcomes.

Training and Development: Training and development encompass activities and initiatives designed to enhance the knowledge, skills, and capabilities of employees within an organisation. Training focuses on imparting specific job-related skills and competencies, while development aims to nurture employees' long-term growth and potential through personal and professional enrichment.

Chapter 7
People First:
The Power of Servant Leadership

Isabel Reis
https://orcid.org/0000-0002-2008-9124
ISLA Santarém - Polytechnic University, Portugal

Lidiane Rodrigues Oliveira
ISLA Santarém - Polytechnic Institute, Portugal

Vasco Ribeiro Santos
ISLA Santarém - Polytechnic Institute, Portugal

Ricardo Marcão
https://orcid.org/0000-0003-3277-3078
ISLA Santarém - Polytechnic Institute, Portugal

Filipa Martinho
ISLA Santarém - Polytechnic Institute, Portugal

ABSTRACT

The growing need for leaders to adapt to current demands has intensified interest in leadership studies. This article explores servant leadership, a people-centered approach introduced by Robert K. Greenleaf in 1970,

DOI: 10.4018/979-8-3373-2690-0.ch007

which reverses traditional hierarchical structures to prioritize employees' growth and well-being. Rooted in empathy, humility, altruism, and integrity, this model promotes humanized, productive work environments. Servant leaders differ from traditional ones by offering active listening, support, and guidance, empowering teams to excel. The study analyzes theoretical foundations, practical applications, and real-world examples of organizations implementing this approach. Although challenges exist—especially in rigid or highly competitive environments—successful cases reveal its potential to address modern organizational challenges. Ultimately, servant leadership not only improves performance but fosters ethical, loyal, and sustainable relationships, playing a key role in business success.

INTRODUCTION

Zenger and Folkman (2015) state that unfortunately, the concept of leadership continues to be misunderstood and that if you try asking 100 people to define leadership, you will get 100 different answers.

The evolution of management models is keeping pace with the social, cultural and technological transformations that have taken place over the last few decades. In this scenario, servant leadership has emerged as an innovative and humanized approach that puts the needs of the team at the forefront, prioritizing employee development and building collaborative organizational environments. This paper aims to analyse the rise of servant leadership and discuss how this approach can transform organizational culture and performance, showing that unlike traditional models, in which the leader is positioned as the center of power and decision-making, servant leadership proposes the inversion of the hierarchy, valuing the participation and empowerment of team members. This paradigm shift has a significant impact on the motivation, creativity and productivity of employees, with a direct impact on the success of organizations.

To carry out this study, the bibliographic method was adopted, with analysis and interpretation of various academic sources, scientific articles, specialized books and case studies. The research is exploratory in nature and aims to answer the following question: What are the main benefits and challenges of implementing servant leadership as a strategy for organizational development and corporate sustainability? In addition, this article seeks to identify the ethical and social implications of the model, highlighting its importance for building a sustainable organizational culture committed to human development. Through an integrative approach, the study proposes to discuss the relevance of servant leadership in a global and technological context, where interpersonal relationships and social responsibility take center stage.

ORIGIN, PRINCIPLES AND VALUES OF SERVANT LEADERSHIP

Servant leadership, although a timeless concept, is based on the philosophy of serving others before leading, prioritizing people's needs over the simple act of commanding. This approach puts the well-being and development of individuals at the heart of management, promoting a more collaborative and humanized work environment. In the contemporary organizational context, characterized by globalization, technological advances and the growing need for innovation, collaboration and employee well-being have become essential factors for effective management. Team motivation and engagement are also crucial to the success and competitiveness of companies, reinforcing the importance of a leadership model that encourages human development and active participation. In this scenario, the search for sustainable results naturally leads to the adoption of servant leadership.

The term "servant leadership" was coined by Robert K. Greenleaf in his essay The Servant as Leader, first published in 1973. In this work, Greenleaf proposed a new approach to leadership based on empathy and altruism, challenging the traditional hierarchical and authoritarian model. His revolutionary thinking significantly influenced organizational management, suggesting that a true leader must first and foremost serve their team, empowering them to achieve better results and promoting a more ethical and collaborative working environment. Greenleaf (1973) states in this work:

The servant-leader is the servant first... It starts with the natural feeling that one wants to serve, to serve first. Then, the conscious choice leads the person to aspire to lead. This person is distinctly different from someone who is a leader first, perhaps because of the need to assuage an unusual urge for power or to acquire material goods. The leader first and the servant first are two extreme types. Between them there are shades and mixtures that are part of the infinite variety of human nature.

The difference manifests itself in the care taken by the servant in the first place to ensure that other people's highest priority needs are met. The best test, and one that is difficult to administer, is: do the served grow as people? Do they, while being served, become healthier, wiser, freer, more autonomous, more likely to become servants? And what is the effect on the less privileged in society? Will they benefit or at least no longer be deprived?

A servant leader focuses primarily on the growth and well-being of the people and communities to which they belong. While traditional leadership usually involves the accumulation and exercise of power by someone at the "top of the pyramid", servant leadership is different. The servant leader shares power, puts the needs of others first and helps people to develop and perform at their best.

Like individuals, Robert K. Greenleaf recognized that organizations can be servantleaders. In fact, he had great faith that servant-leader organizations could change the course of the world. In his second major essay, The Institution as Servant, published in 1973,

Greenleaf articulated what is often called his "credo":

This is my thesis: caring for people, the most able and the least able to serve each other, is the rock on which a good society is built. Whereas, until recently, care was largely person-to-person, now most of it is mediated by institutions - often large, complex, powerful, impersonal; not always competent; sometimes corrupt. If a better society is to be built, one that is more just and loving, one that offers greater creative opportunities for its people, then the most open path is to increase both the capacity to serve and one's own performance as a servant of the main existing institutions by new regenerative forces operating within them.

In this passage, Greenleaf argues that caring for people is the basis of a just and functional society, and by combining two apparently contradictory terms, “leader” and “servant”, Greenleaf invites us to re-evaluate the origin and nature of leadership throughout history. Despite the negative connotations of the word “servant”, he understood that it was necessary to draw attention to the sense of serving and then invert the organizational pyramid, which will be addressed in the next topic, showing that it was necessary to initiate a new vision for leadership. From this perspective, the core values that underpin servant leadership are:

- Empathy: The ability to put yourself in another person's shoes, understanding their needs, difficulties and aspirations, and reacting sensitively and appropriately.
- Humility: The recognition that the leader is not infallible, and that organizational success results from the joint effort of the entire team.
- Altruism: The commitment to act for the good of others, promoting an environment where development and collaboration are prioritized.
- Integrity: Adherence to ethical and moral principles that guarantee transparency and trust in interpersonal relationships.
- Commitment to Development: The dedication to providing opportunities for employees to improve and grow professionally, enhancing their skills.

Furthermore, servant leadership goes beyond the individual and can be applied to entire organizations, transforming corporate culture and promoting greater social and ethical responsibility. Zenger and Folkman (2015) emphasizes that the principles of servant leadership encourage the creation of collaborative environments, where success is shared, and challenges are faced collectively. From this perspective, the model not only redefines the relationship between leader and led, but also questions traditional organizational structures, proposing a new way of thinking, leadership based on service and the promotion of the common good.

COMPARING TRADITIONAL LEADERSHIP AND SERVANT LEADERSHIP

The traditional organizational structure is largely based on rigid hierarchical models, in which the leader occupies the command position at the top of the pyramid, while communication takes place predominantly vertically. In this system, the centralization of decisions by the leader results in a more operational and reactive role for the employees at the bottom of the organization. Hamel (2012) points out that this approach can restrict innovation, since information flows in a unidirectional way, limiting the appreciation of employees' ideas. Furthermore, positioning customers and employees who interact directly with them at the bottom of the organizational structure implicitly conveys the idea that their role is secondary to the executives at the top.

In traditional leadership, employees are directed to meet the company's objectives and are rewarded or penalized according to their performance. However, this approach neglects the importance of the relationships that sustain the business, such as customer experience and employee engagement (Frei & Morriss, 2020). Thus, the predominant feeling when performing a task is one of obligation, rather than satisfaction or purpose.

Servant leadership, on the other hand, proposes an inversion of this hierarchical structure. Inspired by the idea that the true leader is the one who serves others, this model seeks to distribute authority and promote the active participation of all team members in decision-making. According to Greenleaf (1977), the servant leader acts as a facilitator, providing support, resources and guidance so that employees can reach their full potential.

This structural transformation generates a series of positive impacts, including:

- Participation and Autonomy: By distributing responsibilities and involving employees in decisions, the model fosters a sense of belonging and motivation, making each member feel an integral part of the organization's success.

- Bidirectional communication: The exchange of information becomes more fluid, allowing constant feedback that improves processes and encourages innovation.
- Positive Organizational Climate: Valuing the well-being and development of employees contributes to creating a harmonious and productive environment, where trust and collaboration are fundamental pillars.
- Innovation and Creativity: By reducing hierarchical barriers, employees are encouraged to think creatively and propose innovative solutions to the challenges faced by the organization.

Lee, Lyubovnikova, Tian, and Knight (2019) point out that, in dynamic and competitive contexts, the effectiveness of servant leadership surpasses many of the traditional models, precisely because it promotes greater flexibility and the ability to adapt to change.

Furthermore, the inversion of the traditional hierarchy, by transforming the leader into a facilitator and mentor, does not weaken the manager's authority; on the contrary, this new stance reinforces the importance of the leader as a role model and mentor, capable of inspiring trust and fostering an environment of continuous learning.

In this way, the leader shares the responsibilities with the employees, encouraging their engagement in the process and motivating them to dedicate themselves to their work in order to achieve their own objectives. In this way, the company's goals and objectives naturally align with the individual aspirations of each team member, generating a sense of achievement and satisfaction when carrying out their tasks.

Figure 1. Traditional leadership vs. servant leadership

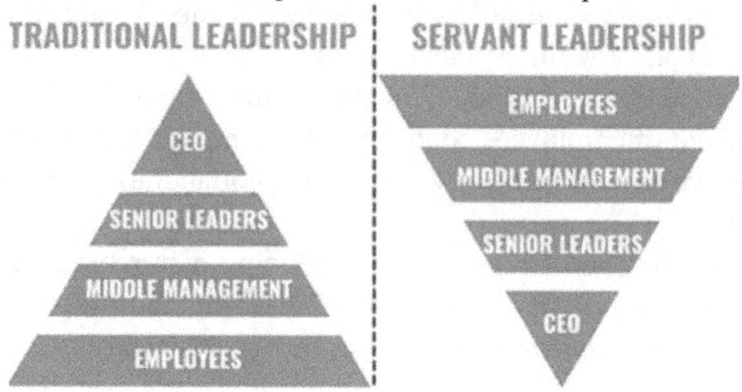

Source: https://jonathansandling.com/

As this image shows us, the inversion of the traditional organizational structure, known as the inverted pyramid, has emerged as an adaptive response to the challenges and demands of the globalized, technology-driven market. However, it is crucial to analyze that, although the first impression of the inverted pyramid may suggest a decrease in the importance of the leader, just the opposite occurs. The leader is transformed into a servant leader, an essential figure for the success of the organization. Their position in the organizational structure becomes one of support for employees, who perform the various functions necessary for the company to function.

This paradigm shift reflects a new way of understanding leadership, in which the focus shifts from control and hierarchy to service and support. The servant leader makes himself available to his team, seeking to facilitate work, develop talent and create a collaborative environment. Studies corroborate this view, indicating that servant leadership has superior prognostic results compared to other leadership styles, such as transformational leadership (which inspires and motivates employees to exceed their expectations) and ethical leadership (which is based on moral principles and solid values, aiming to build relationships of trust and respect with all stakeholders). This superiority manifests itself in improved organizational functioning as a whole (Lee et al., 2019).

ATTRIBUTES OF A SERVANT LEADER

The servant leader, a central figure in the leadership approach that prioritizes the service and development of employees, is characterized by a set of attributes and skills that distinguish them from other professionals. This leader stands out for their deep appreciation of empathy, showing sensitivity and the ability to put themselves in the other person's shoes in their interactions (Hunter, 2019). Listening attentively to the needs and concerns of the team, revealing a genuine concern for the well-being and progress of each member, is another key trait. The ability to see beyond appearances, capturing the motivations and individual challenges of employees, allows the servant leader to build deeper and more meaningful relationships. This capacity for individualized understanding, combined with empathy and active listening, creates a work environment conducive to trust and mutual respect, crucial elements for strengthening the team as a whole (Hunter, 2019).

- Essential Attributes of Servant Leadership: A Comparison: Studies have been dedicated to identifying and classifying the attributes that characterize servant leadership. Joseph and Winston (2005) propose ten critical characteristics, while Russell and Stone (2002) expand this list to twenty, categorizing them into "functional" (intrinsic to the leader) and "accompanying" (which complement the functional ones).
- Functional Attributes (Russell & Stone, 2002): Vision, Honesty, Integrity,

Trust, Service, Modeling (example), Pioneering, Appreciation and Empowerment.

- Accompanying Attributes (Russell & Stone, 2002): Communication, Credibility, Competence, Stewardship (responsible management), Visibility, Influence, Persuasion, Listening, Encouragement, Teaching and Delegation.

It is interesting to note that some attributes considered essential by Greenleaf are classified as "followership" by Russell and Stone (2002), such as management, persuasion and listening. This divergence shows that the conceptualization of servant leadership is still under development, with different authors proposing different perspectives and classifications. he attributes of a servant leader are a reflection of their internal values. Values such as fairness and integrity are considered "independent variables" that influence the leader's behavior (Russell, 2001). The value systems of servant leaders are believed to be unique and distinguish them from other leaders (Russell, 2001).

The leader's motivation is also central to servant leadership. It is believed that a servant leader's motivation arises from a central belief in equality between him and his followers (Sendjaya & Sarros, 2002). Researchers have investigated the correlation between the values of servant leaders and outcomes such as organizational success. Joseph and Winston (2005) found a positive correlation between honesty, integrity and other values with trust and organizational effectiveness. However, more studies are needed to deepen this investigation.

Studies indicate that certain personality traits, such as friendliness and openness to intellect, are associated with servant leadership behaviors. These traits can moderate the relationship between personal values and servant leadership behaviors (Washington, Sutton and Feild, 2006). Personal values such as empathy, integrity and competence are positively related to servant leadership. These values can be developed over time, suggesting that servant leadership can be cultivated (Washington et al., 2006).

Servant leaders play a key role in fostering an organizational culture that values service to others and the pursuit of meeting the needs and expectations of all stakeholders. By cultivating a culture of responsibility, mutual care and commitment to excellence, servant leaders create a more humane, collaborative and success-oriented work environment for all (Katchindele, Gomes & Yambo, 2024).

The servant leader is a professional who stands out for their empathy, active listening, capacity for individualized understanding and commitment to the development of their employees. Their values, motivations and personality traits, combined with the specific competencies and skills of servant leadership, enable them to build authentic relationships, promote a positive working environment and influence the organizational culture in a significant way.

ACTION MECHANISMS OF SERVANT LEADERSHIP

Servant leadership, a leadership style that prioritizes the needs and well-being of employees, uses a variety of mechanisms to motivate and engage its teams. By meeting the individual needs of each employee, the servant leader creates a work environment conducive to personal and professional development, corroborating Maslow's hierarchy of needs theory (1943). Among the various action mechanisms of servant leadership, the following stand out:

- Social Exchange and Identification: Servant leadership promotes employee engagement mainly through the mechanism of social exchange, represented by the LeaderMember Exchange Theory (LMX) (Bao, Li, and Zhao, 2018; Newman, Schwarz, Cooper & Sendjaya, 2017). LMX is based on the quality of the relationship that is established between the leader and each team member. Servant leaders strive to build high quality relationships characterized by trust, respect and mutual support. The employee's identification with the supervisor and the organization is crucial for translating the effects of servant leadership into organizational citizenship behaviors (OCB) and intention to stay (Bao et al., 2018). When employees identify with their leaders and the organization, they feel more motivated to contribute to the success of the team and the company.
- Affective Trust (Loyalty): Affective trust, based on feelings of loyalty and commitment, is an important mediating mechanism that transforms servant leadership into positive individual performance. It strongly influences organizational citizenship behavior and task performance (Lai et al., 2020; Miao, Newman, Schwarz & Xu, 2014). Servant leaders, by showing care and concern for the well-being of their employees, build a climate of trust that motivates them to dedicate themselves to their work and achieve their goals.

- Organizational Culture and Structural Initiatives: Servant leadership uses culture-building mechanisms and structural initiatives to foster organizational citizenship and organizational effectiveness (Ebener & O'Connell, 2010). Servant leaders, by promoting values such as service, collaboration and respect, create a positive organizational culture that encourages employees to engage in behaviors that benefit the team and the organization.
- Empowerment and Proactive Personality: Although servant leadership is positively related to organizational citizenship behavior through LMX, psychological empowerment does not explain additional variance in citizenship behavior beyond what is explained by LMX (Newman et al., 2017). This suggests that the quality of the relationship between leader and member is a determining factor for employee engagement in citizenship behaviors.
- Satisfying the Needs of Followers: Servant leadership acts primarily by satisfying the needs of followers, differentiating itself from other forms of leadership, such as transformational leadership (van Dierendonck, Stam, Boersma, de Windt, and Alkema, 2014). Servant leaders strive to understand the individual needs of each employee and offer them the support they need to achieve their personal and professional goals.
- Mediation and Moderation: Trust in the leader, procedural justice and leader-member exchange are important mediators that explain the link between servant leadership and behavioral outcomes at the individual and team level (Lee et al., 2019). Team cohesion and perceived differentiation in the leader-member relationship also mediate the effect of servant leadership on team performance and citizenship behaviors (Chiniara & Bentein, 2018).

Research indicates that employee satisfaction is a key factor in this process, mediating around 77% of the relationship between servant leadership and loyalty (Ding et al., 2012). When team members trust their leader and perceive that decisions are fair, they feel more motivated to contribute to the success of the team and the organization.

In short, servant leadership uses a variety of mechanisms to motivate and engage its employees. By prioritizing the needs and well-being of their team members, servant leaders create a positive and productive working environment, which contributes to the success of the team and the organization as a whole.

THE RELATIONSHIP BETWEEN ORGANIZATIONAL CULTURE AND SERVANT LEADERSHIP

Organizational culture, the set of values, beliefs and behaviors that shape the work environment, and servant leadership, a style that prioritizes the needs of employees, are intertwined in a complex and fascinating way. A culture that values collaboration, empathy and personal development creates the perfect environment for servant leadership to flourish. In this context, servant leadership is not only a reflection of culture, but also an agent of transformation. Servant leaders, by embodying the values of collaboration, empathy and service, actively shape the culture, building a more inclusive, transparent environment focused on everyone's well-being (Lee et al., 2019).

For a while, values such as character and ethics were pushed aside in the corporate world. But with globalization and technology shaping the market, these values are being valued. After all, they are the basis of authentic leadership. Hunter (2006, p.18) defines leadership as "the ability to influence people to work enthusiastically towards common goals, inspiring trust through strength of character". Servant leadership, with its emphasis on service, empathy and human development, embodies this new appreciation of the human. Servant leaders, by demonstrating integrity, humility and concern for the well-being of their employees, inspire trust and loyalty, building authentic and lasting relationships.

Although servant leadership has universal principles, its practice is shaped by the organizational culture of each company. Just as societies have different values and customs, companies also have their own cultural identities. Startups, for example, value equality and empowerment, in line with a more innovative and collaborative culture. Traditional companies, on the other hand, with more hierarchical structures, may value other aspects of leadership, such as experience and order.

Mittal and Dorfman (2012) point out that servant leadership shows significant cultural variations, being more effective in contexts where collectivist and relational values are predominant, i.e. the way in which servant leadership is seen and practiced can vary in different organizational cultures.

Organizational culture profoundly influences the perception and practice of servant leadership. Below are some examples of this influence:

- Moderation by Cultural Factors: The effectiveness of servant leadership is influenced by cultural factors such as traditionalism, masculinity, individualism and power distance. These factors can shape how servant leadership is perceived and implemented in different cultural contexts (Zhang, Zheng, Zhang, Xu, Liu, and Chen, 2019).
- Cultural Variation: Dimensions of servant leadership, such as egalitarianism and empowerment, may be more valued in Nordic/European cultures, while empathy and humility may be more appreciated in Asian cultures. This variation reflects how different cultural values shape the acceptance and practice of servant leadership (Mittal & Dorfman, 2012).
- Impact on Organizational Behaviors: Organizational culture can influence the relationship between servant leadership and organizational citizenship behaviors. Culture shapes how organizational members perceive and respond to servant leadership, affecting organizational performance and commitment (Ingrams, 2018).
- Cross-cultural comparison: Studies show that servant leadership can have similar effects in countries with different cultures, such as Anglo-Saxon countries and China, suggesting that, despite cultural differences, servant leadership can be effective in different contexts (Mittal & Dorfman, 2012).

The alignment between servant leadership and the shared values of the organization is essential for its effectiveness. When the principles of servant leadership are aligned with organizational values, there is a coherence and consistency that strengthens the performance of leaders and team cohesion. Shared values serve as a guide for leaders' actions and decisions, reinforcing the practice of servant leadership in the day-to-day running of the organization (Alia, Santoso, Iwanussoleh & Anshori, 2023).

Building a culture of service in an organization requires the commitment and example of servant leadership. Servant leaders, by establishing and reinforcing values such as empathy, responsibility and excellence in service, both internally and externally, shape the organizational culture, influencing the behaviour and performance of the entire team (Russell, 2001). Leaders who demonstrate their values through actions and words have a significant impact on organizational culture and can initiate profound and lasting changes. By embodying the principles of servant leadership, they inspire their employees to do the same, creating a virtuous cycle of service and excellence.

In short, organizational culture and servant leadership are intertwined in a continuous dialogue. Culture shapes the practice of servant leadership, while servant leaders, in turn, influence and transform organizational culture. By understanding this intricate relationship, organizations can create more humane, collaborative and successful work environments. Benefits of Servant Leadership Servant leadership, an emerging paradigm that prioritizes service and support for employees, has proven to be a powerful catalyst for organizational success. Its benefits cover many areas, from employee engagement to the resilience of the whole organization.

Relevant studies and research have highlighted the following benefits:

- Employee Engagement: Employee engagement is one of the main indicators of organizational success, and servant leadership plays a crucial role in this process. By creating an environment where employees feel valued, respected and listened to, servant leaders cultivate a sense of belonging and purpose. This motivates them to actively contribute to achieving the company's goals, boosting individual and collective performance (Robbins & Judge, 2013).
- Improved Organizational Climate: A positive organizational climate, characterized by trust, respect and collaboration, is fundamental to the success of servant leadership. Servant leaders act as catalysts for the development of healthy and productive interpersonal relationships, promoting a harmonious and motivating work en-

vironment. By prioritizing the well-being of their employees, they build a strong and cohesive organizational culture (Yukl, 2010).

- Increased Productivity: Research shows that employees who are involved and satisfied with their work tend to be more productive and have a higher level of commitment to the organization (Harter, Schmidt & Hayes, 2002). Servant leadership, by promoting a positive and encouraging work environment, encourages the development of each employee's maximum potential, resulting in an increase in efficiency and quality of work.
- Reducing staff turnover: High staff turnover generates significant costs for organizations and has a negative impact on productivity. Servant leadership, by promoting a positive work environment with opportunities for development and recognition, contributes to retaining talent. Employees who feel valued and supported are more likely to stay with the company, reducing the costs and challenges related to turnover (Bligh et al., 2006).
- New Leaders: Servant leadership encourages the development of new leaders by creating an environment where employees are challenged to take on new responsibilities and grow professionally (Spears, 1998). By sharing knowledge, offering mentoring and delegating challenging tasks, servant leaders train future leaders who will share the same values and principles.
- Greater Innovation and Creativity: A psychologically safe working environment, characteristic of servant leadership, encourages the exchange of ideas, experiences and the generation of new solutions, contributing to the organization's innovation and competitiveness (Amabile, 1998). Servant leaders encourage experimentation, the search for new approaches and freedom of expression, creating fertile ground for creativity and innovation.
- Improved Customer Relations: A culture of customer service, intrinsic to servant leadership, is reflected in the way the organization interacts with its customers, resulting in greater satisfaction and loyalty (Parasuraman, Zeithaml & Berry, 1988). Employees who feel valued and respected tend to replicate this behavior with customers, building lasting and positive relationships.

- Organizational Resilience: Teams led by servant leaders are more resilient, as they are able to deal with changes and challenges more effectively, thanks to mutual trust and commitment to the organization's goals (Weick & Quinn, 1999). Servant leaders cultivate adaptability, collaboration and the ability to learn from mistakes, preparing the organization to face the challenges and uncertainties of the market.
- Employee Development and Empowerment: Servant leadership is characterized by empowering and developing people, expressing humility, authenticity and interpersonal acceptance. This results in a high-quality relationship between leader and member, promoting the initiative of personal actualization and positive attitudes at work (Van Dierendonck, 2011; Canavesi & Minelli, 2021). In addition, servant leadership has been associated with increased employee engagement, through mediators such as empowerment and team cohesion (Canavesi & Minelli, 2021).
- Organizational Performance and Citizen Behavior: Servant leadership positively influences team performance and organizational citizenship behaviors (OCB) by reducing the perceived differentiation in the quality of the leader-member relationship, which strengthens team synergy (Chiniara & Bentein, 2018). Employees who feel part of a cohesive and valued team are more likely to engage in behaviors that benefit the organization.
- Reducing Absenteeism and Turnover: In addition to contributing to increased productivity, servant leadership has been associated with reduced rates of absenteeism and turnover, generating substantial savings for companies and promoting greater organizational stability. Studies indicate that servant leadership can reduce employee turnover by up to 50% (Lee et al., 2019).
- Resilience and Adaptability: Organizations that adopt servant leadership tend to be more resilient and adaptable to market changes, since employees feel more involved and committed to the company's strategic objectives. Servant leadership promotes the creation of high-performance teams capable of dealing with complex challenges and uncertainties (Liden, Wayne, Zhao, and Henderson, 2008).

- Mental health and well-being: Building a safe and welcoming work environment has direct impacts on employees' mental health, reducing stress and anxiety while improving their quality of life and organizational well-being. Research shows that servant leadership is associated with lower levels of burnout and a greater sense of purpose at work (Van Dierendonck, 2011).

Successful examples of servant leadership show that this approach can generate significant results in different sectors and organizational contexts. By prioritizing the service and development of employees, servant leadership contributes to building more humane, collaborative and successful companies In short, the benefits of servant leadership are vast and have a positive impact on all areas of the organization. By prioritizing service and support for employees, servant leaders build a more humane, efficient and motivating work environment. This leadership approach not only improves organizational performance but also contributes to the personal and professional development of employees, creating a virtuous cycle of success and fairer organizations.

EXAMPLES OF SUCCESSFUL SERVANT LEADERSHIP

Servant leadership has shown positive results in various organizational contexts and has proven to be a catalyst for success, whether in specific projects, renowned companies or sectors such as construction, education and health.

The research exemplifies some of the impacts of servant leadership in different sectors:

- Construction projects: In construction projects in China, servant leadership had a positive impact on the success of the projects. This effect was mediated by the strengthening of the learning orientation and the greater agility of the teams, factors enhanced by this leadership approach (Han & Zhang, 2024).
- Catholic parishes: In the religious context, the application of servant leadership in Catholic parishes has been associated with in-

creased organizational citizenship and institutional effectiveness. Mechanisms such as invitation, inspiration and affection have been identified as key elements in promoting an organizational environment based on service to others (Ebener & O'Connell, 2010).

- Education: In the education sector, servant leadership has shown positive effects on teacher morale, job satisfaction and professional engagement. In addition, this approach has fostered the construction of a collaborative and positive organizational culture, promoting an environment conducive to professional and academic development (Kainde & Mandagi, 2023).
- Health: In the health sector, servant leadership has proved fundamental in strengthening the commitment of professionals, which in turn has boosted excellence in organizational performance and improved the quality of the services provided (Demeke, van Engen & Markos, 2024).
- Some companies have adopted servant leadership as a central pillar of their organizational culture, achieving significant results, as an example:
- Zappos: Zappos has established itself as a benchmark by fostering an organizational culture focused on employee autonomy and engagement in customer service. This approach has resulted in high levels of satisfaction and loyalty, reinforcing the importance of empowering employees to deliver excellent service (Hsieh, 2010).
- Southwest Airlines: Southwest Airlines bases its financial success on the premise that motivated and satisfied employees are essential to ensuring customer satisfaction. This strategy has been a determining factor in the company's consolidation in the airline industry (Walsh & Gittell, 2004).

In general, the impacts of servant leadership have been positive in various contexts, promoting psychological empowerment, organizational commitment, the quality of services provided and leadership effectiveness (Zhang et al., 2019). In addition, adopting this approach has been key to strengthening organizational culture and promoting organizational citizenship behaviors, creating a more collaborative work environment that is aligned with the organization's values (Ebener and O'Connell, 2010; Zhang et al., 2019).

CHALLENGES AND CRITICISMS OF SERVANT LEADERSHIP

Servant leadership, a model that prioritizes service and employee development, has gained prominence in the corporate world. However, like any leadership approach, it faces challenges and criticisms that deserve to be analyzed.

Challenges in Implementing Servant Leadership:

- Balance between Service and Authority: One of the main challenges lies in finding the balance between the posture of serving employees and the need to exercise authority and maintain the organizational structure. Servant leaders need to find ways to lead without compromising management effectiveness (Mcquade, Harrison, and Tarbert, 2021; Alia et al., 2023).
- Developing Specific Skills: Servant leadership requires a set of specific skills, such as empathy, active listening, effective communication and the ability to build trust. Developing and honing these skills can be challenging, especially in dynamic and complex work environments (Mcquade et al., 2021).
- Implementation in Competitive Environments: In highly competitive markets, servant leadership can be seen as less aggressive or assertive, which can make it difficult to accept and implement. Leaders who adopt this style need to demonstrate that prioritizing the well-being of employees does not compromise the company's performance and results (Alia et al., 2023).
- Need for Qualitative Research: An important gap in the literature on servant leadership is the lack of qualitative research. This gap makes it difficult to create empirically tested models that can guide the effective practice of servant leadership (Mcquade et al., 2021).
- In addition to the challenges mentioned, uncertainty about the results of implementing servant leadership and fear of the unknown

can generate resistance to change. The transition to this new leadership model requires clear and continuous communication to ensure that all levels of the organization understand and adopt the new philosophy (Carucci, 2021).

However, despite its growing popularity, servant leadership is not immune to criticism. Some authors question the lack of empirical proof of the effectiveness of this leadership model, pointing to the need for more research to validate its results Stone, Russell and Patterson, 2004; Sendjaya & Sarros, 2002).

However, to overcome the challenges and criticisms of servant leadership, it is essential to invest in qualitative research that explores the mechanisms and results of this leadership model in depth. In addition, it is important to develop training programs that enable leaders to develop the skills needed to practice servant leadership, and it is crucial that leaders who adopt this leadership style demonstrate that prioritizing the well-being of employees does not compromise the company's performance and results. On the contrary, effective servant leaders show that investing in people is a key factor in the long-term success of the organization, so by addressing challenges and criticisms transparently and proactively, it is possible to build a solid foundation for implementing servant leadership, reaping the benefits of a more humane, collaborative and success-oriented work environment for all.

FUTURE DIRECTIONS IN SERVANT LEADERSHIP RESEARCH

Research into servant leadership has evolved significantly, but there is still a vast field to be explored in order to improve understanding and strengthen the application of this leadership model. The future directions outlined below represent an invitation to investigate and deepen knowledge in this promising field.

- . Conceptual Clarity and Measurement: Servant leadership, despite its growing popularity, still lacks conceptual clarity and more robust and validated measurement instruments. The literature points to the need for solid empirical frameworks and more standardized definitions to ensure the consistency and comparability of studies (Eva, Robin, Sendjaya, van Dierendonck, and Liden, 2019; Parris and Peachey, 2013; Lee et al., 2019).

- Qualitative and Methodological Research: The predominance of quantitative studies in the literature on servant leadership reveals a gap in the use of qualitative approaches. Future research should invest in qualitative methods, such as interviews, case studies and ethnography, to better understand the internal processes, organizational impacts and mechanisms by which servant leadership influences the behaviour of individuals and teams (McQuade et al., 2021; Parris & Peachey, 2013).
- Exploring Antecedents and Moderators: A promising field for future research lies in exploring the antecedents of servant leadership, i.e. the factors that can influence the development of this leadership style. Identifying personal characteristics, cultural values and aspects of the organizational environment that can facilitate or hinder the practice of servant leadership can provide valuable insights for its implementation (Chon and Zoltan, 2019; Zhang et al., 2019).
- Sectoral and Contextual Applications: Expanding the research to different sectors and cultural contexts is essential to understanding the adaptability and effectiveness of servant leadership in different settings. Sectors such as health, education, social service and non-profit organizations can benefit significantly from servant leadership, considering the centrality of care and service to others in these contexts. Comparative studies between sectors can contribute to a better understanding of the applications and challenges of servant leadership in different realities (Chon and Zoltan, 2019; Demeke et al., 2024).
- Development of theories and practices: Integrating servant leadership with other theoretical approaches, such as transformational leadership, authentic leadership and self-determination theory, can enrich the field and broaden its applications. Comparing different leadership models can help refine concepts and provide new perspectives on the implementation of servant leadership. The develop-

ment of hybrid models and the creation of practical strategies based on evidence can strengthen the application of servant leadership in organizations (Lee et al., 2019; Zhang et al., 2019).

- Servant Leadership and Diversity: The growing diversity in organizations calls for reflection on the relationship between servant leadership and diversity. How can servant leadership promote inclusion and respect for differences? What are the challenges and opportunities for applying servant leadership in multicultural contexts? These are some questions that deserve attention in future research.
- Servant Leadership and Technology: Technology has transformed the way people work and relate to each other. How can servant leadership adapt to this new reality? What are the challenges and opportunities for applying servant leadership in virtual teams and technology-mediated work environments? This is another promising area for future research.

By addressing these future directions, servant leadership research will be able to evolve in a more structured way, providing relevant contributions to academia and organizational practice. We believe that servant leadership has the potential to transform organizations, creating work environments that are more humane, collaborative and oriented towards everyone's success.

CONCLUSION

Servant leadership, based on altruism and the vocation to serve, represents an innovative and humanized approach to managing people and organizations. By reconfiguring the traditional hierarchical structure and prioritizing the needs of employees and the community, this leadership model cultivates a more collaborative, engaging organizational environment geared towards sustainable long-term results.

Its implementation, however, comes up against significant challenges. In many organizations, the corporate culture remains strongly anchored in rigid hierarchical structures and conventional management models, making it difficult to adopt servant leadership. Resistance to change, the undefined roles and responsibilities of servant leaders and the complexity of measuring the impact of this style of leadership represent obstacles that require effective strategies to overcome.

Furthermore, servant leadership requires managers to develop high levels of self-awareness, empathy and humility, skills that require time and continuous effort to improve. The lack of widely disseminated models of success in this approach can also generate uncertainty and hesitation on the part of organizations in adopting this leadership model.

Despite these difficulties, servant leadership offers transformative potential for organizations aiming for a more sustainable and humanized future. Investing in the development of servant leaders can provide a series of benefits, including greater employee engagement, increased customer satisfaction and improved organizational innovation. To consolidate servant leadership as an effective practice, it is essential to adopt the following strategies: Fostering an organizational culture aligned with servant leadership: Creating values, norms and practices that encourage collaboration, empathy and a commitment to serving others.; Providing ongoing training and development for leaders: Offering specific training so that managers acquire the necessary skills to exercise servant leadership effectively; Establish metrics for evaluating impact: Develop indicators that go beyond traditional financial metrics, including employee engagement, customer satisfaction and innovation capacity; Create support networks for servant leaders: Establish learning communities that allow managers who adopt this approach to share experiences, overcome challenges and grow together.

In this way, servant leadership presents itself as a promising model for building more humanized, resilient and sustainable organizations. Although its implementation requires cultural changes and the development of specific skills, its benefits are widely recognized and have a positive impact on productivity, employee well-being and organizational longevity. Therefore, for servant leadership to generate significant results, it is essential that managers commit themselves both to improving their skills and to creating an organizational environment that values the well-being and development of employees. With efforts aimed at overcoming challenges, companies can not only make significant gains in performance and innovation but also contribute to a more humane and sustainable future, where work is a place of growth and fulfillment for everyone.

In light of the evidence presented, it becomes clear that servant leadership is not a one-size-fits-all model, but rather a dynamic and context-sensitive approach that requires intentional alignment with organizational structures, values, and goals. Its flexibility allows it to be adapted across industries and cultures, but this same versatility calls for thoughtful implementation tailored to each organization's unique reality. An essential step toward mainstreaming servant leadership is the development of organizational ecosystems that sustain it over time. This goes beyond individual leaders and touches on systemic change—embedding servant values into performance appraisal systems, leadership pipelines, recruitment criteria, and internal communication strategies. Leaders should not only be trained in technical competencies but also nurtured in emotional and ethical intelligence, resilience, and a mindset of lifelong service.

Moreover, the presence of servant leadership should not be limited to the upper echelons of management. For the model to truly flourish, it must be cultivated at all levels of the organization. Empowering middle managers and frontline supervisors with the tools and autonomy to serve their teams is crucial. This vertical integration ensures consistency in values and enhances psychological safety, which in turn leads to greater openness to innovation, error-sharing, and constructive feedback. Another important dimension that deserves attention is the intersection of servant leadership and digital transformation. As organizations embrace automation, artificial intelligence, and virtual workspaces, there is a risk of dehumanizing work. Servant leadership acts as a counterbalance to this trend by reminding organizations that technological advancement must go hand in hand with human-centric values. Digital transformation should enhance, not replace, the relational and ethical core of organizational life.

Future-oriented organizations must consider the role of servant leadership in environmental and social governance (ESG) agendas. As stakeholders increasingly demand responsible corporate behavior, servant leaders are well-positioned to lead sustainability initiatives with authenticity and purpose. Their long-term perspective, ethical commitment, and community orientation naturally align with broader societal goals, from climate responsibility to social inclusion.

Servant leadership also has profound implications for employee well-being. In the face of growing concerns over mental health in the workplace, burnout, and disengagement, servant leaders can be key agents in promoting healthy, supportive work environments. By placing employees' needs at the forefront and creating space for dialogue, flexibility, and recognition, they contribute to higher levels of satisfaction and psychological flourishing. To further strengthen the impact of this leadership style, academia and industry must collaborate. Universities can play a vital role in integrating servant leadership into curricula across management, psychology, education, and public administration. At the same time, organizations should be encouraged to open their practices to case studies, field research, and impact assessments that provide a deeper understanding of the model's real-world effectiveness.

Ultimately, servant leadership invites a reframing of what it means to lead. It challenges conventional metrics of success and authority and instead promotes a model where influence is measured by how much others grow, thrive, and contribute. This redefinition of leadership speaks to a profound ethical shift—one that prioritizes dignity over dominance, contribution over control, and shared success over individual acclaim. The adoption of servant leadership is not only an organizational strategy but a cultural and moral commitment. It requires courage, humility, and persistence, especially in environments resistant to change. However, as demonstrated throughout this study, the returns of embracing this model are both tangible and transformative: more engaged teams, more ethical organizations, and a more sustainable vision for the future of leadership.

The road ahead calls for action: to move beyond discourse and into widespread application, with servant leadership embedded not only in vision statements but in daily practices, strategic decisions, and organizational DNA. Only then can we truly speak of a leadership paradigm that serves not just organizations, but humanity as a whole.

REFERENCES

Alia, M., Santoso, P. M., Iwanussoleh, I., & Anshori, M. I. (2023). Kepemimpinan yang melayani menghadapi tantangan dan manfaat dalam era bisnis yang berkembang. *Jurnal Riset Dan Inovasi Manajemen, 1*(3), 224–237. DOI: 10.59581/jrim-widyakarya.v1i3.801

Amabile, T. M. (1998, September). *How to kill creativity.* Harvard Business Review. https://hbr.org/1998/09/how-to-kill-creativity

Bao, Y., Li, C., & Zhao, H. (2018). Servant leadership and engagement: A dual mediation model. *Journal of Managerial Psychology, 33*(6), 406–417. DOI: 10.1108/JMP-12-2017-0435

Bligh, M. C., Pearce, C. L., & Kohles, J. C. (2006). The importance of self-and shared leadership in team based knowledge work: A meso-level model of leadership dynamics. Journal of managerial Psychology, 21(4), 296-318.

Canavesi, A., & Minelli, E. (2021). Servant leadership and employee engagement: A qualitative study. *Employee Responsibilities and Rights Journal, 34*(4), 413–435. DOI: 10.1007/s10672-021-09389-9 PMID: 40477632

Carucci, R. A. (2021). *To be honest: Lead with the power of truth, justice and purpose.* Kogan Page Limited.

Chiniara, M., & Bentein, K. (2018). The servant leadership advantage: When perceiving low differentiation in leader-member relationship quality influences team cohesion, team task performance and service OCB. *The Leadership Quarterly, 29*(2), 333–345. DOI: 10.1016/j.leaqua.2017.05.002

Chon, K. K.-S., & Zoltan, J. (2019). Role of servant leadership in contemporary hospitality. *International Journal of Contemporary Hospitality Management, 31*(8), 3371–3394. DOI: 10.1108/IJCHM-11-2018-0935

Demeke, G. K., van Engen, M., & Markos, S. (2024). Servant Leadership in the Healthcare Literature: A Systematic Review. *Journal of Healthcare Leadership, 16*(16), 1–14. https://www.ncbi.nlm.nih.gov/pmc/articles/PMC10771778/. DOI: 10.2147/JHL.S440160 PMID: 38192640

Ding, D., Lu, H., Song, Y., & Lu, Q. (2012). Relationship of servant leadership and employee loyalty: The mediating role of employee satisfaction. *IBusiness*, *4*(3), 208–215. DOI: 10.4236/ib.2012.43026

Ebener, D. R., & O'Connell, D. J. (2010). How might servant leadership work? *Nonprofit Management & Leadership*, *20*(3), 315–335. DOI: 10.1002/nml.256

Eva, N., Robin, M., Sendjaya, S., van Dierendonck, D., & Liden, R. C. (2019). Servant leadership: A systematic review and call for future research. *The Leadership Quarterly*, *30*(1), 111–132. DOI: 10.1016/j.leaqua.2018.07.004

Frei, F., & Morriss, A. (2020). *Unleashed: the unapologetic leader's guide to empowering everyone around you*. Harvard Business Review Press.

Greenleaf, R.K. (1973). The servant as leader. In *Internet Archive*. Greenleaf Center. https://archive.org/details/20200601-the-servant-as-leader

Hamel, G. (2012). *What matters now*. John Wiley & Sons. DOI: 10.1108/sd.2012.05628iaa.012

Han, H., & Zhang, X. (2024). Servant leadership and project success: The mediating roles of team learning orientation and team agility. *Frontiers in Psychology*, *15*, 1417604. Advance online publication. DOI: 10.3389/fpsyg.2024.1417604 PMID: 39149700

Harter, J. K., Schmidt, F. L., & Hayes, T. L. (2002). Business-unit-level Relationship between Employee satisfaction, Employee engagement, and Business outcomes: A meta-analysis. *The Journal of Applied Psychology*, *87*(2), 268–279. https://www.researchgate.net/publication/11367971_Business-Unit-Level_Relationship_Between_Employee_Satisfaction_Employee_Engagement_and_Business_Outcomes_A_Meta-Analysis. DOI: 10.1037/0021-9010.87.2.268 PMID: 12002955

Hsieh, T. (2010). *Delivering happiness: A path to profits, passion, and purpose*. Business Plus.

Hunter, J. C. (2006). *The world's most powerful leadership principle: How to become a servant leader*. Crown Business.

Hunter, J. C. (2019). *Como se tornar um líder servidor*. Sextante.

Ingrams, A. (2018). Comportamento de Cidadania Organizacional nos Setores Público e Privado: Um Teste Multinível de Motivação para o Serviço Público e Antecedentes Tradicionais. *Revisão da Administração de Pessoal Público, 40*(2), 0734371X1880037. https://doi.org/DOI: 10.1177/0734371X18800372

Joseph, E. E., & Winston, B. E. (2005). Uma correlação de liderança servidora, confiança do líder e confiança organizacional. *Revista de Desenvolvimento de Liderança e Organização*, *26*(1), 6–22. DOI: 10.1108/01437730510575552

Kainde, S. J. R., & Mandagi, D. (2023). A systematic review of servant leadership outcomes in education context. *EDUKASIA: Jurnal Pendidikan Dan Pembelajaran*, *4*(2), 2563–2574. DOI: 10.62775/edukasia.v4i2.627

Katchindele, M., Gomes, R., & Yambo, N. (2024). Liderança Organizacional: Uma Revisão Integrativa. *Revista Academicus: Revista Multidisciplinar*, *2*(2), 29–41. DOI: 10.4314/academicus.v2i2.2

Lai, F.-Y., Tang, H.-C., Lu, S.-C., & Cheng-Chen Timothy Lin. (2020, January 6). *Transformational leadership and job performance: The mediating role of work engagement*. ResearchGate; SAGE. https://www.researchgate.net/publication/338427319_Transformational_Leadership_and_Job_Performance_The_Mediating_Role_of_Work_Engagement

Lee, A., Lyubovnikova, J., Tian, A. W., & Knight, C. (2019). Servant leadership: A Meta-analytic Examination of Incremental contribution, moderation, and Mediation. *Journal of Occupational and Organizational Psychology*, *93*(1), 1–44. Advance online publication. DOI: 10.1111/joop.12265

Liden, R. C., Wayne, S. J., Zhao, H., & Henderson, D. (2008). Servant leadership: Development of a multidimensional measure and multi-level assessment. *The Leadership Quarterly*, *19*(2), 161–177. DOI: 10.1016/j.leaqua.2008.01.006

Maslow, A. H. (1943). A theory of human motivation. *Psychological Review*, *50*(4), 370–396. DOI: 10.1037/h0054346

Mcquade, K. E., Harrison, C., & Tarbert, H. (2021). Systematically reviewing servant leadership. *European Business Review*, *33*(3), 465–490. DOI: 10.1108/EBR-08-2019-0162

Miao, Q., Newman, A., Schwarz, G., & Xu, L. (2014). Servant leadership, trust, and the organizational commitment of public sector employees in China. *Public Administration*, *92*(3), n/a, n/a. DOI: 10.1111/padm.12091

Mittal, R., & Dorfman, P. W. (2012). Servant leadership across cultures. *Journal of World Business*, *47*(4), 555–570. DOI: 10.1016/j.jwb.2012.01.009

Newman, A., Schwarz, G., Cooper, B., & Sendjaya, S. (2017). How servant leadership influences organizational citizenship behavior: The roles of LMX, empowerment, and proactive personality. *Journal of Business Ethics*, *145*(1), 49–62. DOI: 10.1007/s10551-015-2827-6

Parasuraman, A. P., Zeithaml, V. A., & Berry, L. L. (1988, January). *SERVQUAL: A multiple- item scale for measuring consumer perceptions of service quality*. ResearchGate. https://www.researchgate.net/publication/225083802_SERVQUAL_A_multiple-_Item_Scale_for_measuring_consumer_perceptions_of_service_quality

Parris, D. L., & Peachey, J. W. (2013). A systematic literature review of servant leadership theory in organizational contexts. *Journal of Business Ethics*, *113*(3), 377–393. DOI: 10.1007/s10551-012-1322-6

Robbins, S. P., & Judge, T. A. (2013). *Organizational behavior* (15th ed.). Pearson., https://digilib.stekom.ac.id/assets/dokumen/ebook/feb_c5d15cc7c32d4985a70c200bad26dc576781601d_1648649445.pdf

Russell, B. (2001). *The problems of philosophy*. Oxford University Press.

Russell, R. F., & Stone, A. G. (2002). A review of servant leadership attributes: Developing a practical model. *Leadership and Organization Development Journal*, *23*(3), 145–157. DOI: 10.1108/01437730210424

Sendjaya, S., & Sarros, J. C. (2002). Servant leadership: Its origin, development, and application in organizations. *Journal of Leadership & Organizational Studies*, *9*(2), 57–64. DOI: 10.1177/107179190200900205

Spears, L. C. (1998). *Insights on leadership*. John Wiley & Sons.

Stone, A. G., Russell, R. F., & Patterson, K. (2004). Transformational versus Servant leadership: A Difference in Leader Focus. *Leadership and Organization Development Journal, 25*(4), 349–361. DOI: 10.1108/01437730410538671

Van Dierendonck, D. (2011). Servant leadership: A review and synthesis. *Journal of Management, 37*(4), 1228–1261. DOI: 10.1177/0149206310380462

van Dierendonck, D., Stam, D., Boersma, P., de Windt, N., & Alkema, J. (2014). Same difference? Exploring the differential mechanisms linking servant leadership and transformational leadership to follower outcomes. *The Leadership Quarterly, 25*(3), 544–562. DOI: 10.1016/j.leaqua.2013.11.014

Walsh, D. J., & Gittell, J. H. (2004). The southwest airlines way: Using the power of relationships to achieve high performance. *Industrial & Labor Relations Review, 57*(3), 474. DOI: 10.2307/4126671

Washington, R. R., Sutton, C. D., & Feild, H. S. (2006). Diferenças individuais na liderança servidora: Os papéis dos valores e da personalidade. *Revista de Desenvolvimento de Liderança e Organização, 27*(8), 700–716. DOI: 10.1108/01437730610709309

Weick, K. E., & Quinn, R. E. (1999). Organisational change and development. *Annual Review of Psychology, 50*(1), 361–386. DOI: 10.1146/annurev.psych.50.1.361 PMID: 15012461

Yukl, G. (2010). *Leadership in organizations* (7th ed.). Pearson Education.

Zenger, J., & Folkman, J. (2015). *O líder inspirador desvendando o segredo por trás de como os líderes extraordinários motivam*. https://zengerfolkman.com/wp-content/uploads/2019/04/White-Paper_-Unlocking-The-Secret-Behind-How-Extraordinary-Leaders-Motivate.pdf

Zhang, Y., Zheng, Y., Zhang, L., Xu, S., Liu, X., & Chen, W. (2019). A meta-analytic review of the consequences of servant leadership: The moderating roles of cultural factors. *Asia Pacific Journal of Management, 38*(1), 371–400. Advance online publication. DOI: 10.1007/s10490-018-9639-z

Chapter 8
The Role of Digital Platforms in Shaping Competitive Intelligence Strategies

Mustafa Kayyali
https://orcid.org/0000-0003-3300-262X
Maaref University of Applied Sciences, Syria

ABSTRACT

In the rapidly evolving digital economy, competitive intelligence (CI) has moved beyond traditional market monitoring to become a dynamic, platform-driven capability. This chapter explores how digital platforms—from social media to enterprise SaaS and data analytics ecosystems—are reshaping the way organizations gather, interpret, and act upon intelligence. It unpacks the transformation of CI strategies as businesses increasingly rely on real-time, algorithmic, and participatory forms of knowledge extraction. Rather than treating digital platforms merely as tools, the chapter considers them as active environments that shape competitive behaviors, enable new forms of collaboration, and challenge conventional notions of information control. Drawing from contemporary cases, the analysis emphasizes the critical role of digital literacy, ethical reflexivity, and

DOI: 10.4018/979-8-3373-2690-0.ch008

adaptive leadership in harnessing these platforms effectively. Ultimately, it argues for a reimagined model of CI—one that is agile, inclusive, and grounded in a nuanced understanding of digital realities.

INTRODUCTION

In today's economy, where volatility is no longer an exception but a defining feature, competitive intelligence (CI) has evolved from a behind-the-scenes activity into a mission-critical function deeply woven into the fabric of strategic leadership. The rise of digital platforms has been one of the most transformative developments in this evolution. What began as a shift in tools—moving from printed reports and manually compiled datasets to real-time dashboards and AI-powered analytics—has turned into a more profound transformation in how organizations perceive, pursue, and practice intelligence (Cano-Marin et al, 2023). No longer confined to static information retrieval, CI is increasingly shaped by platforms that are dynamic, participatory, and algorithmically driven. These platforms do not merely deliver data; they mediate how data is created, shared, and acted upon. This shift demands a rethinking of foundational assumptions. Traditional CI frameworks often rested on a linear model: data is collected, analyzed, then translated into decisions. But in a platform-mediated world, that sequence is no longer linear. Platforms accelerate cycles, dissolve boundaries between internal and external intelligence, and blur the distinction between signal and noise. Consider the instantaneous ripple effects of a tweet from a CEO, the strategic insights buried in customer reviews across e-commerce platforms, or the geopolitical implications discernible through platform-driven disinformation campaigns. Intelligence now flows in real-time, often unstructured, and sometimes manipulated—yet it remains essential. The challenge is not merely how to access data, but how to make sense of it meaningfully and ethically.

Digital platforms are also changing the nature of competition itself (Kayyali, 2025 a). Companies are no longer just competing in markets—they're competing within ecosystems, where visibility, velocity, and the ability to harness user-generated content can determine a brand's rise or fall. In this new terrain, CI is not an optional luxury but an adaptive survival skill. It requires organizations to become both observers and participants in digital spaces—monitoring competitors, yes, but also listening to sentiment, watching behaviors, and anticipating shifts that may not yet be quantifiable. Digital platforms democratize access to intelligence—but with that democratization comes noise, bias, and the challenge of filtering. While there is more data than ever, much of it is fragmented, overwhelming, and shaped by invisible algorithms. Organizations must now invest not only in tools but in talent—people who can interpret ambiguity, challenge assumptions, and draw insight from complexity. In that sense, CI is becoming less about possession of data and more about the *ability to think intelligently with data*—to contextualize, to synthesize, and to act.

This chapter takes a deep dive into this emergent landscape. It explores how digital platforms are reshaping the competitive intelligence paradigm and what that means for strategists, analysts, and decision-makers. Drawing on case examples, theoretical insights, and critical reflections, it examines not only what platforms offer but also what they demand: new competencies, new ethics, and a new understanding of strategy itself. As the digital age continues to unfold, the role of CI will not diminish—it will only grow more central, more complex, and more human in its demands.

Digital Platforms as Catalysts for Competitive Intelligence Evolution

There was a time—not too long ago—when competitive intelligence was a cloistered activity. It belonged in the quiet corners of strategy departments, carried out through spreadsheets, trade publications, and market reports. Executives would wait for quarterly updates, analysts would meticulously scan regulatory filings, and product teams would rely on industry gossip whispered at conferences. It was a world where information trickled slowly and decision-making followed in thoughtful, often deliberate steps. That world has been irreversibly transformed.

Digital platforms—spanning social media, search engines, digital marketplaces, data aggregators, and enterprise collaboration tools—have not simply changed how information is accessed; they have altered the very nature of intelligence (Ali, 2023). These platforms are not neutral channels. They are dynamic, self-reinforcing ecosystems that shape what we see, when we see it, and how we interpret its significance. They don't just accelerate the flow of information—they direct it, color it, and often distort it. And it is in this complex landscape that competitive intelligence has found new momentum, new relevance, and new challenges. To speak of platforms as "catalysts" is not a metaphor. A catalyst, in chemical terms, speeds up a reaction without being consumed in the process. Likewise, digital platforms accelerate the processes of information production, circulation, and interpretation—while remaining structurally intact and often invisible in the background. They serve as the unseen architects of perception, enabling organizations to move from hindsight to foresight almost in real time.

Take, for example, the evolution of consumer sentiment tracking. In the past, gauging how the public felt about a product required formal surveys, costly focus groups, and weeks of lag time. Today, a well-trained algorithm can sift through millions of tweets, Reddit threads, TikTok comments, or app store reviews to extract not only sentiment but also patterns of behavior, emerging preferences, and emotional tones (Vargo, 2025). The speed, scale, and granularity of this insight are unprecedented. But what's even more compelling is how this data isn't just passively received—it's actively shaped by the platforms that host it. Trending hashtags, algorithmic amplification, and platform-specific cultures all influence what becomes visible and what remains in the shadows. And so, the CI professional is no longer a quiet analyst working from static documents. They have become an interpreter of signals, a digital ethnographer, and often, a detective working across layers of information, noise, and nuance. The work has become faster, yes—but also more uncertain, more relational, and more interdisciplinary.

Another dimension of this evolution is the blurring of boundaries between internal and external intelligence. Digital collaboration platforms like Slack, Microsoft Teams, and Trello were once seen primarily as tools for internal communication and project management (Emmanuel et al, 2024). But they have become informal archives of strategic thought. Within these platforms lie trails of product discussions, competitor mentions, customer feedback loops, and strategic shifts—all of which can be analyzed, visualized, and acted upon. Intelligence is no longer "out there" in the market; it is also "in here," woven into the daily rhythms of organizational life. Digital platforms have introduced a participatory layer to intelligence gathering. Through open innovation platforms, online communities, and real-time customer interaction channels, companies now draw insights directly from their users, partners, and even competitors—sometimes without realizing it. Crowdsourced data, feedback loops, and co-creation initiatives have turned the market itself into a kind of living intelligence system. Every interaction, review, or comment can become a datapoint—if one knows how to listen.

Yet, amidst this abundance, lies a paradox: more data does not always mean more clarity. In fact, the sheer volume of information often leads to saturation, overwhelm, and decision fatigue. Digital platforms can generate echo chambers, reinforce biases, and flood strategists with irrelevant signals disguised as insights (Pansanella, 2024). The role of the CI professional, therefore, is not just to collect data—but to make meaning of it. This calls for a deeper literacy, not just in tools, but in critical thinking. It demands the ability to ask: *What are we seeing, and what are we missing? Who controls this information? What filters are shaping our view?*

Platforms also change the temporal logic of intelligence. In a pre-digital age, the pace of decision-making followed the rhythm of quarterly reports, annual plans, and five-year visions. Today, strategy is shaped by moments—viral posts, breaking news, shifts in online discourse, or the sudden emergence of a new market entrant halfway across the globe. Competitive threats can materialize in days, and opportunities can vanish just as quickly (Adner, R., & Lieberman, 2021). Speed is now a competitive advantage—but it must be tempered with strategic depth. Interestingly, digital platforms also influence how organizations understand their competitors. It's no longer just about benchmarking against product offerings or market share. It's about analyzing digital presence, engagement quality, brand sentiment, hiring patterns (as seen on LinkedIn), investor signals, public statements, and even the narratives companies craft about themselves online. A company's website, social media voice, and digital footprint now reveal more than any formal press release ever could. Competitive intelligence, in this context, becomes an exercise in reading between the lines—decoding tone, intention, trajectory.

But perhaps one of the most subtle yet profound shifts is the way platforms reframe the role of *power* in intelligence. In traditional CI, power was rooted in access—access to proprietary reports, exclusive databases, and specialized expertise. In the digital platform era, power lies in interpretation. Everyone has access to the same ocean of data—but not everyone knows how to navigate it. The edge comes from the capacity to extract insight, to ask the right questions, and to see what others overlook. This marks a democratization of CI, but also an elevation of its most human qualities: intuition, contextual reasoning, and strategic foresight. And still, there are ethical layers we cannot ignore. As companies monitor competitors, engage with users, and mine platform data, they must confront questions of privacy, consent, and transparency (Wu, 2024). Surveillance masquerading as intelligence can backfire—not only in reputation but in trust (Garrido, 2021). The platforms themselves are not immune from manipulation. Bots can skew sentiment, paid promotions can masquerade as organic trends, and algorithmic biases can silence entire perspectives. For CI to remain credible and constructive, it must evolve with a sense of ethical responsibility. Intelligence should not be weaponized, and it should never dehumanize the very people it seeks to understand.

Furthermore, the evolution of CI on digital platforms is not uniform across sectors or geographies. While some industries—like tech, retail, and finance—have embraced platform-based CI tools with agility, others—like healthcare, energy, or public administration—are slower to adapt due to regulation, legacy systems, or cultural resistance. The journey to platform-enabled CI is therefore uneven, requiring tailored strategies, change management, and cross-functional collaboration. In this unfolding reality, leadership plays a pivotal role. Organizations that excel in CI are those that recognize it not as a departmental function, but as a cultural asset (Fannon et al, 2022). They create environments where curiosity is encouraged, where data is not hoarded but shared, where insights flow horizontally and vertically. They invest not only in platforms and dashboards, but in the people who can animate them with strategic intelligence. They know that while technology offers tools, it is human discernment that makes them meaningful. Digital platforms have redefined what competitive intelligence means, where it happens, and who participates in it. They have shifted intelligence from being a product to being a process—from a report to a conversation. This transformation is still in motion. As platforms evolve, as data becomes more decentralized, and as AI and machine learning further automate pattern recognition, the role of the CI professional will continue to change. But the essence will remain: to see clearly, to think critically, and to act wisely. What we are witnessing is not just the digitization of intelligence, but its re-humanization through new modes of connectivity, participation, and reflection. The platforms may be digital, but the strategy is—and must always remain—profoundly human.

The Convergence of Data, Strategy, and Speed in the Digital Landscape

There is a quiet, almost imperceptible shift that has taken place in the way modern organizations think about strategy. Where once the key to competitive success lay in careful long-term planning, shaped by historical data and steady market trends, today's decision-making lives in the moment, moves at the speed of thought, and hinges on the ability to sense, interpret, and act on data almost as it emerges. The era we inhabit is not merely digital—it is accelerated, hyperconnected, and continuously redefined by the convergence of three interwoven forces: data, strategy, and speed. These are not just buzzwords. They are not loosely affiliated concepts. They form a living ecosystem in which one cannot function without the other. Data without strategy is noise. Strategy without speed is obsolescence (Rust, 2021). Speed without data is recklessness. Together, they create a new paradigm—one that favors organizations capable of both sensing and responding, of analyzing with depth and acting with agility, of seeing not just what *is* but what *could be.*

The digital landscape is not kind to those who hesitate. Today, decisions that once took weeks or months now demand to be made in hours. Competitive threats do not arrive with warning signs; they appear, sometimes silently, through shifts in customer behavior, changes in algorithmic rankings, or quiet movements by nimble startups testing ideas in digital shadows. The very structure of competition has changed—from traditional market segments to digitally mediated, fast-moving ecosystems. In this context, data becomes more than information—it becomes oxygen. Without it, organizations suffocate in irrelevance. Yet the irony is that we are swimming in more data than we can possibly use. From transactional logs and sensor outputs to customer reviews, social media conversations, and third-party market feeds, organizations now face what can only be described as a flood. The challenge is no longer how to gather data, but how to *tame it, interpret it*, and *embed it meaningfully* within a living, breathing strategy (Cochrane et al, 2022). Strategic intelligence, once confined to isolated departments or quarterly reports, is now a daily practice. It has moved from the boardroom to the browser, from polished decks to real-time dashboards. But the shift is not purely technological—it is cognitive. Leaders and teams are being called upon to think differently, to look for signals amid the noise, to challenge outdated assumptions, and to resist the comfort of the known. Because in the digital age, yesterday's insight is already losing relevance, and tomorrow's opportunity will not wait for your analysis to catch up.

This is where speed becomes existential. Not speed for the sake of it, but speed as *responsiveness*. Speed as the capacity to translate intelligence into action before the window closes. It is not about being impulsive or reactive—it is about being *prepared.* It is about building systems, processes, and mental models that allow organizations to *sense early, decide quickly, and adapt continuously.* We can already see this shift playing out across industries. In retail, supply chains are being recalibrated in near real-time based on demand signals gathered through platform data and customer behavior analytics (Neuman, 2023). In finance, microsecond decisions are made on trading floors driven by predictive algorithms. In healthcare, digital diagnostics and patient feedback platforms are altering treatment plans within days, not months. What these examples reveal is that speed, when anchored in data and shaped by strategy, does not lead to chaos—it leads to resilience. But this convergence is not without its tensions. Speed can create pressure. Data can be overwhelming. Strategy can become performative rather than purposeful. There is a fine line between agility and panic, between responsiveness and reactivity. It is not enough to act fast; one must act *wisely*. This requires a new kind of discipline—a fusion of analytical thinking and strategic patience (Prokushenkov, 2023). It demands leaders who can hold complexity without rushing to simplify, who can tolerate ambiguity without being paralyzed by it. The question then becomes: how do organizations build this capacity? How do they create environments where data, strategy, and speed reinforce each other rather than pull in different directions?

Part of the answer lies in culture. A data-rich organization is not one that simply hoards analytics—it is one that cultivates curiosity. It encourages questions, fosters exploration, and resists the instinct to treat dashboards as gospel. Strategy is no longer confined to a few senior executives—it must be conversational, distributed, and iterative (Prashantham & Madhok, 2023). It must invite voices from across the organization, especially those closest to the data and the customers. Speed must not be forced—it must be enabled. This means removing bureaucratic bottlenecks, flattening decision hierarchies, and trusting people to act in alignment with shared strategic intent. Technology plays a role, of course. But the most advanced tools in the world are useless without the human capacity to frame questions, interpret patterns, and make judgment calls. Artificial intelligence can recommend, but it cannot *choose* in context. Machine learning can predict, but it cannot *prioritize* in values. These remain fundamentally human functions (Kayyali, 2025 b). The convergence of data, strategy, and speed, therefore, is not about replacing human insight—it is about augmenting it. It is about equipping humans to think faster, see wider, and act smarter. In many ways, we are witnessing a return to first principles. Strategy, at its core, has always been about making choices in conditions of uncertainty. What digital platforms and data technologies offer is not certainty—but *clarity*. They help illuminate the landscape, surface emerging trends, and test assumptions. But it is still up to humans to decide what matters, why it matters, and how to respond. The convergence we are describing is not mechanical; it is philosophical. It asks: What kind of organization do you want to be? How do you define intelligence? And how do you balance the need for speed with the responsibility of impact?

This is especially relevant in the age of reputational volatility. A poorly informed decision, amplified across social media, can cause lasting damage. A rushed response, made without sufficient context, can undermine trust. In the race to move fast, organizations must not lose sight of their values. Strategy must remain anchored in purpose. Data must be interpreted with empathy. Speed must be grounded in readiness, not reaction. There is also a geopolitical dimension to this convergence. Digital platforms operate across borders, shaping perceptions and preferences in ways that are difficult to regulate or fully understand (Popiel & Sang, 2021). In this environment, intelligence is not just about competitors—it's about ecosystems, alliances, cultures, and narratives. It is about understanding how global events ripple through digital channels and affect local realities. For international organizations, this means CI must now be multilingual, multicultural, and media-savvy. It must account for digital influence, not just digital presence.

What we see emerging is a new literacy. A fluency not just in data science or strategic frameworks, but in systems thinking. A capacity to connect dots across disciplines, timelines, and contexts. This is the new competitive advantage—not data alone, not speed alone, not strategy alone, but the ability to weave them together into coherent, dynamic action. Organizations that can do this are not just more agile—they are more *aware*. They move with purpose, not just pace (Ray, 2023). As we look ahead, the convergence of data, strategy, and speed will only deepen. Technologies will become more intelligent. Platforms will grow more immersive. Expectations for responsiveness will rise. But the essential task will remain the same: to make meaning in motion. To act decisively without becoming hasty. To think deeply without becoming slow. This is not easy work. It requires humility, experimentation, and constant learning. It requires organizations to see strategy not as a plan on a slide deck but as a living dialogue. It requires them to treat data not as truth but as a signal. It requires them to treat speed not as a metric but as a mindset. The digital landscape rewards those who can move fast without losing their way. Who can see clearly without seeing only what they want to see. Who can act with urgency while still honoring the complexity of the moment. The convergence of data, strategy, and speed is not a trend—it is a test. A test of adaptability. A test of judgment. And above all, a test of leadership.

Case Insights: Platform-Driven Intelligence in Action

There is something profoundly revealing about watching theory unfold in the real world—when abstract concepts collide with practical constraints and come alive through human choices, organizational risk, and unpredictable digital dynamics. In the realm of competitive intelligence (CI), no amount of strategic frameworks or analytical models can substitute for the raw clarity that case insights provide (Cavallo et al, 2021). Real-world scenarios force us to confront ambiguity, to acknowledge context, and to respect the layered nature of decision-making. When it comes to digital platforms and their role in shaping CI strategies, the power of the case study lies not in illustrating perfection, but in illuminating complexity. The digital landscape, for all its sophistication, remains an environment shaped by people—by how they use, misuse, interpret, and challenge technology. Platforms do not create intelligence; they amplify the capacity to generate and mobilize it. The following narratives, drawn from diverse sectors and geographies, illustrate how organizations have navigated digital platforms not just to gather information, but to craft insight, challenge assumptions, and stay strategically alert in real time.

One of the most instructive cases in recent years involves Nike—a company long known for its marketing prowess, but whose evolution in the digital CI space is both subtle and profound. In 2019, Nike began transitioning from its traditional retail distribution model toward a direct-to-consumer (DTC) approach (Bodley et al, 2021). But this wasn't simply a logistical decision; it was rooted in deep platform-driven intelligence. Nike had been quietly leveraging insights from its own apps—like Nike Training Club and SNKRS—and tracking digital engagement patterns, micro-trends, and user behaviors across social platforms. Through this, it recognized that consumer loyalty was increasingly tied not to product availability, but to digital experience and narrative connection. The decision to scale back partnerships with certain retailers and prioritize their own digital ecosystem wasn't a gut move. It was informed by months of platform listening—understanding which stories resonated, which influencers held trust in specific demographics, how product drops performed in different regions, and even which emojis customers used when describing their excitement or disappointment. It was CI—but not in the conventional sense. There was no espionage, no industrial secrets. Just relentless curiosity, interpretive rigor, and the ability to synthesize digital signals into strategic action.

A different, but equally rich case can be found in Zara, the Spanish fast-fashion powerhouse. Long before "real-time retail" became a buzzword, Zara had mastered a system of micro-collection experimentation—releasing small product batches, tracking their performance, and iterating quickly (Nguyen, 2023). But what accelerated their foresight was the way they embedded digital intelligence into every layer of decision-making. Zara doesn't just monitor fashion bloggers or scroll through Pinterest mood boards. It actively mines Instagram for emerging aesthetics, tracks geographic variations in color preferences, and observes which influencers are generating the most reposts—not just likes. Their strategic brilliance lies in connecting the dots. When a spike in lavender-colored blouses in Seoul coincides with a K-pop artist's appearance, Zara doesn't just see a trend—it sees a window. That product, or a variation of it, shows up in store within weeks, sometimes days. The intelligence isn't just about *what* people are wearing, but *why* they are wearing it, *when* they want it, and *how* it reflects something deeper—a cultural moment, a generational mood, an emotional resonance. This is competitive intelligence in the age of platforms—not driven by spreadsheets but by living insight.

Consider now a very different kind of platform case—the rise of Clubhouse during the COVID-19 pandemic (Kayyali, 2020). Though short-lived in its peak, Clubhouse offered an unexpected playground for CI practitioners. Without formal structures, users from across industries, geographies, and expertise levels were suddenly engaging in candid, unscripted conversations. Early adopters from venture capital firms, startup founders, academics, and even policy makers were openly discussing trends, anxieties, and emerging technologies in voice-only rooms. For those listening closely—not with intent to copy, but to understand—Clubhouse became a source of anticipatory insight. Some tech companies began assigning analysts to silently participate in thematic rooms—not to extract information covertly, but to *listen to sentiment*. The emotional tone of conversations, the cadence of excitement around certain topics, the kinds of questions being asked repeatedly—all of these became strategic inputs. It wasn't about harvesting trade secrets. It was about detecting energy: Where is curiosity building? What terms are becoming sticky? Who is framing the future in compelling ways?

The lesson from Clubhouse wasn't that every new platform is a goldmine. It was that *early attention is data*. The very act of where innovators choose to gather, how they talk, and what stories they tell can reveal tomorrow's priorities. Competitive intelligence here moved from content analysis to *conversation analysis*, from metrics to meaning (Köseoglu et al, 2021). We also see the inverse of platform-driven foresight in cases where companies failed to act on available intelligence. Kodak, often cited as a cautionary tale, actually had the data. It pioneered digital photography. It understood the disruption ahead. But what it lacked was the cultural willingness to listen to what its own platform data was telling it. Internal reports flagged changes in consumer behavior, test launches revealed a growing appetite for digital storage, and early online forums signaled a shift in how people talked about photography. But the information was dismissed, because it clashed with entrenched identities and business models. The failure wasn't technological. It was interpretive. Contrast this with Spotify, a company that has continually used platform intelligence not just to survive, but to lead. Beyond streaming data, Spotify gathers micro-insights from user-generated playlists, skip rates, social sharing, and even the time of day certain tracks are played. But the real magic lies in how this intelligence is applied strategically. Spotify doesn't just recommend music; it shapes taste (Seaver, 2022). It uses platform intelligence to subtly guide user journeys, test content placement, and identify potential podcast themes or original content investments. Its competitive intelligence doesn't simply follow what's trending—it anticipates what *could* trend, and positions the company as a tastemaker, not a passive distributor.

Then there's the case of Tesla, whose CI strategy is not built on secrecy but on *visibility*. Elon Musk's tweets, often controversial and impulsive, are themselves part of a deliberate platform intelligence play (Zhang et al, 2024). They serve not only as communication but as data generators—each response, retweet, and media reaction becomes a feedback loop. Tesla watches how narratives evolve in real time, adapts communication, and leverages its digital tribe to test ideas, provoke media cycles, and crowd-source energy around its brand. Whether one agrees with the ethics of this model or not, its effectiveness is undeniable. It's a masterclass in *narrative-driven intelligence*—where the platform is not just a place to observe the market, but to *shape it*. From these cases, a few powerful themes emerge.

First, platform-driven CI is participatory. Intelligence is no longer the result of isolated observation—it is the product of interaction. Whether it's brands co-creating with users, companies engaging with communities, or strategists listening to open conversations, intelligence is increasingly drawn from dialogue, not distance. Second, context is everything. Data is meaningless without cultural and strategic context (Karaboga et al, 2023). Lavender blouses only matter if you understand why they matter *now.* Skip rates mean nothing if you can't interpret what users are skipping *toward.* Strategic value lies in pattern recognition, not just pattern detection. Third, platform CI is dynamic, not archival. Unlike traditional competitive intelligence that relied on static benchmarking, digital CI is fluid. Insights have half-lives. Windows of opportunity are brief. The pace of change means intelligence must be living, adaptive, and continuously updated—not filed away in quarterly decks. Fourth, ethical boundaries matter more than ever. As organizations increase their digital intelligence capacities, they walk a thin line between strategic listening and intrusive monitoring (Gitelman et al, 2021). Trust—both internal and external—will increasingly become a differentiator. Transparency, accountability, and cultural sensitivity must anchor how intelligence is gathered and used.

And finally, human interpretation remains irreplaceable. Tools can help, algorithms can accelerate, but insight—the kind that moves strategy—is a human craft. It is shaped by experience, empathy, intuition, and imagination. The most successful organizations don't just invest in platforms—they invest in people who know how to ask the right questions of those platforms. These case insights show us that CI in the digital age is not about being omniscient. It's about being attuned. It's about listening deeply, thinking holistically, and acting with strategic humility. Platforms offer access. Intelligence is what we make of that access. And perhaps most importantly, these stories remind us that in a world of noise, the competitive advantage lies not in hearing more, but in *hearing what matters most—and knowing what to do with it.*

Ethical, Strategic, and Human-Centered Futures of CI in the Digital Age

As we move deeper into an era defined by platforms, automation, and real-time data flows, competitive intelligence (CI) faces a paradox (Adewusi et al, 2024). On one hand, the technological tools available have never been more powerful. We can track market signals with astounding granularity, parse sentiment in multiple languages, detect weak signals across emerging markets, and anticipate trends that haven't yet become mainstream. On the other hand, this very power has given rise to new complexities—ethical ambiguities, strategic dilemmas, and a subtle erosion of the human element in decision-making. The future of competitive intelligence will not be decided by technology alone. Nor will it be shaped purely by data analytics or artificial intelligence. It will be carved out in the tension between what we *can* do and what we *should* do; between speed and responsibility, efficiency and empathy, automation and human wisdom. It is in this space that the ethical, strategic, and human-centered future of CI must be envisioned—and consciously designed.

Ethics is no longer a footnote in intelligence practices. It has become the main stage. As digital ecosystems become more saturated with surveillance tools, predictive models, and platform intermediaries, questions of data ownership, consent, manipulation, and bias move to the forefront. The ethical contours of CI are not simply about avoiding corporate espionage or respecting intellectual property—though those remain essential. They now extend to how we collect data, how transparently we disclose our intent, how respectfully we interpret human behavior online, and how accountable we are when our insights are wrong—or harmful. We are entering a world where invisible algorithms decide what information we see, where deepfakes blur the boundary between fiction and truth, and where data extracted from users—often without their awareness—fuels hyper-targeted strategies (Kayyali, 2024). In this context, CI professionals must ask themselves hard questions. Are we listening, or are we intruding? Are we interpreting behavior, or are we exploiting vulnerability? Are we surfacing insight, or are we reinforcing bias? These are not philosophical musings; they are strategic imperatives. Because in a future where trust is currency, ethical lapses are not just moral failures—they are competitive risks.

Ethical CI demands more than compliance with regulation. It demands an internal culture of discernment. It calls for teams who can recognize when a dataset, though technically public, should not be used. It requires leaders willing to question whether a strategic move enabled by intelligence also aligns with the values the company claims to uphold. In short, it requires integrity—not as an abstract virtue, but as an operational principle. But ethics alone is not enough. The strategic dimension of CI must evolve alongside the ethical. Too often, CI has been used defensively—to track competitors, to avoid threats, to follow the market. The future belongs to organizations that use intelligence *creatively*—to imagine new possibilities, to reframe challenges, and to generate not just competitive advantage, but competitive relevance. Strategic intelligence in the digital age is not merely about predicting what others will do. It is about anticipating what is *possible*, and being prepared to act before others even realize that the ground is shifting.

This shift requires a new orientation. Strategy can no longer be divorced from complexity. The world is no longer shaped by linear cause-and-effect chains. It is shaped by feedback loops, tipping points, and interdependencies. A protest in one country can ripple into supply chain disruptions across continents. A policy change in data privacy can rewrite the rules of digital engagement overnight (Brown & Marsden, 2023). A viral moment can undo years of brand-building—or catapult a small company into the spotlight. In such a world, CI must become a living, adaptive system—not a static report. It must help organizations not only *know* what is happening, but *understand* why it matters, and *imagine* what could come next. Strategic intelligence in this form is not a snapshot—it's a moving picture. It's not just about who's ahead and who's behind. It's about sensing the future, interpreting ambiguity, and making choices with foresight rather than fear.

Herein lies the final and perhaps most important dimension: the human-centered future of CI. For all the sophistication of AI tools and digital platforms, the real value of intelligence lies in how humans use it. Insight does not arise from data alone. It arises from interpretation, context, emotion, and experience (Kayyali, 2025 c). It arises from seeing patterns others miss, asking questions others don't think to ask, and making connections others don't yet understand. This human dimension has often been treated as secondary—as a soft skill in a hard-data world. But in truth, it is the foundation. Technology can find the signal. Only humans can give it meaning. Technology can highlight an anomaly. Only humans can see whether that anomaly is a threat, an opportunity, or a mirage. Technology can accelerate the pace of decisions. Only humans can weigh their consequences (Darioshi & Lahav, 2021). The future of CI must therefore prioritize human development alongside technical innovation. It must invest in the training of analysts not only in tools, but in critical thinking, systems awareness, narrative understanding, and ethical discernment. It must build teams that are diverse—not just demographically, but cognitively and experientially. It must recognize that true intelligence is not just about the capacity to know more—it's about the courage to know differently.

A human-centered CI approach also means designing intelligence processes that are inclusive. Too often, intelligence is centralized—hoarded by a few, reported upwards, and rarely shared laterally. But some of the best insights come from the periphery—from frontline workers, from overlooked customer comments, from minor market fluctuations that only someone with ground-level familiarity might notice. Creating systems that listen to these voices, integrate their perspectives, and treat them as legitimate sources of foresight is not only more democratic—it is more effective (Vesnic-Alujevic, 2021). A human-centered CI approach demands space for reflection. In a world obsessed with speed, pausing to think deeply can feel like a luxury. But it is a necessity. Insight emerges not from constant motion, but from moments of stillness—where patterns cohere, where contradictions are held, and where new mental models are allowed to form. Organizations that value insight must create time and space for it. They must protect the contemplative amid the urgent.

There is also a need for humility. Intelligence work is often associated with confidence—clear answers, decisive conclusions, actionable insights. But the most profound insights are often tentative. They live in ambiguity. They require iteration. The most dangerous intelligence is not incomplete data—it is overconfidence in flawed interpretation. The future demands a kind of epistemological humility: a willingness to say "we don't know yet," and the discipline to keep listening until we do. As we consider the ethical, strategic, and human-centered future of CI, it becomes clear that we are not merely updating an old practice. We are redefining it. We are moving from intelligence as control to intelligence as conversation. From intelligence as surveillance to intelligence as sensemaking. From intelligence as secrecy to intelligence as shared understanding (Kane et al, 2023). This is not a future that will be built quickly, nor without resistance. It challenges many of the assumptions that have shaped CI for decades. But it is a future worth building—a future where intelligence does not just serve power, but also serves understanding. Where insight is not just used to outperform, but to outlearn, outadapt, and outimagine. Where strategy is not just efficient, but ethical. Where data is not just harvested, but honored. Where the human remains at the center—not just as a user, but as a meaning-maker, a steward of values, and a shaper of futures.

In this future, CI professionals are not merely analysts. They are interpreters of complexity, facilitators of learning, and guardians of ethical strategy. Their work is not just about knowing what's coming—it's about helping organizations become the kind of entities that can meet the future with integrity, intelligence, and imagination. That is not only a competitive advantage. It is a moral and strategic necessity.

CONCLUSION

As we stand at the intersection of technological acceleration and strategic adaptation, it becomes clear that competitive intelligence is no longer a peripheral activity, nor is it the exclusive domain of large corporations with dedicated analysis teams. Instead, it is becoming a pervasive organizational mindset—one shaped, fed, and filtered through digital platforms that now define the contours of modern competition. From social media to cloud-based collaboration hubs, from data aggregators to crowdsourced content engines, platforms are not just environments in which intelligence happens—they are co-creators of that intelligence. Yet with this evolution comes a paradox. While digital platforms have expanded the quantity and accessibility of information, they have also introduced new layers of complexity, bias, and ephemerality. Algorithms privilege certain voices while muting others. Attention cycles are shorter, and the boundaries between intelligence gathering and surveillance are increasingly thin. In this context, CI professionals must learn to navigate not only the mechanics of data extraction but also the ethics of platform engagement. Strategy today must be as much about understanding *how* intelligence is produced and shaped as *what* it says. What emerges from this landscape is a call for a new kind of intelligence literacy—one that goes beyond technical proficiency. It requires reflective thinking, critical questioning, and a willingness to interrogate the platforms themselves. Why does a certain trend surface? Whose interests are being amplified or silenced? How do algorithmic logics skew perception and influence decision-making? These are not just analytical questions; they are moral ones, too. The strategist of the future must be as attuned to context and consequence as to calculation.

Additionally, the platformization of CI highlights the growing importance of adaptability. In a world where yesterday's data can become obsolete in hours, where reputations can be built or shattered in tweets, and where strategic advantage lies as much in perception as in performance, static models of intelligence are insufficient. The future belongs to those who can move fluidly—between data and meaning, between automation and intuition, between speed and depth. This chapter has sought to show that digital platforms are not merely tools for intelligence—they are terrains, battlegrounds, and laboratories. They demand not just technical adoption, but cultural and intellectual reorientation. Competitive intelligence in the digital age is as much about *how* we see as *what* we see. It is a relational practice, grounded in context, shaped by platforms, and driven by the need to make meaning amid noise. As businesses and institutions navigate this evolving reality, their success will depend not just on what they know—but on how wisely and humanely they use what they know. And in that space—between information and wisdom—lies the future of competitive strategy.

REFERENCES

Adewusi, A. O., Okoli, U. I., Adaga, E., Olorunsogo, T., Asuzu, O. F., & Daraojimba, D. O. (2024). Business intelligence in the era of big data: A review of analytical tools and competitive advantage. *Computer Science & IT Research Journal*, *5*(2), 415–431. DOI: 10.51594/csitrj.v5i2.791

Adner, R., & Lieberman, M. (2021). Disruption through complements. *Strategy Science*, *6*(1), 91–109. DOI: 10.1287/stsc.2021.0125

Ali, W. (2023). Business Intelligence In The Digital Age: Tools And Techniques. Competitive Research Journal Archive, 1(03), 215-224. https://thecrja.com/index.php/Journal/article/view/21

Bodley, D., Liedtke, A., & Tekin, P. (2021, November). Even Big Brands Need a Direct-to-Consumer Strategy. https://www.bcg.com/publications/2021/direct-to-consumer-strategy-business-benefits

Brown, I., & Marsden, C. T. (2023). *Regulating code: Good governance and better regulation in the information age*. MIT press.

Cano-Marin, E., Sánchez-Alonso, S., & Mora-Cantallops, M. (2023). Unleashing competitive intelligence: News mining analysis on technology trends and digital health driving healthcare innovation. *IEEE Transactions on Engineering Management*, *71*, 12311–12325. DOI: 10.1109/TEM.2023.3326233

Cavallo, A., Sanasi, S., Ghezzi, A., & Rangone, A. (2021). Competitive intelligence and strategy formulation: Connecting the dots. *Competitiveness Review*, *31*(2), 250–275. DOI: 10.1108/CR-01-2020-0009

Cochrane, K., Cao, Y., Girouard, A., & Loke, L. (2022, February). Breathing scarf: using a first-person research method to design a wearable for emotional regulation. In *Proceedings of the Sixteenth International Conference on Tangible, Embedded, and Embodied Interaction* (pp. 1-19). DOI: 10.1145/3490149.3501330

Darioshi, R., & Lahav, E. (2021). The impact of technology on the human decision-making process. *Human Behavior and Emerging Technologies*, *3*(3), 391–400. DOI: 10.1002/hbe2.257

. Emmanuel, O. K., Grace, J., & John, M. (2024). Collaborative Learning Tools.

Fannon, S. R., Munive-Hernandez, J. E., & Campean, F. (2022). Mastering continuous improvement (CI): The roles and competences of mid-level management and their impact on the organisation's CI capability. *The TQM Journal*, *34*(1), 102–124. DOI: 10.1108/TQM-03-2021-0083

. Garrido, M. V. (2021). Why a militantly democratic lack of trust in state surveillance can enable better and more democratic security. Trust and Transparency in an Age of Surveillance, 221-240. DOI: 10.4324/9781003120827-16

Gitelman, L. D., Kozhevnikov, M. V., & Chebotareva, G. S. (2021). *Strategic intelligence of an organization amid uncertainty*. WIT Press., DOI: 10.2495/EQ-V6-N3-294-305

Kane, A. A., Paletz, S. B., Vahlkamp, S. H., Nelson, T., Porter, A., Diep, M., & Carraway, M. (2023, September). Intelligence analysis shift work: Sensemaking processes, tensions, and takeaways. []). Sage CA: Los Angeles, CA: SAGE Publications.]. *Proceedings of the Human Factors and Ergonomics Society Annual Meeting*, *67*(1), 741–746. DOI: 10.1177/21695067231192569

Karaboga, T., Zehir, C., Tatoglu, E., Karaboga, H. A., & Bouguerra, A. (2023). Big data analytics management capability and firm performance: The mediating role of data-driven culture. *Review of Managerial Science*, *17*(8), 2655–2684. DOI: 10.1007/s11846-022-00596-8

Kayyali, M. (2020). Post COVID-19: New era for higher education systems. *International Journal of Applied Science and Engineering*, *8*(2), 131–145. DOI: 10.30954/2322-0465.2.2020.6

Kayyali, M. (2024). Immersive Technologies: Virtual and Augmented Reality in Higher Education. In Reshaping learning with next generation educational technologies (pp. 99-114). IGI Global. DOI: 10.4018/979-8-3693-1310-7.ch007

Kayyali, M. (2025 a). E-Learning Platforms and Their Influence on Lifelong Learning. In Impact of Digitalization on Education and Social Sustainability (pp. 155-176). IGI Global. DOI: 10.4018/979-8-3693-1854-6.ch006

Kayyali, M. (2025 b). The Role of Artificial Intelligence in Transforming Business Models. In *AI-Driven Business Model Innovation* (pp. 71–98). IGI Global Scientific Publishing., DOI: 10.4018/979-8-3693-9571-4.ch003

Kayyali, M. (2025 c). Ethical Implications of Generative AI in Education: Privacy, Bias, and Integrity. In Transformative AI Practices for Personalized Learning Strategies (pp. 185-218). IGI Global Scientific Publishing. DOI: 10.4018/979-8-3693-8744-3.ch008

Köseoglu, M. A., Mehraliyev, F., Altin, M., & Okumus, F. (2021). Competitor intelligence and analysis (CIA) model and online reviews: Integrating big data text mining with network analysis for strategic analysis. *Tourism Review*, *76*(3), 529–552. DOI: 10.1108/TR-10-2019-0406

Neuman, W. R. (2023). *Evolutionary intelligence: How technology will make us smarter*. MIT Press. DOI: 10.7551/mitpress/15049.001.0001

Nguyen, T. (2023). Zara's organization apparatus: what is the key behind Zara's fast fashion success? https://urn.fi/URN:NBN:fi:amk-2023051811620

Pansanella, V. (2024). Biased Echoes: Unraveling Mechanisms of Opinion Dynamics and their Impacts in Online Social Networks. DOI: 10.25429/pansanella-valentina_phd2024-01-30

. Popiel, P., & Sang, Y. (2021). Platforms' governance: analyzing digital platforms' policy preferences. Global Perspectives, 2(1).

Prashantham, S., & Madhok, A. (2023). Corporate-startup partnering: Exploring attention dynamics and relational outcomes in asymmetric settings. *Strategic Entrepreneurship Journal*, *17*(4), 770–801. DOI: 10.1002/sej.1475

Prokushenkov, P. (2023). Strategy formation as narrative-driven performative praxis. *International Journal of Management and Decision Making*, *22*(3), 310–333. DOI: 10.1504/IJMDM.2023.131734

Ray, S. K. S. (2023). Moving towards agile leadership to help organizations succeed. *The IUP Journal of Soft Skills*, *17*(1), 5–17.

Rust, R. (2021). A Framework for Mitigating Obsolescence in Military Based Systems. https://purls.library.ucf.edu/go/DP0025458

Seaver, N. (2022). Computing taste: Algorithms and the makers of music recommendation. In *Computing Taste*. University of Chicago Press. DOI: 10.7208/chicago/9780226822969.001.0001

Vargo, C. J. (2025). *The Computational Content Analyst: Using Machine Learning to Classify Media Messages*. Taylor & Francis., DOI: 10.4324/9781003514237

Vesnic-Alujevic, L. (2021). Imagining democratic societies of the future: Insights from a foresight study. *Futures & Foresight Science*, *3*(1), ffo2.60. Advance online publication. DOI: 10.1002/ffo2.60

Wu, C. (2024). Data privacy: From transparency to fairness. *Technology in Society*, *76*, 102457. DOI: 10.1016/j.techsoc.2024.102457

Zhang, X., Tu, Y., Long, Y., Shan, L., Elsaadani, M. A., Fu, K., & Hei, X. (2024, May). From Virtual Touch to Tesla Command: Unlocking Unauthenticated Control Chains From Smart Glasses for Vehicle Takeover. In *2024 IEEE Symposium on Security and Privacy (SP)* (pp. 2366-2384). IEEE. DOI: 10.1109/SP54263.2024.00231

Compilation of References

Adeola, O. (2024). Leveraging Ubuntu-inspired values to promote sustainable digital entrepreneurship in Africa. *Africa Journal of Management*, *10*(2), 120–149. DOI: 10.1080/23322373.2024.2349484

Adewusi, A. O., Okoli, U. I., Adaga, E., Olorunsogo, T., Asuzu, O. F., & Daraojimba, D. O. (2024). Business intelligence in the era of big data: A review of analytical tools and competitive advantage. *Computer Science & IT Research Journal*, *5*(2), 415–431. DOI: 10.51594/csitrj.v5i2.791

Adner, R., & Lieberman, M. (2021). Disruption through complements. *Strategy Science*, *6*(1), 91–109. DOI: 10.1287/stsc.2021.0125

Afeltra, G., Alerasoul, S., Minelli, E., Vecchio, Y., & Montalvo, C. (2022). Assessing the integrated impact of sustainable innovation on organisational performance: An empirical evidence from manufacturing firms. *Journal of Small Business Strategy*, *32*(4). Advance online publication. DOI: 10.53703/001c.38515

Aguinis, H. (2009). *Performance management* (2nd ed.). Pearson Prentice Hall.

Aldoseri, A., Al-Khalifa, K. N., & Hamouda, A. M. (2023). Re-thinking data strategy and integration for artificial intelligence: Concepts, opportunities, and challenges. *Applied Sciences (Basel, Switzerland)*, *13*(12), 7082. DOI: 10.3390/app13127082

Ali, W. (2023). Business Intelligence In The Digital Age: Tools And Techniques. Competitive Research Journal Archive, 1(03), 215-224. https://thecrja.com/index.php/Journal/article/view/21

Alia, M., Santoso, P. M., Iwanussoleh, I., & Anshori, M. I. (2023). Kepemimpinan yang melayani menghadapi tantangan dan manfaat dalam era bisnis yang berkembang. *Jurnal Riset Dan Inovasi Manajemen, 1*(3), 224–237. DOI: 10.59581/jrim-widyakarya.v1i3.801

Allen, T. D., Eby, L. T., & Lentz, E. (2019). *The Blackwell handbook of mentoring: A multiple perspectives approach.* John Wiley & Sons.

Al-Omoush, K., Ribeiro-Navarrete, B., & McDowell, W. (2023). The impact of digital corporate social responsibility on social entrepreneurship and organizational resilience. *Management Decision, 62*(8), 2621–2640. DOI: 10.1108/MD-11-2022-1613

Amabile, T. M. (1998, September). *How to kill creativity*. Harvard Business Review. https://hbr.org/1998/09/how-to-kill-creativity

Amaral, R., Faria, L., Oprime, P., Gregolin, J., & Alliprandini, D. (2012). Perfis de competências relativas à inteligência competitiva: Um estudo exploratório no brasil. *Ciência da Informação, 40*(2). Advance online publication. DOI: 10.18225/ci.inf.v40i2.1306

Anlesinya, A., & Abugre, J. (2021). Strategic CSR practices, strategic orientation and business value creation among multinational subsidiaries in Ghana. *Society and Business Review, 17*(2), 257–279. DOI: 10.1108/SBR-02-2021-0021

Anokye, C., Hajmasy, G., & Raffay-Danyi, Á. (2022, November). The impacts of CSR of hotels on the socio-economic development of the South Tongu District of Ghana. *Euro-Asia Tourism Studies Journal, 3*(November 2022). Advance online publication. DOI: 10.58345/MELK1969

Anshari, M., Almunawar, M. N., Lim, S. A., & Al-Mudimigh, A. (2019). Customer relationship management and big data enabled: Personalization & customization of services. *Applied Computing and Informatics, 15*(94), 101. DOI: 10.1016/j.aci.2018.05.004

Ardiansyah, M., & Alnoor, A. (2024). Integrating corporate social responsibility into business strategy: Creating sustainable value. *IIJB*, *1*(1), 29–42. DOI: 10.62569/iijb.v1i1.5

Austin, R. D. (1996). *Measuring and managing performance in organizations*. Dorset House Publishing.

Avolio, B. J., & Bass, B. M. (2004). *Multifactor Leadership Questionnaire: Manual and sampler set*. Mind Garden.

Ayres, I. (2007). *Super crunchers: Why thinking-by-numbers is the new way to be smart*. Bantam Books.

Bajpai, G., Schildmeijer, M., Mishra, M., & Piwosz, P. (2024). *CI/CD Design Patterns: Design and implement CI/CD using proven design patterns*. Packt Publishing Ltd.

Bakker, A. B., & Demerouti, E. (2008). Towards a model of work engagement. *Career Development International*, *13*(3), 209–223. DOI: 10.1108/13620430810870476

Bao, Y., Li, C., & Zhao, H. (2018). Servant leadership and engagement: A dual mediation model. *Journal of Managerial Psychology*, *33*(6), 406–417. DOI: 10.1108/JMP-12-2017-0435

Barrena-Martínez, J., López-Fernández, M., & Fernández, P. (2018). Drivers and barriers in socially responsible human resource management. *Sustainability (Basel)*, *10*(5), 1532. DOI: 10.3390/su10051532

Bartes, F. (2015). The objectives of competitive intelligence as a part of corporate development strategy. *Acta Universitatis Agriculturae et Silviculturae Mendelianae Brunensis*, *62*(6), 1243–1250. DOI: 10.11118/actaun201462061243

Bass, B. M. (1985). Leadership: Good, better, best. *Organizational Dynamics*, *13*(3), 26–40. DOI: 10.1016/0090-2616(85)90028-2

Bass, B. M., & Avolio, B. J. (1993). Transformational leadership and organizational culture. *Public Administration Quarterly*, *17*(1), 112–121.

Bass, B. M., & Bass, R. (2008). *The Bass handbook of leadership: Theory, research, and managerial applications*. Free Press.

Bass, B. M., & Riggio, R. E. (2006). *Transformational leadership*. Routledge. DOI: 10.4324/9781410617095

Battagello, F. M., Cricelli, L., & Grimaldi, M. (2016). Benchmarking strategic resources and business performance via an open framework. *International Journal of Productivity and Performance Management, 65*(3), 324–350. DOI: 10.1108/IJPPM-08-2014-0129

Battaglia, M., Testa, F., Bianchi, L., Iraldo, F., & Frey, M. (2014). Corporate social responsibility and competitiveness within SMES of the fashion industry: Evidence from Italy and France. *Sustainability (Basel), 6*(2), 872–893. DOI: 10.3390/su6020872

Becker, B. E., & Huselid, M. A. (2006). Strategic human resources management: Theory and practice. In *The handbook of human resource management* (pp. 3–26). Blackwell Publishing.

Becker, B. E., Huselid, M. A., & Ulrich, D. (2001). *The HR scorecard: Linking people, strategy, and performance*. Harvard Business School Press.

Belu, C., & M nescu, C. (2013). Strategic corporate social responsibility and economic performance. *Applied Economics, 45*(19), 2751–2764. DOI: 10.1080/00036846.2012.676734

Benyaminova, A., Mathews, M., Langley, P., & Rieple, A. (2019). The impact of changes in stakeholder salience on corporate social responsibility activities in russian energy firms: A contribution to the divergence/convergence debate. *Corporate Social Responsibility and Environmental Management, 26*(6), 1222–1234. DOI: 10.1002/csr.1743

Bersin, J. (2014). Big data in human resources: The future of HR analytics. *Deloitte University Press*. https://www2.deloitte.com/us/en/insights/deloitte-review/issue-14/dr14-big-data-in-human-resources.html

Bharti, S. S., & Aryal, S. K. (2023). The right to privacy and an implication of the EU General Data Protection Regulation (GDPR) in Europe: Challenges to the companies. *Journal of Contemporary European Studies*, *31*(4), 1391–1402. DOI: 10.1080/14782804.2022.2130193

Bhattacharyya, S., & Jha, S. (2020). Explicating micro foundations of corporate social responsibility: A moderated-mediation study of customer, investor and employee roles. *International Journal of Ethics and Systems*, *36*(4), 619–640. DOI: 10.1108/IJOES-05-2020-0073

Bhavya, K. R., Dharmaraj, A., Pareek, P., Sathe, M. A., Tiwari, M., & Manoharan, G. (2023). Application of soft computing techniques for predictive analytics in financial markets. In *2023 6th International Conference on Contemporary Computing and Informatics (IC3I)* (pp. 1756–1760). IEEE. DOI: 10.1109/IC3I59117.2023.10397684

Biran, D., Zack, M., & Briotta, R. (2013). Competitive intelligence and information quality. *ACM Journal of Data and Information Quality*, *4*(3), 1–20. DOI: 10.1145/2458517.2458520

Bisht, N. S., Noronha, E., & Tripathy, A. K. (2025). Digital technologies exacerbating mission drift in microfinance institutions: Evidence from India. *Information and Organization*, *35*(1), 100541. DOI: 10.1016/j.infoandorg.2024.100541

Bititci, U. S., Carrie, A. S., & McDevitt, L. (2012). Dynamic performance measurement systems. *International Journal of Production Economics*, *139*(1), 238–248. DOI: 10.1108/01443570010321676

Bligh, M. C., Pearce, C. L., & Kohles, J. C. (2006). The importance of self-and shared leadership in team based knowledge work: A meso-level model of leadership dynamics. Journal of managerial Psychology, 21(4), 296-318.

Bobylev, T. (2023). Dashboard for data-driven decision support in small and medium enterprises: a web-based approach.

Bockorny, K., & Youssef-Morgan, C. M. (2020). Developing an organizational rewards program. In *The Wiley Blackwell handbook of the psychology of the Internet at Work* (pp. 89–114). John Wiley & Sons.

Bodley, D., Liedtke, A., & Tekin, P. (2021, November). Even Big Brands Need a Direct-to-Consumer Strategy. https://www.bcg.com/publications/2021/direct-to-consumer-strategy-business-benefits

Boudreau, J. W., & Ramstad, P. M. (2007). *Beyond HR: The new science of human capital*. Harvard Business Review Press.

Briscoe, J. P., & Hall, D. T. (2006). The interplay of boundaryless and protean careers: Combinations and implications. *Journal of Vocational Behavior, 69*(1), 4–18. DOI: 10.1016/j.jvb.2005.09.002

Broo, D. G., & Schooling, J. (2023). Digital twins in infrastructure: Definitions, current practices, challenges and strategies. *International Journal of Construction Management, 23*(7), 1254–1263. DOI: 10.1080/15623599.2021.1966980

Brown, I., & Marsden, C. T. (2023). *Regulating code: Good governance and better regulation in the information age*. MIT press.

Burns, J. M. (1978). *Leadership*. Harper & Row.

Cameron, J., & Pierce, W. D. (2002). *Rewards and intrinsic motivation: Resolving the controversy*. Greenwood Publishing Group. DOI: 10.5040/9798216008569

Cameron, J., & Quinn, R. E. (2011). *Diagnosing and changing organizational culture: Based on the competing values framework*. John Wiley & Sons.

Campbell, J. P., McHenry, J. J., & Wise, L. L. (1990). Modeling job performance in a population of jobs. *Personnel Psychology, 43*(2), 313–333. DOI: 10.1111/j.1744-6570.1990.tb01561.x

Canada, P. (2015). *PwC Saratoga human capital effectiveness survey (HCES) - 2015 PwC Saratoga Canada metric list*. PwC Canada.

Canavesi, A., & Minelli, E. (2021). Servant leadership and employee engagement: A qualitative study. *Employee Responsibilities and Rights Journal, 34*(4), 413–435. DOI: 10.1007/s10672-021-09389-9 PMID: 40477632

Cano-Marin, E., Sánchez-Alonso, S., & Mora-Cantallops, M. (2023). Unleashing competitive intelligence: News mining analysis on technology trends and digital health driving healthcare innovation. *IEEE Transactions on Engineering Management, 71*, 12311–12325. DOI: 10.1109/TEM.2023.3326233

Carte, T. A., Schwarzkopf, A. B., Shaft, T. M., & Zmud, R. W. (2005). Advanced business intelligence at Cardinal Health. *MIS Quarterly Executive, 4*(4), 413–424.

Carucci, R. A. (2021). *To be honest: Lead with the power of truth, justice and purpose*. Kogan Page Limited.

Cascio, W. F. (1987). *Costing human resources: The financial impact of behavior in organizations* (2nd ed.). Kent Publishing.

Cavallo, A., Sanasi, S., Ghezzi, A., & Rangone, A. (2020). Competitive intelligence and strategy formulation: Connecting the dots. *Competitiveness Review, 31*(2), 250–275. DOI: 10.1108/CR-01-2020-0009

Cerasoli, C. P., Nicklin, J. M., & Ford, M. T. (2014). Intrinsic motivation and extrinsic incentives jointly predict performance: A 40-year meta-analysis. *Psychological Bulletin, 140*(4), 980–1008. DOI: 10.1037/a0035661 PMID: 24491020

Chakrabarty, S. (2020). Value creation in industrial clusters: The strategic nature of relationships with stakeholders and the policy environment. *Journal of Strategy and Management, 13*(4), 535–550. DOI: 10.1108/JSMA-04-2020-0084

Chang, Y., & Yoo, J. (2023). When csr matters: The moderating effect of industrial growth rate on the relationship between csr and firm performance. *Sustainability (Basel), 15*(18), 13677. DOI: 10.3390/su151813677

Charlwood, A., & Guenole, N. (2022). Can HR adapt to the paradoxes of artificial intelligence? *Human Resource Management Journal, 32*(4), 2022. DOI: 10.1111/1748-8583.12433Chen, H., Chiang, R. H., & Storey, V. C. (2012). Business intelligence and analytics: From big data to big impact. *Management Information Systems Quarterly, 36*(4), 1165–1188. DOI: 10.2307/41703503

Chaudhuri, A., Datta, P., Fernandes, K., & Xiong, Y. (2021). Optimal pricing strategies for manufacturing-as-a service platforms to ensure business sustainability. *International Journal of Production Economics, 234*, 108065. DOI: 10.1016/j.ijpe.2021.108065

Chernev, A., & Blair, S. (2015). Doing well by doing good: The benevolent halo of corporate social responsibility. *The Journal of Consumer Research, 41*(6), 1412–1425. DOI: 10.1086/680089

Chiniara, M., & Bentein, K. (2018). The servant leadership advantage: When perceiving low differentiation in leader-member relationship quality influences team cohesion, team task performance and service OCB. *The Leadership Quarterly, 29*(2), 333–345. DOI: 10.1016/j.leaqua.2017.05.002

Choi, D., Chung, C., & Young, J. (2019). An economic analysis of corporate social responsibility in korea. *Sustainability (Basel), 11*(9), 2676. DOI: 10.3390/su11092676

Chon, K. K.-S., & Zoltan, J. (2019). Role of servant leadership in contemporary hospitality. *International Journal of Contemporary Hospitality Management, 31*(8), 3371–3394. DOI: 10.1108/IJCHM-11-2018-0935

Chourasia, S., Dhama, A., & Bhardwaj, G. (2024). AI-Driven Organizational Culture Evolution: A Critical Review. In *2024 International Conference on Communication, Computer Sciences and Engineering (IC3SE)* (pp. 1839-1844). IEEE. DOI: 10.1109/IC3SE62002.2024.10592949

Chung, C., Jung, S., & Young, J. (2018). Do CSR activities increase firm value? evidence from the Korean market. *Sustainability (Basel), 10*(9), 3164. DOI: 10.3390/su10093164

Cioffi, R., Travaglioni, M., Piscitelli, G., Petrillo, A., & Felice, F. (2020). Artificial intelligence and machine learning applications in smart production: Progress, trends, and directions. *Sustainability (Basel), 12*(2), 492. DOI: 10.3390/su12020492

Cochrane, K., Cao, Y., Girouard, A., & Loke, L. (2022, February). Breathing scarf: using a first-person research method to design a wearable for emotional regulation. In *Proceedings of the Sixteenth International Conference on Tangible, Embedded, and Embodied Interaction* (pp. 1-19). DOI: 10.1145/3490149.3501330

Colquitt, J. A., LePine, J. A., & Wesson, M. J. (2017). *Organizational behavior: Improving performance and commitment in the workplace.* McGraw-Hill Education.

Cronquist, B. (2004). *Organizational intelligence: A dynamic knowledge creating activity embedded in organizational routines. Informatics Research Group*. Kristiansted University.

Cruickshank, P. (2021). Evaluation of engagement with hyperlocal e-participation systems by citizens and representatives (Doctoral dissertation).

D'Amato, A., & Falivena, C. (2019). Corporate social responsibility and firm value: Do firm size and age matter? empirical evidence from European listed companies. *Corporate Social Responsibility and Environmental Management, 27*(2), 909–924. DOI: 10.1002/csr.1855

Dahiya, N., Sheifali, G., & Sartajvir, S. (2022). A Review Paper on Machine Learning Applications, Advantages, and Techniques. *ECS Transactions, 107*(1), 6137–6150. DOI: 10.1149/10701.6137ecst

Dam, N. A. K., Le Dinh, T., & Menvielle, W. (2020b). *A Service-based Model for Customer Intelligence in the Age of Big Data.* Academic Press.

Darioshi, R., & Lahav, E. (2021). The impact of technology on the human decision-making process. *Human Behavior and Emerging Technologies, 3*(3), 391–400. DOI: 10.1002/hbe2.257

Darnall, N., Henriques, I., & Sadorsky, P. (2010). Adopting a proactive environmental strategy: The influence of stakeholders and firm size. *Journal of Management Studies*, *47*(6), 1072–1094. DOI: 10.1111/j.1467-6486.2009.00873.x

Davenport, T. H., & Spanyi, A. (2019). Digital Transformation Should Start With Customers. *MIT Sloan Management Review*.

Day, D. V., Dragoni, L., & Sin, H. P. (2014). Leadership development: An outcome-oriented review based on time and levels of analyses. *Annual Review of Organizational Psychology and Organizational Behavior*, *1*(1), 109–131.

de Kervenoael, R., Hasan, R., Schwob, A., & Goh, E. (2020). Leveraging human-robot interaction in hospitality services: Incorporating the role of perceived value, empathy, and information sharing into visitors' intentions to use social robots. *Tourism Management*, *78*, 104042. DOI: 10.1016/j.tourman.2019.104042

De Pelsmacker, P., Muller, M. L., Viviers, W., Saayman, A., Cuyvers, L., & Jegers, M. (2005). Competitive intelligence practices of South African and Belgian exporters. *Marketing Intelligence & Planning*, *23*(6), 606–620. DOI: 10.1108/02634500510624156

de Waal, A., Weaver, M., Day, T., & van der Heijden, B. (2019). Silo-busting: Overcoming the greatest threat to organizational performance. *Sustainability (Basel)*, *11*(23), 6860. DOI: 10.3390/su11236860

Deci, E. L., & Ryan, R. M. (2008). Self-determination theory: A macrotheory of human motivation, development, and health. *Canadian Psychology*, *49*(3), 182–185. DOI: 10.1037/a0012801

DeGroot, S. J. (2013). *Workforce effectiveness: A practical guide*. Self-published.

Deitiana, T. (2015). The determinant of CSR disclosure of the mining industry listed in the Indonesia Stock Exchange. *Asian Business Review*, *5*(3), 141–148. DOI: 10.18034/abr.v5i3.66

Dela, E., Ye, J., & Berhe, H. (2024). The impact of corporate social responsibility on financial performance in highly polluted Indonesian industries: Mediating role of industry competitiveness. *SAGE Open*, *14*(4). Advance online publication. DOI: 10.1177/21582440241259479

Demeke, G. K., van Engen, M., & Markos, S. (2024). Servant Leadership in the Healthcare Literature: A Systematic Review. *Journal of Healthcare Leadership*, *16*(16), 1–14. https://www.ncbi.nlm.nih.gov/pmc/articles/PMC10771778/. DOI: 10.2147/JHL.S440160 PMID: 38192640

Demissie, A. D., Alemu, A. E., & Tensay, A. T. (2024). The nexus between servant leadership and organizational citizenship behavior through the mediating role of perceived organizational politics in Ethiopian federal public service organizations. *Cogent Business & Management*, *11*(1), 2336653. Advance online publication. DOI: 10.1080/23311975.2024.2336653

Ding, D., Lu, H., Song, Y., & Lu, Q. (2012). Relationship of servant leadership and employee loyalty: The mediating role of employee satisfaction. *IBusiness*, *4*(3), 208–215. DOI: 10.4236/ib.2012.43026

Dionne, S. D., Yammarino, F. J., Atwater, L. E., & Spangler, W. D. (2004). Transformational leadership and team performance. *Journal of Organizational Change Management*, *17*(2), 177–193. DOI: 10.1108/09534810410530601

Dmytriyev, S., Freeman, R., & Hörisch, J. (2021). The relationship between stakeholder theory and corporate social responsibility: Differences, similarities, and implications for social issues in management. *Journal of Management Studies*, *58*(6), 1441–1470. DOI: 10.1111/joms.12684

Dubiel, M. (2022). The blind side of art: Visual impairment as a resource in the work of Mexican artists. *Przegląd Socjologii Jakościowej*, *18*(3), 120–137. DOI: 10.18778/1733-8069.18.3.07

Durai, S., Krishnaveni, K., & Manoharan, G. (2022a). Designing entrepreneurial performance metric (EPM) framework for entrepreneurs owning small and medium manufacturing units (SME) in Coimbatore. In *AIP Conference Proceedings* (Vol. 2418, No. 1). AIP Publishing. DOI: 10.1063/5.0081941

Durai, S., Krishnaveni, K., & Manoharan, G. (2022b). Leveraging HR metrics for effective recruitment & selection process in IT industries in Chennai and Coimbatore, Tamil Nadu. In *AIP Conference Proceedings* (Vol. 2418, No. 1). AIP Publishing. DOI: 10.4018/979-8-3693-1343-5.ch010

Durai, S., Krishnaveni, K., & Manoharan, G. (2022c). Metric based performance management of employees: A case study of MSME unit in Coimbatore, Tamil Nadu. In *AIP Conference Proceedings* (Vol. 2418, No. 1). AIP Publishing. DOI: 10.1063/5.0081943

Duressa, W. T., & Kidane, B. Z. (2024). Indirect effects of leadership behaviors on departmental performance via organizational learning in Ethiopian public research universities. *Cogent Education*, *11*(1), 2354969. Advance online publication. DOI: 10.1080/2331186X.2024.2354969

Eagly, A. H., & Chin, J. L. (2010). Diversity and leadership in a changing world. *The American Psychologist*, *65*(3), 216–224. DOI: 10.1037/a0018957 PMID: 20350020

Ebener, D. R., & O'Connell, D. J. (2010). How might servant leadership work? *Nonprofit Management & Leadership*, *20*(3), 315–335. DOI: 10.1002/nml.256

Eby, L. T., Allen, T. D., & Evans, S. C. (2013). Are mentoring and coaching the same? *Annual Review of Organizational Psychology and Organizational Behavior*, *1*(1), 449–481.

ElAlfy, A., Palaschuk, N., El-Bassiouny, D., Wilson, J., & Weber, O. (2020). Scoping the evolution of corporate social responsibility (CSR) research in the Sustainable Development Goals (SDGS) era. *Sustainability (Basel)*, *12*(14), 5544. DOI: 10.3390/su12145544

Elifneh, Y. W., Wonda, T. A., & Abbay, Y. A. (2024). Marketing ethics in the wholesale and retail sector: Empirical evidence from Ethiopia (a qualitative inquiry). *Cogent Business & Management*, *11*(1), 2373353. Advance online publication. DOI: 10.1080/23311975.2024.2373353

Esposito, E. (2022). *Artificial communication: How algorithms produce social intelligence*. MIT Press. DOI: 10.7551/mitpress/14189.001.0001

Eva, N., Robin, M., Sendjaya, S., van Dierendonck, D., & Liden, R. C. (2019). Servant leadership: A systematic review and call for future research. *The Leadership Quarterly*, *30*(1), 111–132. DOI: 10.1016/j.leaqua.2018.07.004

Fannon, S. R., Munive-Hernandez, J. E., & Campean, F. (2022). Mastering continuous improvement (CI): The roles and competences of mid-level management and their impact on the organisation's CI capability. *The TQM Journal*, *34*(1), 102–124. DOI: 10.1108/TQM-03-2021-0083

Faoziyah, S. (2022). Corporate social responsibility to reduce community rejection of a company existence: Analysis of business ethics perspective. *Journal of Scientech Research and Development*, *4*(1), 162–175. DOI: 10.56670/jsrd.v4i1.119

Feng, P., & Ngai, C. (2020). Doing more on the corporate sustainability front: A longitudinal analysis of CSR reporting of global fashion companies. *Sustainability (Basel)*, *12*(6), 2477. DOI: 10.3390/su12062477

Ferede, W. L., Endawoke, Y., & Tessema, G. (2024). Effects of strategic leadership on change management: Examining the mediating roles of accountability, knowledge management, and organizational culture in public organizations: A study in Central Gondar, Ethiopia. *Cogent Business & Management*, *11*(1), 2416613. Advance online publication. DOI: 10.1080/23311975.2024.2416613

Fernández-Kranz, D., & Santaló, J. (2010). when necessity becomes a virtue: The effect of product market competition on corporate social responsibility. *Journal of Economics & Management Strategy*, *19*(2), 453–487. DOI: 10.1111/j.1530-9134.2010.00258.x

Fitz-enz, J. (2010). *The new HR analytics: Predicting the economic value of your company's human capital investments*. AMACOM.

Fitz-enz, J., & Davidson, B. (2002). *How to measure human resources management* (3rd ed.). McGraw-Hill.

France, S. L., & Ghose, S. (2018). Marketing analytics: Methods, practice, implementation, and links to other fields. *Expert Systems with Applications, 119*, 456–475. DOI: 10.1016/j.eswa.2018.11.002

Frei, F., & Morriss, A. (2020). *Unleashed: the unapologetic leader's guide to empowering everyone around you*. Harvard Business Review Press.

Frishammar, J., Lichtenthaler, U., & Rundquist, J. (2012). Identifying technology commercialization opportunities: The importance of integrating product development knowledge. *Journal of Product Innovation Management, 29*(4), 573–589. DOI: 10.1111/j.1540-5885.2012.00926.x

Frynas, J., & Yamahaki, C. (2016). Corporate social responsibility: Review and roadmap of theoretical perspectives. *Business Ethics (Oxford, England), 25*(3), 258–285. DOI: 10.1111/beer.12115

Gabber, H. (2007). Competitive intelligence topology analyze for improved plan operation. *Industrial Management & Data Systems, 107*(2), 198–236.

Gabriel, A. K. (2024). *Cultural Intelligence for Marketers: Building an inclusive marketing strategy*. Kogan Page Publishers.

Geissdoerfer, M., Savaget, P., Bocken, N., & Hultink, E. (2017). The circular economy – a new sustainability paradigm? *Journal of Cleaner Production, 143*, 757–768. DOI: 10.1016/j.jclepro.2016.12.048

Giannoni, C., Alarcón, L., & Vera, S. (2017). Diagnosis of sustainable business strategies implemented by Chilean construction companies. *Sustainability (Basel), 10*(1), 82. DOI: 10.3390/su10010082

Gitelman, L. D., Kozhevnikov, M. V., & Chebotareva, G. S. (2021). *Strategic intelligence of an organization amid uncertainty*. WIT Press., DOI: 10.2495/EQ-V6-N3-294-305

Gkeredakis, M., Lifshitz-Assaf, H., & Barrett, M. (2021). Crisis as opportunity, disruption and exposure: Exploring emergent responses to crisis through digital technology. *Information and Organization, 31*(1), 100344. DOI: 10.1016/j.infoandorg.2021.100344

Glavas, A. (2016). Corporate social responsibility and employee engagement: Enabling employees to employ more of their whole selves at work. *Frontiers in Psychology*, *7*. Advance online publication. DOI: 10.3389/fpsyg.2016.00796 PMID: 27303352

Goleman, D. (2000). Leadership that gets results. *Harvard Business Review*, *78*(2), 78–90.

Gopinathan, R., & Manoharan, G. (2022). Work-life balance practices and organizational performance for achieving superior performance. In *The changing role of human resource management in the global competitive environment* (pp. 217–230). Book Rivers.

Grant, A. M. (2012). Leading with meaning: Beneficiary contact, prosocial impact, and the performance effects of transformational leadership. *Academy of Management Journal*, *55*(2), 458–476. DOI: 10.5465/amj.2010.0588

Grant, O. (2024). The influence of corporate social responsibility on supplier relationship management in e-commerce. https://doi.org/DOI: 10.20944/preprints202407.1079.v1

Greenleaf, R.K. (1973). The servant as leader. In *Internet Archive*. Greenleaf Center. https://archive.org/details/20200601-the-servant-as-leader

Greenleaf, R. K. (1977). *Servant leadership: A journey into the nature of legitimate power and greatness*. Paulist Press.

Griffeth, R. W., Hom, P. W., & Gaertner, S. (2000). A meta-analysis of antecedents and correlates of employee turnover: Update, moderator tests, and research implications for the next millennium. *Journal of Management*, *26*(3), 463–488. DOI: 10.1177/014920630002600305

Grumbach, J. (2015). Polluting industries as climate protagonists: Cap and trade and the problem of business preferences. *Business and Politics*, *17*(4), 633–659. DOI: 10.1515/bap-2015-0012

Guessoum, M. A., Djiroun, R., & Boukhalfa, K. (2022, May). Causality analysis method and model related to why-question answering in business intelligence context. In *International Conference on Computing Systems and Applications* (pp. 15-26). Cham: Springer International Publishing. DOI: 10.1007/978-3-031-12097-8_2

Guo, H. (2020). The evolution of strategic social responsibility of Chinese enterprises and the design of a decision support system. Destech Transactions on Social Science Education and Human Science, (ecemi). https://doi.org/DOI: 10.12783/dtssehs/ecemi2020/34702

Gupta, A., & Govindarajan, V. (2020). Cultivate Leadership with the 'Covid-19 Leadership Compass'. Harvard Business Review.

Hall, S. (2022). *Innovative B2B marketing: new models, processes and theory*. Kogan Page Publishers.

Hamel, G. (2012). *What matters now*. John Wiley & Sons. DOI: 10.1108/sd.2012.05628iaa.012

Han, H., & Zhang, X. (2024). Servant leadership and project success: The mediating roles of team learning orientation and team agility. *Frontiers in Psychology*, *15*, 1417604. Advance online publication. DOI: 10.3389/fpsyg.2024.1417604 PMID: 39149700

Harter, J. K., Schmidt, F. L., & Hayes, T. L. (2002). Business-unit-level relationship between employee satisfaction, employee engagement, and business outcomes: A meta-analysis. *The Journal of Applied Psychology*, *87*(2), 268–279. https://psycnet.apa.org/doi/10.1037/0021-9010.87.2.268. DOI: 10.1037/0021-9010.87.2.268 PMID: 12002955

Heath, J. B. (2022). Making sense of security. *The American Journal of International Law*, *116*(2), 289–339. DOI: 10.1017/ajil.2021.63

Hinz, J., Stephens, J. P., & Van Oosten, E. B. (2022). Toward a pedagogy of connection: A critical view of being relational in listening. *Management Learning*, *53*(1), 76–97. DOI: 10.1177/13505076211047506

Hoffman, B. J., Bynum, B. H., Piccolo, R. F., & Sutton, A. W. (2011). Person-organization value congruence: How transformational leaders influence work group effectiveness. *Academy of Management Journal, 54*(4), 779–796. DOI: 10.5465/amj.2011.64870139

Hollmann, R. W. (2002). Absenteeism: Analyzing work absences (SHRM White Paper). Society for Human Resource Management.

Hörisch, J., Freeman, R., & Schaltegger, S. (2014). Applying stakeholder theory in sustainability management. *Organization & Environment, 27*(4), 328–346. DOI: 10.1177/1086026614535786

Hsieh, T. (2010). *Delivering happiness: A path to profits, passion, and purpose*. Business Plus.

Hunter, J. C. (2006). *The world's most powerful leadership principle: How to become a servant leader*. Crown Business.

Hunter, J. C. (2019). *Como se tornar um líder servidor*. Sextante.

Ilić, M., Ranković, M., Dobrilović, M., Bucea-Manea- oni , R., Mihoreanu, L., Ghe a, M., & Simion, V. (2022). Challenging novelties within the circular economy concept under the digital transformation of society. *Sustainability (Basel), 14*(2), 702. DOI: 10.3390/su14020702

Impact of marketing intelligence on effectiveness of decision making: an Empirical study. (2023). *Journal of Informatics Education and Research.* https://doi.org/DOI: 10.52783/jier.v3i1.64

Ingrams, A. (2018). Comportamento de Cidadania Organizacional nos Setores Público e Privado: Um Teste Multinível de Motivação para o Serviço Público e Antecedentes Tradicionais. *Revisão da Administração de Pessoal Público, 40*(2), 0734371X1880037. https://doi.org/DOI: 10.1177/0734371X18800372

Ismaeel, B., Alkhawaldeh, B., & Alafi, K. (2023). The role of marketing intelligence in improving the efficiency of the organization: An empirical study on Jordanian hypermarkets. *Journal of Intelligence Studies in Business, 13*(2), 32–42. DOI: 10.37380/jisib.v13i2.1082

Jaén, J., Guijarro, A., & Lema, D. (2021). The impact of corporate social responsibility on innovation in small and medium-sized enterprises: The mediating role of debt terms and human capital. *Corporate Social Responsibility and Environmental Management*, *28*(4), 1200–1215. DOI: 10.1002/csr.2125

Jaichandran, R., Krishna, S. H., Madhavi, G. M., Mohammed, S., Raj, K. B., & Manoharan, G. (2023). Fuzzy evaluation method on the financing efficiency of small and medium-sized enterprises. In *2023 International Conference on Artificial Intelligence and Knowledge Discovery in Concurrent Engineering (ICECONF)* (pp. 1–7). IEEE. DOI: 10.1109/ICECONF57129.2023.10083731

Jiang, B. (2022). How consumers' response on CSR affects brand competitiveness in the fast fashion industry——case study of Zara (Inditex) and H&m. *Academic Journal of Business & Management*, *4*(1). Advance online publication. DOI: 10.25236/AJBM.2022.040117

Jia, X. (2019). Corporate social responsibility activities and firm performance: The moderating role of strategic emphasis and industry competition. *Corporate Social Responsibility and Environmental Management*, *27*(1), 65–73. DOI: 10.1002/csr.1774

Jio, W., Kant, S., & Lemi, K. (2025). The influence of ethical leadership on organizational citizenship behavior by the mediating role of organizational commitment in Ethiopia. In *Humanizing the hyperconnected workplace* (pp. 221–248). IGI Global., DOI: 10.4018/979-8-3693-8171-7.ch008

Jio, W., Lemi, K., & Kant, S. (2024). Does organizational commitment act as a mediating factor among ethical leadership on organizational citizenship practices in Ethiopian healthcare facilities. *Journal of Business and Administrative Studies*, *16*(2), 18–33.

Joo, J., Eom, M., & Shin, M. (2017). Finding the missing link between corporate social responsibility and firm competitiveness through social capital: A business ecosystem perspective. *Sustainability (Basel)*, *9*(5), 707. DOI: 10.3390/su9050707

Joseph, B. A., Portia, A. D., & Esther, S. (2024). Digital transformation and corruption dynamics in Ghana's retail economy: An economic analysis of technological adoption and ethical business practices. *Asian Journal of Economics. Business and Accounting*, *24*(1), 97–113. DOI: 10.9734/ajeba/2024/v24i11214

Joseph, E. E., & Winston, B. E. (2005). Uma correlação de liderança servidora, confiança do líder e confiança organizacional. *Revista de Desenvolvimento de Liderança e Organização*, *26*(1), 6–22. DOI: 10.1108/01437730510575552

Judge, T. A., & Piccolo, R. F. (2004). Transformational and transactional leadership: A meta-analytic test of their relative validity. *The Journal of Applied Psychology*, *89*(5), 755–768. DOI: 10.1037/0021-9010.89.5.755 PMID: 15506858

Kahn, W. A. (1990). Psychological conditions of personal engagement and disengagement at work. *Academy of Management Journal*, *33*(4), 692–724. DOI: 10.2307/256287

Kainde, S. J. R., & Mandagi, D. (2023). A systematic review of servant leadership outcomes in education context. *EDUKASIA: Jurnal Pendidikan Dan Pembelajaran*, *4*(2), 2563–2574. DOI: 10.62775/edukasia.v4i2.627

Kai-xing, W. & Sun, Q. (2021). Corporate social responsibility and cash holdings.. https://doi.org/DOI: 10.2991/assehr.k.211209.152

Kane, A. A., Paletz, S. B., Vahlkamp, S. H., Nelson, T., Porter, A., Diep, M., & Carraway, M. (2023, September). Intelligence analysis shift work: Sensemaking processes, tensions, and takeaways. []. Sage CA: Los Angeles, CA: SAGE Publications.]. *Proceedings of the Human Factors and Ergonomics Society Annual Meeting*, *67*(1), 741–746. DOI: 10.1177/21695067231192569

Kanellopoulos, A. N., & Ioannidis, A. (2024). Leveraging competitive intelligence in offensive cyber counterintelligence: An operational approach for the Shipping industry. *Security and Defence Quarterly*, *48*(4), 80–92.

Kang, Y., & Chiu, C. (2016). How corporate social responsibility indicators influence organization identification? the perspective of labor relations. *Ibusiness, 08*(04), 61–69. DOI: 10.4236/ib.2016.84007

Kan, L., & Xiang, H. (2023). Corporate social responsibility, advertising competition and consumer welfare: A research on the model of oligopoly competition theory. *American Journal of Industrial and Business Management, 13*(03), 140–153. DOI: 10.4236/ajibm.2023.133010

Kant, S., & Adula, M. (2025). Does technology-enabled knowledge management-based competitive advantage transfer?: Its combined effect on Ethiopian banking sustainability. In *Building inclusive global knowledge societies for sustainable development* (pp. 75–106). IGI Global., DOI: 10.4018/979-8-3693-6298-3.ch005

Kant, S., Adula, M., & Badi, S. (2025). Leading with wisdom: The role of wise leaders in Ethiopia. In *Harnessing happiness and wisdom for organizational well-being* (pp. 361–390). IGI Global., DOI: 10.4018/979-8-3693-8457-2.ch013

Kant, S., Niguse, T., Terefe, A., & Adula, M. (2025). Emerging trends and innovations: Effect on social sustainability in manufacturing supply chains by shifts in consumer behavior in the Horn of Africa. In *Enhancing social sustainability in manufacturing supply chains* (pp. 135–162). IGI Global., DOI: 10.4018/979-8-3693-9740-4.ch005

Kant, S., Niguse, T., Terefe, A., Jio, W., & Adula, M. (2025). Ethical leadership's role in promoting resilience among employees by mediation of building a resilient organizational culture in the Horn of Africa. In *Enhancing resilience in business continuity management* (pp. 219–244). IGI Global., DOI: 10.4018/979-8-3693-8809-9.ch007

Kaplan, R. S., & Norton, D. P. (1992). The balanced scorecard: Measures that drive performance. *Harvard Business Review, 70*(1), 71–79. PMID: 10119714

Kaplan, R. S., & Norton, D. P. (1996). *The balanced scorecard: Translating strategy into action*. Harvard Business School Press.

Karaboga, T., Zehir, C., Tatoglu, E., Karaboga, H. A., & Bouguerra, A. (2023). Big data analytics management capability and firm performance: The mediating role of data-driven culture. *Review of Managerial Science*, *17*(8), 2655–2684. DOI: 10.1007/s11846-022-00596-8

Karmaker, C. L., Al Aziz, R., Ahmed, T., Misbauddin, S. M., & Moktadir, M. A. (2023). Impact of industry 4.0 technologies on sustainable supply chain performance: The mediating role of green supply chain management practices and circular economy. *Journal of Cleaner Production*, *419*, 138249. DOI: 10.1016/j.jclepro.2023.138249

Kartikasary, M., Wijanarko, H., Tihar, A., & Zaldin, A. (2023). The effect of financial distress and firm size on carbon emission disclosure. E3S Web of Conferences, 426, 02093. https://doi.org/DOI: 10.1051/e3sconf/202342602093

Katchindele, M., Gomes, R., & Yambo, N. (2024). Liderança Organizacional: Uma Revisão Integrativa. *Revista Academicus: Revista Multidisciplinar*, 2(2), 29–41. DOI: 10.4314/academicus.v2i2.2

Kayyali, M. (2024). Immersive Technologies: Virtual and Augmented Reality in Higher Education. In Reshaping learning with next generation educational technologies (pp. 99-114). IGI Global. DOI: 10.4018/979-8-3693-1310-7.ch007

Kayyali, M. (2025 a). E-Learning Platforms and Their Influence on Lifelong Learning. In Impact of Digitalization on Education and Social Sustainability (pp. 155-176). IGI Global. DOI: 10.4018/979-8-3693-1854-6.ch006

Kayyali, M. (2025 c). Ethical Implications of Generative AI in Education: Privacy, Bias, and Integrity. In Transformative AI Practices for Personalized Learning Strategies (pp. 185-218). IGI Global Scientific Publishing. DOI: 10.4018/979-8-3693-8744-3.ch008

Kayyali, M. (2025). E-Learning Platforms and Their Influence on Lifelong Learning. In Impact of Digitalization on Education and Social Sustainability (pp. 155-176). IGI Global.

Kayyali, M. (2020). Post COVID-19: New era for higher education systems. *International Journal of Applied Science and Engineering*, *8*(2), 131–145. DOI: 10.30954/2322-0465.2.2020.6

Kayyali, M. (2025 b). The Role of Artificial Intelligence in Transforming Business Models. In *AI-Driven Business Model Innovation* (pp. 71–98). IGI Global Scientific Publishing., DOI: 10.4018/979-8-3693-9571-4.ch003

Kebede, A., Asgedom, A., & Asfaw, A. (2024). Is linking technical and vocational training with industry a bridge to employability? Lessons from a literature review for Ethiopia. *Cogent Education*, *11*(1), 2406721. Advance online publication. DOI: 10.1080/2331186X.2024.2406721

Kellen, V. (2003). Measuring performance: The key to achieving better results. *International Journal of Productivity and Performance Management*, *52*(2), 179–194. DOI: 10.1108/17410400310469192

Khatri, V., & Brown, C. V. (2010). Designing data governance. *Communications of the ACM*, *53*(1), 148–152. DOI: 10.1145/1629175.1629210

Khương, M., & Nguyen, A. (2022). The impact of corporate social responsibility performance on competitive advantage and business success. *International Journal of Asian Business and Information Management*, *12*(3), 1–15. DOI: 10.4018/IJABIM.294095

Khương, M., Nguyen, A., & Nguyen, T. (2021). Implementation of corporate social responsibility strategy to enhance firm reputation and competitive advantage. *Journal of Competitiveness*, *13*(4), 96–114. DOI: 10.7441/joc.2021.04.06

Kim, B., Quaquebeke, N., Chang, Y., & Kim, T. (2024). When and how corporate social responsibility promotes innovation: A multi-level moderated mediation model. *Corporate Social Responsibility and Environmental Management*, *32*(1), 1325–1345. DOI: 10.1002/csr.2984

Kluger, A. N., & Itzchakov, G. (2022). The power of listening at work. *Annual Review of Organizational Psychology and Organizational Behavior*, *9*(1), 121–146. DOI: 10.1146/annurev-orgpsych-012420-091013

Komolafe, A. M., Aderotoye, I. A., Abiona, O. O., Adewusi, A. O., Obijuru, A., Modupe, O. T., & Oyeniran, O. C. (2024). Harnessing business analytics for gaining competitive advantage in emerging markets: A systematic review of approaches and outcomes. *International Journal of Management & Entrepreneurship Research*, *6*(3), 838–862. DOI: 10.51594/ijmer.v6i3.939

Köseoglu, M. A., Mehraliyev, F., Altin, M., & Okumus, F. (2021). Competitor intelligence and analysis (CIA) model and online reviews: Integrating big data text mining with network analysis for strategic analysis. *Tourism Review*, *76*(3), 529–552. DOI: 10.1108/TR-10-2019-0406

Kotter, J. P. (1996). *Leading change*. Harvard Business Review Press.

Kraiger, K., Salas, E., & Cannon-Bowers, J. A. (2019). *Training and development: A handbook for practitioners*. Routledge.

Krieger, F., Drews, P., & Velte, P. (2021). Explaining the (non-) adoption of advanced data analytics in auditing: A process theory. *International Journal of Accounting Information Systems*, *41*, 100511. DOI: 10.1016/j.accinf.2021.100511

Kucharska, W., & Bedford, D. A. D. (2020). Love your mistakes!—They help you adapt to change. How do knowledge, collaboration and learning cultures foster organizational intelligence? *Journal of Organizational Change Management*, *33*(7), 1329–1354. DOI: 10.1108/JOCM-02-2020-0052

Kuosa, T. (2011). Different approaches of pattern management and strategic intelligence. *Technological Forecasting and Social Change*, *42*(6), 458–467. DOI: 10.1016/j.techfore.2010.06.004

Kurniawan, I., & Arief, N. (2023). Creating shared value in an upstream oil and gas company and the community: A case study of CSR implementation in PT Pertamina EP Tarakan field. *European Journal of Business Management and Research*, *8*(4), 282–292. DOI: 10.24018/ejbmr.2023.8.4.2091

Kwon, K., & Lee, J. (2021). Corporate social responsibility advertising in social media: A content analysis of the fashion industry's CSR advertising on Instagram. *Corporate Communications, 26*(4), 700–715. DOI: 10.1108/CCIJ-01-2021-0016

Lagerborg, A., Pappa, E., & Ravn, M. O. (2023). Sentimental business cycles. *The Review of Economic Studies, 90*(3), 1358–1393. DOI: 10.1093/restud/rdac053

Lai, F.-Y., Tang, H.-C., Lu, S.-C., & Cheng-Chen Timothy Lin. (2020, January 6). *Transformational leadership and job performance: The mediating role of work engagement*. ResearchGate; SAGE. https://www.researchgate.net/publication/338427319_Transformational_Leadership_and_Job_Performance_The_Mediating_Role_of_Work_Engagement

Lailiyah, N. (2021). *Media relations and corporate reputations in the corporate social responsibility (CSR) activities of PT.* Indonesia Power Semarang Up Generation., DOI: 10.4108/eai.9-10-2020.2304798

Latif, A., Hadi, N., & Khurshid, J. (2020). Does CSR add value to service innovation performance via HRM? A conceptual framework and future research agenda. Global Management Sciences Review, V(III), 73-83. https://doi.org/DOI: 10.31703/gmsr.2020(V-III).08

Lazarenko, Y., Garafonova, O., Marhasova, V., & Grigashkina, S. (2021). Gaining a competitive advantage through sustainability strategy: managerial applications for the mining sector. E3S Web of Conferences, 278, 03036. https://doi.org/DOI: 10.1051/e3sconf/202127803036

Lee, E. A. (2024, October). Certainty vs. Intelligence. In International Conference on Bridging the Gap between AI and Reality (pp. 20-32). Cham: Springer Nature Switzerland.

Lee, A., Lyubovnikova, J., Tian, A. W., & Knight, C. (2019). Servant leadership: A Meta-analytic Examination of Incremental contribution, moderation, and Mediation. *Journal of Occupational and Organizational Psychology, 93*(1), 1–44. Advance online publication. DOI: 10.1111/joop.12265

Lee, H., & Choi, B. (2003). Knowledge Management enablers, processes and organizational knowledge: An integrative view and empirical investigation. *Journal of Management Information Systems*, *20*(1), 179–228. DOI: 10.1080/07421222.2003.11045756

Levine, D. K. (2021). The reputation trap. *Econometrica*, *89*(6), 2659–2678. DOI: 10.3982/ECTA17891

Lewin, K., Lippitt, R., & White, R. K. (1939). Patterns of aggressive behavior in experimentally created social climates. *The Journal of Social Psychology*, *10*(2), 271–301. DOI: 10.1080/00224545.1939.9713366

Liden, R. C., Wayne, S. J., Zhao, H., & Henderson, D. (2008). Servant leadership: Development of a multidimensional measure and multi-level assessment. *The Leadership Quarterly*, *19*(2), 161–177. DOI: 10.1016/j.leaqua.2008.01.006

Lies, J. (2019). Marketing intelligence and big data: Digital marketing techniques on their way to becoming social engineering techniques in marketing. *International Journal of Interactive Multimedia and Artificial Intelligence*, *5*(5), 134. DOI: 10.9781/ijimai.2019.05.002

Li, J., Qin, X., & Lin, Y. (2024). Strategy, corporate social responsibility and investment efficiency: The role of substitute and complement. *Business & Society*, *64*(4), 757–803. DOI: 10.1177/00076503241254544

Li, K., Khalili, N., & Cheng, W. (2019). Corporate social responsibility practices in China: Trends, context, and impact on company performance. *Sustainability (Basel)*, *11*(2), 354. DOI: 10.3390/su11020354

Lin, X. (2025). A Model of Big Data-Based Governance: China's National Government Big Data Platform and an Analysis of Its Governance Competence. *Chinese Political Science Review*, •••, 1–40. DOI: 10.1007/s41111-025-00279-1

Liu, Y., & Xu, H. (2022). Strategic corporate social responsibility with spillover effect in innovation. *Nankai Business Review International*, *13*(2), 318–339. DOI: 10.1108/NBRI-04-2021-0025

Locke, E. A., & Latham, G. P. (2019). New directions in goal-setting theory. *Current Directions in Psychological Science*, *28*(2), 154–160.

Longo, F., Nicoletti, L., & Padovano, A. (2017). Smart operators in industry 4.0: A human-centered approach to enhance operators' capabilities and competencies within the new smart factory context. *Computers & Industrial Engineering*, *113*, 144–159. DOI: 10.1016/j.cie.2017.09.016

Lu, J., Ren, L., Yao, S., Qiao, J., Mikalauskienė, A., & Štreimikis, J. (2020). Exploring the relationship between corporate social responsibility and firm competitiveness. *Ekonomska Istrazivanja*, *33*(1), 1621–1646. DOI: 10.1080/1331677X.2020.1761419

Lyu, C., Yang, J., Zhang, F., Teo, T. S. H., & Mu, T. (2020). How do knowledge characteristics affect a firm's knowledge sharing intention in inter firm cooperation? An empirical study. *Journal of Business Research*, *115*(381), 48–60. DOI: 10.1016/j.jbusres.2020.04.045

Madureira, L., Popovič, A., & Castelli, M. (2023). Competitive intelligence empirical validation and application: Foundations for knowledge advancement and relevance to practice. *Journal of Information Science*, •••, 01655515231191221. DOI: 10.1177/01655515231191221

Mael, F. A., O'Shea, P. G., Smith, M. A., Burling, A. S., Carman, K. L., Haas, A., & Rogers, K. S. (2010). Development of a model and measure of process-oriented quality of care for substance abuse treatment. *The Journal of Behavioral Health Services & Research*, *37*(1), 4–24. DOI: 10.1007/s11414-009-9180-4 PMID: 19462245

Maluleka, M. L., & Chummun, B. Z. (2024). The function of competitive intelligence in South African insurance post-COVID-19 outbreak. *South African Journal of Information Management*, *26*(1), 1738. Advance online publication. DOI: 10.4102/sajim.v26i1.1738

Manoharan, G., Ashtikar, S. P., Durai, S., & Selvaraj, F. J. (2022). Work-Life Balance Perceptions of Women in the IT and ITeS Sectors in Kerala: A Research Study. *European Journal of Molecular and Clinical Medicine*, *9*(7), 4764+. https://link.gale.com/apps/doc/A737509380/AONE?u=anon~92871157&sid=googleScholar&xid=0e0a5afe

Manoharan, G., Ashtikar, S. P., Durai, S., & Selvaraj, F. J. (2022). Work-Life Balance Perceptions of Women in the IT and ITeS Sectors in Kerala: A Research Study. *European Journal of Molecular and Clinical Medicine, 9*(7), 4764+. https://link.gale.com/apps/doc/A737509380/AONE?u=anon~e39eb447&sid=googleScholar&xid=70aae9af

Manoharan, G., Durai, S., & Rajesh, G. A. (2022). Identifying performance indicators and metrics for performance measurement of the workforce is the need of the hour: A case of a retail garment store in Coimbatore. In *AIP Conference Proceedings* (Vol. 2418, No. 1). AIP Publishing. DOI: 10.1063/5.0081821

Manoharan, G., Jalaja, V., Sathe, M. A., Lourens, M., & Suresh, K. (2023). Machine learning and data privacy in human resource management. In *2023 4th International Conference on Computation, Automation and Knowledge Management (ICCAKM)* (pp. 1–6). IEEE. DOI: 10.1109/ICCAKM58659.2023.10449576

Manoharan, G., Durai, S., Rajesh, G. A., & Ashtikar, S. P. (2023a). Credit and risk analysis in the financial and banking sectors: An investigation. In *Artificial intelligence for capital markets* (pp. 57–72). Chapman and Hall/CRC., DOI: 10.1201/9781003327745-5

Manoharan, G., Durai, S., Rajesh, G. A., Razak, A., Rao, C. B., & Ashtikar, S. P. (2023b). A study on the perceptions of officials on their duties and responsibilities at various levels of the organizational structure in order to accomplish artificial intelligence-based smart city implementation. In *Artificial intelligence and machine learning in smart city planning* (pp. 1–10). Elsevier., DOI: 10.1016/B978-0-323-99503-0.00007-7

Manoharan, G., & Rajoli, S. B. (2024). Leveraging technology for enhancing performance appraisal. In Rajapakshe, W. (Ed.), *Employee performance management for improved workplace motivation* (pp. 289–310). IGI Global., DOI: 10.4018/979-8-3693-4387-6.ch012

Manoharan, G., Razak, A., Rajchandar, K., Nithya, G., Durai, S., & Ashtikar, S. P. (2024). Digital learning for professional development in varied fields of service sectors: Embracing technological advancements. In *Embracing technological advancements for lifelong learning* (pp. 111–137). IGI Global., DOI: 10.4018/979-8-3693-1410-4.ch006

Marco, D. (2006). Understanding data governance and stewardship, part 1. *DM Review*, *16*(9), 2006.

Marr, B. (2012). *Key performance indicators: The 75+ measures every manager needs to know*. Pearson.

Marr, B. (2018). *Artificial Intelligence in Practice: How 50 Successful Companies Used AI and Machine Learning to Solve Problems*. John Wiley & Sons.

Mas, F., Tucker, W., Massaro, M., & Bagnoli, C. (2021). Corporate social responsibility in the retail business: A case study. *Corporate Social Responsibility and Environmental Management*, *29*(1), 223–232. DOI: 10.1002/csr.2198

Maslow, A. H. (1943). A theory of human motivation. *Psychological Review*, *50*(4), 370–396. DOI: 10.1037/h0054346

Mattera, M., González, F., Ruiz-Morales, C., & Gava, L. (2021). Facing a global crisis - how sustainable business models helped firms overcome COVID-19. *Corporate Governance (Bradford)*, *21*(6), 1100–1116. DOI: 10.1108/CG-07-2020-0309

McAfee, A., Brynjolfsson, E., Davenport, T. H., Patil, D. J., & Barton, D. (2012). Big data: The management revolution. *Harvard Business Review*, *90*(10), 60–68. PMID: 23074865

McClelland, D. C. (1961). *The achieving society*. D. Van Nostrand Company. DOI: 10.1037/14359-000

McKinsey & Company. (2015). *Why diversity matters*. https://www.mckinsey.com/business-functions/people-and-organizational-performance/our-insights/why-diversity-matters

Mcquade, K. E., Harrison, C., & Tarbert, H. (2021). Systematically reviewing servant leadership. *European Business Review*, *33*(3), 465–490. DOI: 10.1108/EBR-08-2019-0162

Mesu, J., Sanders, K., & Riemsdijk, M. V. (2015). Transformational leadership and organisational commitment in manufacturing and service small to medium-sized enterprises: The moderating effects of directive and participative leadership. *Personnel Review*, *44*(6), 970–990. DOI: 10.1108/PR-01-2014-0020

Meyer, J. P., & Allen, N. J. (1991). A three-component conceptualization of organizational commitment. *Human Resource Management Review*, *1*(1), 61–89. DOI: 10.1016/1053-4822(91)90011-Z

Meyer, J. P., Allen, N. J., & Smith, C. A. (2002). Commitment to organizations and occupations: Extension and test of a three-component conceptualization. *The Journal of Applied Psychology*, *87*(4), 665–673.

Miao, Q., Newman, A., Schwarz, G., & Xu, L. (2014). Servant leadership, trust, and the organizational commitment of public sector employees in China. *Public Administration*, *92*(3), n/a, n/a. DOI: 10.1111/padm.12091

Mittal, R., & Dorfman, P. W. (2012). Servant leadership across cultures. *Journal of World Business*, *47*(4), 555–570. DOI: 10.1016/j.jwb.2012.01.009

Mohammadalian, S., Nazemi, E., & Tarokh, M. (2013). Propose a conceptual model of adaptive competitive intelligence (aci). *International Journal of Business Intelligence Research*, *4*(4), 22–32. DOI: 10.4018/ijbir.2013100102

Mohammed, I. A. (2025, February). Managing AI-Driven Innovations: Aligning Technological Advancements with Strategic Business Objectives. In *2025 First International Conference on Advances in Computer Science, Electrical, Electronics, and Communication Technologies (CE2CT)* (pp. 950-955). IEEE DOI: 10.1109/CE2CT64011.2025.10941386

Muhandi, A. (2024). Corporate social responsibility practices and stakeholder perceptions: A cross-cultural analysis in Kenya. *International Journal of Leadership and Governance*, *4*(2), 49–60. DOI: 10.47604/ijlg.2695

Mullins, L. J. (2016). *Management and organizational behaviour*. Pearson Education.

Muntean, M. (2018). Business intelligence issues for sustainability projects. *Sustainability (Basel)*, *10*(2), 335. DOI: 10.3390/su10020335

Nasri, W. (2011). Competitive intelligence in Tunisian companies. *Journal of Enterprise Information Management*, *24*(1), 53–67. DOI: 10.1108/17410391111097429

Nawangsari, L., & Sutawidjaya, A. (2021). How can SMES achieve sustainable business? *Business and Entrepreneurial Review (Ber)*, *21*(1), 153–170. DOI: 10.25105/ber.v21i1.9271

Neely, A., Adams, C., & Crowe, P. (2002). *The performance prism: The scorecard for measuring and managing business success*. Cambridge University Press.

Nenzhelele, T. (2016). Competitive intelligence practice challenges in the South African property sector. *Problems and Perspectives in Management*, *14*(2), 298–305. DOI: 10.21511/ppm.14(2-2).2016.05

Neuman, W. R. (2023). *Evolutionary intelligence: How technology will make us smarter*. MIT Press. DOI: 10.7551/mitpress/15049.001.0001

Newman, A., Schwarz, G., Cooper, B., & Sendjaya, S. (2017). How servant leadership influences organizational citizenship behavior: The roles of LMX, empowerment, and proactive personality. *Journal of Business Ethics*, *145*(1), 49–62. DOI: 10.1007/s10551-015-2827-6

Nguyen, T. (2023). Zara's organization apparatus: what is the key behind Zara's fast fashion success? https://urn.fi/URN:NBN:fi:amk-2023051811620

Nixon, M., & Thato, M. (2016). Linking business intelligence to a knowledge-based sustainable competitive advantage in organizations. *African Journal of Business Management, 10*(19), 459–468. DOI: 10.5897/AJBM2016.8059

Noe, R. A. (2017). *Employee training and development* (7th ed.). McGraw-Hill Education.

Northouse, P. G. (2016). *Leadership: Theory and practice* (7th ed.). Sage.

Obonyo, M., & Kilika, J. (2020). Competitive intelligence and corresponding outcome in a strategic management process: A review of literature. *Journal of Economics and Business, 3*(4). Advance online publication. DOI: 10.31014/aior.1992.03.04.313

Olah, D. (2024). Subversion as the Modus Operandi-China's integration of influence operations into the Belt and Road Initiative as a mode of disrupting geopolitical powers in Vietnam and Pakistan.

Omale, S. A., Yusuf, S. O., Oyenuga, M. O., Ikemefuna, M., Ojo, S. S., & Momodu, I. D. (2024). Organizational Learning in the Post-COVID-19 Era: A Prerequisite for Stakeholder Satisfactions. Twist 19(3), 265-272 https://twistjournal.net/twist/article/view/339

Oosthuizen, J. H. (2022). A fourth industrial revolution integrated intelligence taxonomy and measurement framework for top management.

Oyedele, M. O., Marcus, G. O., & Ahungwa, A. I. (2023). Do Consumers Care About Green Marketing Practices? Insight From A Developing Nation. *Budapest International Research and Critics Institute Journal(BIR-CIJournal)* 6(3), (1424-1436)_https://bircu-journal.com/index.php/birci/article/view/7665

Oyedele, O. M. (2025). Digital Circular Economy: Driving Sustainable Innovation Through Stakeholder Synergy. In Singh, R., & Kumar, V. (Eds.), *Sustainable Innovations and Digital Circular Economy*. Springer., DOI: 10.1007/978-981-96-1064-8_4

Oyenuga, M. O., Ahungwa, A. I., & Onoja, E. (2021). Effect of Brand Equity on consumer behaviour among students of Veritas University, Nigeria: A Study of Apple Smartphones. *Marketing and Branding Research*, *8*, 48–64. DOI: 10.33844/mbr.2021.60329

Oyenuga, M. O., & Fredrick, E. (2023). Managing Product Features and Customer Satisfaction via Product Development, Product Branding, and Product Packaging: Evidence from CWAY Table Water. *Marketing and Branding Research*, *10*(1), 28–44. DOI: 10.32038/mbr.2023.10.01.03

Oyetunde, T. O., Oyenuga, M. O., & Adoga, G. J. (2023). Green Management Practices and Organisational Efficiency in Higher Institutions. *Budapest International Research and Critics in Linguistics and Education (BirLE). Journal*, *6*(3), 276–290. https://bircu-journal.com/index.php/birle/article/view/7716

Padgett, R., & Moura-Leite, R. (2012). Innovation with high social benefits and corporate financial performance. *Journal of Technology Management & Innovation*, *7*(4), 59–69. DOI: 10.4067/S0718-27242012000400005

Palilingan, V. & Batmetan, J. (2019). Competitive intelligence framework for increasing competitiveness in vocational high school management.. https://doi.org/DOI: 10.2991/ictvet-18.2019.52

Pansanella, V. (2024). Biased Echoes: Unraveling Mechanisms of Opinion Dynamics and their Impacts in Online Social Networks. DOI: 10.25429/pansanella-valentina_phd2024-01-30

Pan, X., Sinha, P., & Chen, X. (2020). Corporate social responsibility and eco-innovation: The triple bottom line perspective. *Corporate Social Responsibility and Environmental Management*, *28*(1), 214–228. DOI: 10.1002/csr.2043

Parasuraman, A. P., Zeithaml, V. A., & Berry, L. L. (1988, January). *SERVQUAL: A multiple- item scale for measuring consumer perceptions of service quality*. ResearchGate. https://www.researchgate.net/publication/225083802_SERVQUAL_A_multiple-_Item_Scale_for_measuring_consumer_perceptions_of_service_quality

Parmenter, D. (2015). *Key performance indicators: Developing, implementing, and using winning KPIs* (3rd ed.). Wiley. DOI: 10.1002/9781119019855

Parris, D. L., & Peachey, J. W. (2013). A systematic literature review of servant leadership theory in organizational contexts. *Journal of Business Ethics, 113*(3), 377–393. DOI: 10.1007/s10551-012-1322-6

Pellissier, R., & Nenzhelele, T. E. (2013). Towards a universal definition of competitive intelligence. *South African Journal of Information Management, 15*(2). Advance online publication. DOI: 10.4102/sajim.v15i2.559

Phillips, J. J., & Gully, S. M. (2015). *Strategic staffing* (3rd ed.). Pearson.

Prashantham, S., & Madhok, A. (2023). Corporate-startup partnering: Exploring attention dynamics and relational outcomes in asymmetric settings. *Strategic Entrepreneurship Journal, 17*(4), 770–801. DOI: 10.1002/sej.1475

Prokushenkov, P. (2023). Strategy formation as narrative-driven performative praxis. *International Journal of Management and Decision Making, 22*(3), 310–333. DOI: 10.1504/IJMDM.2023.131734

Ramachandran, K. K., Mary, S. S. C., Painoli, A. K., Satyala, H., Singh, B., & Manoharan, G. (2022). Assessing the full impact of technological advances on business management techniques. *The British Journal of Administrative Management, 58*(Special Issue 06). https://tbjam.org/vol58-special-issue-06

Ramaswamy, V., & Ozcan, K. (2019). Digitalized Interactive Platforms: Turning Goods and Services into Retail Co-Creation Experiences. *NIM Marketing Intelligence Review, 11*(1), 18–23. DOI: 10.2478/nimmir-2019-0003

Rayed, C. (2019). Using business intelligence solutions for forecasting in marketing researches. International Journal of Informatics and Communication Technology (Ij-Ict), 8(2), 102. https://doi.org/DOI: 10.11591/ijict.v8i2.pp102-110

Ray, S. K. S. (2023). Moving towards agile leadership to help organizations succeed. *The IUP Journal of Soft Skills*, *17*(1), 5–17.

Rith, R., & Spinelli, R. (2024). Examining the x factor of corporate social responsibility in professional football clubs: An integrative literature review. *Corporate Social Responsibility and Environmental Management*, *31*(4), 3487–3501. DOI: 10.1002/csr.2750

Robbins, S. P., & Judge, T. A. (2013). *Organizational behavior* (15th ed.). Pearson., https://digilib.stekom.ac.id/assets/dokumen/ebook/feb_c5d15cc7c32d4985a70c200bad26dc576781601d_1648649445.pdf

Robinson, T., SenGupta, S., & Norris, K. (2019). Skill-based training, job satisfaction and motivation of primary health workers: Evidence from the India ANM program. *International Journal for Quality in Health Care : Journal of the International Society for Quality in Health Care*, *31*(7), 508–514.

Russell, B. (2001). *The problems of philosophy*. Oxford University Press.

Russell, R. F., & Stone, A. G. (2002). A review of servant leadership attributes: Developing a practical model. *Leadership and Organization Development Journal*, *23*(3), 145–157. DOI: 10.1108/01437730210424

Russom P. (2011). Big data analytics. TDWI best practices report, *fourth quarter. 19*(4):1-34.

Rust, R. (2021). A Framework for Mitigating Obsolescence in Military Based Systems. https://purls.library.ucf.edu/go/DP0025458

Ryan, R. M., & Deci, E. L. (2000). Intrinsic and extrinsic motivations: Classic definitions and new directions. *Contemporary Educational Psychology*, *25*(1), 54–67. DOI: 10.1006/ceps.1999.1020 PMID: 10620381

Saks, A. M. (2006). Antecedents and consequences of employee engagement. *Journal of Managerial Psychology*, *21*(7), 600–619. DOI: 10.1108/02683940610690169

Sambharya, R. (2024). Are discrete dimensions of corporate social responsibility disclosures global, regional or hybrid? *Cross Cultural & Strategic Management, 31*(4), 725–747. DOI: 10.1108/CCSM-03-2024-0066

Sangeetha, M., Gupta, R., Reddy, K. S., Nanda, S. K., Mannar, B. R., Manoharan, G., & Liudmyla, I. (2024). Detailed investigation of digital transformational strategies to enhance business productivity. In *Proceedings of recent advances in management and engineering* (pp. 45–51). CRC Press. DOI: 10.1201/9781003532026-8

Sarjana, S. & Khayati, N. (2016). CSR strategy in industrial city to achieve competitive advantage. https://doi.org/DOI: 10.2991/gcbme-16.2016.152

Schein, E. H. (2010). *Organizational culture and leadership* (4th ed.). Jossey-Bass.

Seaver, N. (2022). Computing taste: Algorithms and the makers of music recommendation. In *Computing Taste*. University of Chicago Press. DOI: 10.7208/chicago/9780226822969.001.0001

Selvaraj, F. J., Singh, R., Manoharan, G., Razak, A., Kukreja, J., & Ashtikar, S. P. (2024). Evaluation of customer loyalty and customer relationship management in mobile communication lesson from new normal. In *2024 3rd International Conference on Computational Modelling, Simulation and Optimization (ICCMSO)* (pp. 216–221). IEEE. DOI: 10.1109/ICCMSO61761.2024.00052

Sendjaya, S., & Sarros, J. C. (2002). Servant leadership: Its origin, development, and application in organizations. *Journal of Leadership & Organizational Studies, 9*(2), 57–64. DOI: 10.1177/107179190200900205

Sendjaya, S., Sarros, J. C., & Santora, J. C. (2019). *Servant leadership: Its origin, development, and application in organizations*. Springer.

Shameem, A., Ramachandran, K. K., Sharma, A., Singh, R., Selvaraj, F. J., & Manoharan, G. (2023). The rising importance of AI in boosting the efficiency of online advertising in developing countries. In *2023 3rd International Conference on Advance Computing and Innovative Technologies in Engineering (ICACITE)* (pp. 1762–1766). IEEE. DOI: 10.1109/ICACITE57410.2023.10182754

Silva, E. S., & Bonetti, F. (2021). Digital humans in fashion: Will consumers interact? *Journal of Retailing and Consumer Services*, *60*, 102430. DOI: 10.1016/j.jretconser.2020.102430

Singireddy, J. (2025). *Smart Finance: Harnessing Artificial Intelligence to Transform Tax, Accounting, Payroll, and Credit Management for the Digital Age*. Deep Science Publishing.

Spears, L. C. (1998). *Insights on leadership*. John Wiley & Sons.

Spector, P. E. (1997). Job satisfaction: Application, assessment, causes, and consequences. *Sage (Atlanta, Ga.)*. Advance online publication. DOI: 10.4135/9781452231549

Srivastava, M., Franklin, A., & Martinette, L. (2013). Building a sustainable competitive advantage. *Journal of Technology Management & Innovation*, *8*(2), 7–8. DOI: 10.4067/S0718-27242013000200004

Stone, A. G., Russell, R. F., & Patterson, K. (2004). Transformational versus Servant leadership: A Difference in Leader Focus. *Leadership and Organization Development Journal*, *25*(4), 349–361. DOI: 10.1108/01437730410538671

Stoyanova, T., & Angelova, M. (2018). From sustainable to transient competitive advantage. *International Conference Knowledge-Based Organization*, 24(2), 134-139. https://doi.org/DOI: 10.1515/kbo-2018-0078

Suh, B. (2021). Workplace learning: How to build a culture of continuous employee development. *The Learning Organization*, *28*(4), 457–459. DOI: 10.1108/TLO-05-2021-269

Szegedi, K., Németh, T., & Körtvési, D. (2023). Employer branding in the fashion industry: CSR actions by fashion SMES. *Sustainability (Basel), 15*(3), 1827. DOI: 10.3390/su15031827

Szirmai, A., & Verspagen, B. (2015). Manufacturing and economic growth in developing countries, 1950–2005. *Structural Change and Economic Dynamics, 34*, 46–59. DOI: 10.1016/j.strueco.2015.06.002

Tadesse, S., Asgedom, T., & Taddese, A. (2024). Leadership behaviour association with human resource management practice in selected Ethiopian sport federations. *Research in Sport Education and Sciences, 26*(1), 9–15. DOI: 10.62425/rses.1460061

Tanev, S. (2024). Design Thinking for Competitive Intelligence in a Digital Business Transformation Context. Journal of Intelligence Studies in Business, 14(Special Issue 1), 57-85.

Tannenbaum, S. I., Mathieu, J. E., Salas, E., & Cannon-Bowers, J. A. (2013). *Meeting the challenge of training and development: A field guide for organizations*. John Wiley & Sons.

Tarnovskaya, V. (2023). Sustainability as the source of competitive advantage. how sustainable is it?., 75-89. https://doi.org/DOI: 10.1108/S1876-066X20230000037005

Taylor, J., Vithayathil, J., & Yim, D. (2018). Are corporate social responsibility (CSR) initiatives such as sustainable development and environmental policies value enhancing or window dressing? *Corporate Social Responsibility and Environmental Management, 25*(5), 971–980. DOI: 10.1002/csr.1513

Tinonetsana, F. & Musariwa, P. (2024). Integration of sustainability marketing into business strategies: challenges during adoption. International Journal of Research in Business and Social Science (2147-4478), 13(2), 23-30. https://doi.org/DOI: 10.20525/ijrbs.v13i2.3011

Tolbert, P. S., & Hall, R. H. (2009). *Organizations: Structures, processes, and outcomes*. Routledge.

Trabucco, T. G. (2024). Artificial intelligence as a tool for research and development in European patent law.

Trivellas, P., Rafailidis, A., Polychroniou, P., & Dekoulou, P. (2019). Corporate social responsibility (CSR) and its internal consequences on job performance. *International Journal of Quality and Service Sciences*, *11*(2), 265–282. DOI: 10.1108/IJQSS-12-2017-0117

Tu n, L. (2013). Competitive intelligence and other levers of brand performance. *Journal of Strategic Marketing*, *21*(3), 217–239. DOI: 10.1080/0965254X.2013.765501

Turban, E., Sharda, R., Aronson, J. E., & King, D. (2008). *Business Intelligence: A Managerial Approach*. Pearson Prentice Hall.

Van Dierendonck, D. (2011). Servant leadership: A review and synthesis. *Journal of Management*, *37*(4), 1228–1261. DOI: 10.1177/0149206310380462

van Dierendonck, D., Stam, D., Boersma, P., de Windt, N., & Alkema, J. (2014). Same difference? Exploring the differential mechanisms linking servant leadership and transformational leadership to follower outcomes. *The Leadership Quarterly*, *25*(3), 544–562. DOI: 10.1016/j.leaqua.2013.11.014

Vargo, C. J. (2025). *The Computational Content Analyst: Using Machine Learning to Classify Media Messages*. Taylor & Francis., DOI: 10.4324/9781003514237

Vázquez, B., & Fornés, G. (2015). Corporate social responsibility in emerging markets: Case studies of Spanish MNCS in Latin America. *European Business Review*, *27*(2), 214–230. DOI: 10.1108/EBR-03-2013-0053

Vesnic-Alujevic, L. (2021). Imagining democratic societies of the future: Insights from a foresight study. *Futures & Foresight Science*, *3*(1), ffo2.60. Advance online publication. DOI: 10.1002/ffo2.60

Virmani, N., Sharma, S., Kumar, A., & Luthra, S. (2023). Adoption of industry 4.0 evidence in emerging economy: Behavioral reasoning theory perspective. *Technological Forecasting and Social Change*, *188*, 122317. DOI: 10.1016/j.techfore.2023.122317

Vorozheykina, T., Muravitskaya, N., Lukyanenko, G., Antonova, O., Lyalkova, E., & Basova, M. (2019). Technologies of corporate social responsibility in accounting and statistics. *International Journal of Recent Technology and Engineering*, *8*(2), 3871–3876. DOI: 10.35940/ijrte.B3075.078219

Waithaka, P. (2021). Key vulnerabilities and the competitive advantage among commercial banks in Kenya. *Journal of Contemporary Research in Social Sciences*, *3*(4), 114–124. DOI: 10.33094/26410249.2021.34.114.124

Walsh, D. J., & Gittell, J. H. (2004). The southwest airlines way: Using the power of relationships to achieve high performance. *Industrial & Labor Relations Review*, *57*(3), 474. DOI: 10.2307/4126671

Wang, Z. (2021). Business analysis on sustainable competitive advantages. E3S Web of Conferences, 235, 03009. https://doi.org/DOI: 10.1051/e3sconf/202123503009

Wang, J., Tian, Y., Wang, Y., Yang, J., Wang, X., Wang, S., & Kwan, O. (2023). A framework and operational procedures for metaverses-based industrial foundation models. *IEEE Transactions on Systems, Man, and Cybernetics. Systems*, *53*(4), 2037–2046. DOI: 10.1109/TSMC.2022.3226755

Washington, R. R., Sutton, C. D., & Feild, H. S. (2006). Diferenças individuais na liderança servidora: Os papéis dos valores e da personalidade. *Revista de Desenvolvimento de Liderança e Organização*, *27*(8), 700–716. DOI: 10.1108/01437730610709309

Weick, K. E., & Quinn, R. E. (1999). Organisational change and development. *Annual Review of Psychology*, *50*(1), 361–386. DOI: 10.1146/annurev.psych.50.1.361 PMID: 15012461

Wing, C. (2025). *Four Future Seasons: How to anticipate and prepare for multiple potential futures*. Penguin Random House South Africa.

Wixom, B. H., Watson, H. J., & Werner, T. (2011). Developing an enterprise business intelligence capability. *MIS Quarterly Executive*, *10*, 2.

Wu, C. (2024). Data privacy: From transparency to fairness. *Technology in Society*, *76*, 102457. DOI: 10.1016/j.techsoc.2024.102457

Xia, T., Luo, X., Liao, Y., & Liu, W. (2018). Corporate governance, corporate social responsibility and corporate performance study.. https://doi.org/DOI: 10.2991/sshr-17.2018.10

Yadav, M., & Sinha, N. (2021). Investigating the impact of corporate social responsibility on competitive performance: An empirical study based on panel data analysis. *Fiib Business Review*, *11*(2), 165–173. DOI: 10.1177/23197145211015443

Yang, L., Ngai, C., & Lu, W. (2020). Changing trends of corporate social responsibility reporting in the world-leading airlines. *PLoS One*, *15*(6), e0234258. DOI: 10.1371/journal.pone.0234258 PMID: 32511253

Yan, Y., Huang, C., Wang, Q., & Hu, B. (2020). Data mining of customer choice behavior in internet of things within relationship network. *International Journal of Information Management*, *50*, 566–574. DOI: 10.1016/j.ijinfomgt.2018.11.013

Yin, Y., Zhang, Z., Da, K., & Wen, X. (2023). Sustainable influence mechanism of technological innovation diffusion on intelligent transformation of manufacturing enterprises based on competitive advantage and value chain can regulate mediation effect analysis. *Polish Journal of Environmental Studies*, *33*(2), 1429–1441. DOI: 10.15244/pjoes/173439

Yousfi, O., Elkateb, M., & Omri, A. (2023). Perspective chapter: Rethinking CSR strategies in the era of COVID-19.. https://doi.org/DOI: 10.5772/intechopen.106248

Yu, H., Kuo, L., & Kao, M. (2017). The relationship between CSR disclosure and competitive advantage. *Sustainability Accounting Management and Policy Journal*, *8*(5), 547–570. DOI: 10.1108/SAMPJ-11-2016-0086

Yukl, G. (2010). *Leadership in organizations* (7th ed.). Pearson Education.

Yu, S., & Liang, W. (2020). Exploring the determinants of strategic corporate social responsibility: An empirical examination. *Sustainability (Basel), 12*(6), 2368. DOI: 10.3390/su12062368

Zenger, J., & Folkman, J. (2015). *O líder inspirador desvendando o segredo por trás de como os líderes extraordinários motivam*. https://zengerfolkman.com/wp-content/uploads/2019/04/White-Paper_-Unlocking-The-Secret-Behind-How-Extraordinary-Leaders-Motivate.pdf

Zerbato, G. (2024). Relative Valuation for Value Investing: theoretical aspects and empirical evidence.

Zerbino, P., Aloini, D., Dulmin, R., & Mininno, V. (2018). Big Data-enabled customer relationship management: A holistic approach. *Information Processing & Management, 54*(5), 818–846. DOI: 10.1016/j.ipm.2017.10.005

Zhang, X., Tu, Y., Long, Y., Shan, L., Elsaadani, M. A., Fu, K., & Hei, X. (2024, May). From Virtual Touch to Tesla Command: Unlocking Unauthenticated Control Chains From Smart Glasses for Vehicle Takeover. In *2024 IEEE Symposium on Security and Privacy (SP)* (pp. 2366-2384). IEEE. DOI: 10.1109/SP54263.2024.00231

Zhang, Y., Zheng, Y., Zhang, L., Xu, S., Liu, X., & Chen, W. (2019). A meta-analytic review of the consequences of servant leadership: The moderating roles of cultural factors. *Asia Pacific Journal of Management, 38*(1), 371–400. Advance online publication. DOI: 10.1007/s10490-018-9639-z

Zhao, L. & Du, J. (2017). Certification of environmental corporate social responsibility activities in a differentiated duopoly market. Mathematical Problems in Engineering, 2017(1). https://doi.org/DOI: 10.1155/2017/2597159

Zhao, J., Wang, X., Yao, X., & Xi, X. (2024). Digital-intelligence transformation, for better or worse? The roles of pace, scope and rhythm. *Internet Research*. Advance online publication. DOI: 10.1108/INTR-12-2023-1125

About the Contributors

Ricardo Marcão, PhD, MBA, PMP, is a global expert in Project Management, Strategy, Finance, and Healthcare Innovation, with experience in Pharma, MedTech, IT, and Professional Services. He is Chairman of ICoE Portugal at SCIP, Senior PM at Feedzai, and Professor at ISLA Santarém - Polytechnic University. His work spans Grand Strategy, Democracy, and International Relations, focusing on how geopolitics and competitive intelligence shape global business. He has led major transformations, implemented gamification for engagement and sales, and introduced a risk control model that improved project margins by 20%. From 2022–2023, he led global CRM projects for top pharma firms. Currently combating fraud, Ricardo is also an academic, editor, and speaker, with several books on strategy and innovation. As coordinator of MBA and graduate programs at ISLA Santarém, he develops future leaders at the intersection of business and technology.

Vasco Santos PhD, is a seasoned academic and researcher with expertise in Tourism, Marketing, and Innovation. He holds two PhDs - one in Business Sciences with a focus on Marketing (Fernando Pessoa University) and another in Tourism (University of Seville) - as well as a Post-Doc in Innovation Management for Sustainable Luxury Tourism (University of Aveiro) and an Habilitation in Management (European University, Portugal). He also holds an MSc in Marketing and Tourism Promotion and a BA in Hospitality Management. Vasco lectures at the Polytechnic University of Tomar and ISLA Santarém - Polytechnic University, and is a full researcher at GOVCOPP, University of Aveiro. A founding member of the National Tourism Platform (PNT), he has authored several scientific papers and book chapters. His research focuses on tourism, marketing, employer branding, and management, contributing to strategic thinking and innovation in the global hospitality and tourism landscape.

***

João Farinha PhD is an Associate Professor at ISLA Santarém – Polytechnic University, where he coordinates the MBA in Commercial Management and Marketing, the undergraduate degree in Business Processes and Operations Management, and a higher technical course in Industrial Organization. He holds a PhD in Management from Universidade Europeia and an Executive Master's in Marketing Management, alongside certifications in Leadership and Entrepreneurship from Case Western Reserve, Maryland, and Wharton. He is also a member of the GOVCOPP research unit (University of Aveiro) and CinTurs (University of Algarve), actively contributing to research and teaching in management, operations, HR, and marketing.

Muhammad Nawaz Iqbal is an Academician, Researcher and Philosopher. He have almost 13 years of corporate experience and now serving as an Assistant Professor in department of Business Administration of Sir Syed university of Engineering and Technology, Karachi, Pakistan. He credited numerous publications in local and international journals and also credited two books in the field of Business Management.

Geetha Manoharan is an Assistant Professor at SR University, Telangana, India, where she also serves as the university-level PhD Program Coordinator and Director of Publications and Patents under the Research Division. Her academic leadership promotes interdisciplinary collaboration and research excellence. She plays a key role in supporting doctoral scholars and advancing the institution's publishing and innovation agenda.

Rui Martins PhD is a Professor at ISLA Santarém – Polytechnic University and holds a PhD in Management from the University of

Beira Interior, where he was affiliated with the NECE-UBI Research Centre. His research focuses on the internationalization strategies of SMEs, entrepreneurship, business creation, and business networks. He combines academic rigor with practical relevance, fostering innovation and international competitiveness in business education and applied research.

Amalia Nedelcut PhD is a lecturer at Babe -Bolyai University, where she teaches Management, Project Management, Business Ethics, and Organizational Behavior in English, Romanian, and German. Holding a PhD in Cultural Management and a Master's in Business Engineering, she brings an interdisciplinary perspective to her academic work. She actively leads international projects focused on personal development and global collaboration, promoting inclusive education and empowering individuals to reach their full potential.13663790-faad-4208-aa7f-d7a39468b5ea)

Lidiane Rodrigues de Oliveira é uma profissional com mais de 25 anos de experiência nas áreas de Recursos Humanos, Gestão Hospitalar e Formação Empresarial. Atua no desenvolvimento de lideranças, fortalecimento da cultura organizacional e gestão estratégica de pessoas, com foco em excelência operacional e bem-estar no trabalho.

Oyenuga Michael Oyedele PhD is an Associate Professor and Assistant Dean of International Relations at Woxsen University, India. He is a Manaaki New Zealand Scholar and a Carbon Literacy Certificate recipient from Nottingham Business School & PRME. His work focuses on marketing, consumer behavior, digital sustainability, and climate governance. Educated across Nigeria, the US, India, and Malaysia, he brings a global and multidisciplinary approach to sustainability, technology, and policy, contributing to the advancement of net-zero economic models.

Maria de Fátima Pina PhD is an Adjunct Professor at ISLA Santarém – Polytechnic University and holds a PhD in Mathematics from the University of Coimbra and the University of Porto. She is a member of the Portuguese Mathematical Society, the Portuguese Association for Automatic Control, and IFAC. A researcher at ISR-UC, her work spans Control Theory, Robotics, Data Science, and Medical Engineering. She contributes to academic innovation through interdisciplinary research that integrates systems theory, computing, and applied science.

Index

L

M

O

S

T

www.ingramcontent.com/pod-product-compliance
Lightning Source LLC
LaVergne TN
LVHW061543290926
849162LV00004B/893